The Media and the Internet

The Media and the Internet

Final report of the British Library funded research project
*The changing information environment:
the impact of the Internet on information
seeking behaviour in the media*

David Nicholas, Peter Williams, Helen Martin
and Peter Cole

Department of Information Science
City University

March 1998

British Library Research and Innovation Report 110

Routledge
Taylor & Francis Group

LONDON AND NEW YORK

First published 1998 by Aslib

Published 2020 by Routledge
2 Park Square, Milton Park, Abingdon, Oxon OX14 4RN
52 Vanderbilt Avenue, New York, NY 10017

Routledge is an imprint of the Taylor & Francis Group, an informa business

RIC/G/371
ISSN 1366-8218
ISBN 13: 978-0-85142-415-6 (pbk)

Contents

Project information

The Changing Information Environment project, known in its short-hand form as the 'Journalists and the Internet' study, ran from April 1997 to March 1998. It was funded by the British Library Research and Innovation Centre (BLRIC) and based at City University. The research team was led by Dr David Nicholas, Senior Tutor for Research at the Department of Information Science at City University, London. Peter Williams was the Research Assistant on the project. Helen Martin, Information Manager, *The Guardian/Observer*, and Professor Peter Cole, Head, Department of Journalism, University of Central Lancashire, were external members of the research team. Nat Lievesley, Network Manager, Centre for Policy on Ageing, was the project's technical consultant.

The project was generously supported by the members of its Advisory Board – Gertrud Erbach, Reference Librarian, News International; Peter Chapman, Information Manager, Newsquest NorthEast, and Graham Jetcoate, BLRIC. Thanks also to: Robin Hunt, arehause; Tony Ageh, VirginNet and Richard Withey, News International; for their thoughts and suggestions.

The preliminary results of this study have been widely disseminated: on the Net in the project's own web site (*http://www.soi.city.ac.uk/~pw/ji_home.html*); at an international conference (Online 97); and in the professional press (see Appendix 4 for list of publications). Reports on the final results were given at: The Social Context Of Information Use In Museums, Libraries & Galleries (York, June 1998); NetMedia 98 (City University, July 1998); and at Information Seeking in Context: An International Conference on Information Needs, Seeking and Use in Different Contexts (Sheffield University, August 1998).

Data for this report was collected up until February 1998. This fact is important especially when reading of some of the statistical data presented in the literature review – undoubtedly the situation has changed.

Abstract

Its sheer functionality, connectivity and accessibility make the Internet an information force to be reckoned with. However, there is very little qualitative data on how the Internet is impacting upon information seeking in the workplace. Using largely unstructured interviewing techniques, the impact on the media – mainly the press – was assessed. More than three hundred journalists and media librarians were surveyed. It was found that amongst traditional print journalists use was light, unsophisticated and uneven and there was disagreement as to its future significance. Poor access to the Internet – and good access to other information resources – were largely the reasons for this. In general it was the older and more senior journalists who availed themselves of the facility. Librarians and the New Media journalists however made extensive use of the Internet.

Use tended to concentrate on searching the World Wide Web and was generally conservative in character. Newspapers and official sites were those favoured and searches were mainly of a fact-checking and background-collecting nature. Email was being used on a very limited scale and was not regarded as a serious journalistic tool – nor too were newsgroups. Non-users were partly put off by the Internet's potential for overloading them with information and its reputation for producing information of suspect quality. Users were not so concerned, dealing with the overload and quality problems where they arose largely by sticking to authoritative sites and exploiting the lower quality data where circumstances allowed. Use of the Internet has generally not been at the expense of other information sources or communication channels, although data is beginning to emerge of a threat to commercial online hosts and fax. In general, media librarians have pioneered the use of the Internet and this has enhanced their position. And even in the case of the most avid Internet users – the New Media journalists – information professionals appear to have an important role to play. Information management is seen as the key to news management.

Chapter 1

Introduction

New forces are threatening to alter, perhaps permanently, the information landscape. These forces are being released by the seemingly irresistible growth of the Internet. They are forces which all types of information provider will have to confront as a matter of urgency, for it is quite possible that they will bring about fundamental changes in the relationship between information user, information intermediary, information provider and information system. Patently, the greatest force of all – and potentially the most disruptive – will be the effect of millions of end-users entering the information market in a short space of time; perhaps more than 40 million joining the ranks of Internet (online) users in little more than four years (Gilster, 1997). Most will be first time users and many will be searching the system from home or for personal use. Among other major forces to be dealt with are the information deluge the Internet brings with it (the number of sites is forecasted to exceed the population of the planet), and the spectacular leap towards electronic information retrieval and communication which the Internet appears to be bringing about.

Plainly the Internet poses many strategic and searching questions, and the answers to many of them will massively affect people, products and companies in the information industry. It is hardly surprising that the Internet has become the information world's obsession. Information professionals, and those whose work involves the collection and processing of information, talk continuously about the Internet. However, despite all the rhetoric and debate, there is very little qualitative data to provide us with the answers we need. Worryingly, in the information vacuum, hype and hot air are influencing many an agenda and marketing plan. What in-roads the Internet is making, and what challenges are to be faced, can really only be guessed at – and guessing is not good enough with something as big as the Internet. This project sets out to collect and evaluate data to obtain answers to some very important questions. For instance: does the Internet represent the information equivalent of the financial services big bang, and is it, indeed, powerful enough to change work patterns, restructure organisations and reshape industries?

The chosen ground for the investigation was the media. There were good reasons for focusing on the media:

- With information so central to and often the reason for its activities, it might be expected that journalists would be the 'early leaders' in the adoption and adaptation of the new technology. Plainly when such a huge and powerful communication and information retrieval system as the Internet gate-crashes media workplaces there is much at stake.

- The pressurised and demanding nature of news rooms offered an ideal environment in which to investigate the issues unobtrusively. In the media, events are telescoped, resources are relatively plentiful and impacts (if any) are relatively immediate, thus providing ideal laboratory conditions for impact research and an early warning of what is in store for others not so close to the technological front-line.

- The media was visited in a previous British Library Research and Innovation Centre study[1] to provide early warning as to how end-user access to full-text, natural language databases would impact upon the industry and its information professionals. That research concluded – correctly, as it turned out – that end-use would not prove the information turning point that many commentators had thought. The impact on the information seeking behaviour of journalists was light, patchy and fairly insignificant, and the threat to the intermediary proved to be largely bogus (Nicholas et al, 1987; 1988). But would things be different this time around – a decade later, and with a much, much more powerful information system in play?

Aims and objectives

Expressed simply, the aim of the research project was to examine very closely and comprehensively the impact of the Internet on a strategic information community to whom it appeared to be of immense significance. Of paramount concern was the exploitation of the Internet for information retrieval and communication rather than as a medium for disseminating the news or advertising it. Such a broad brief was inevitable, given the massive functionality of the Internet, the potentially enormous area of impact, the fact that the claims made for it were so great, and that the situation was changing so fast. In such circumstances it would be only too easy to artificially constrain such a study. The (unavoidably overlapping) research questions forefront in our minds were these:

- How much of an impact was the Internet having or going to have – did the Internet really mark the dawn of a new information age,

---

[1]Information seeking in an information society: the end-user. 1985–1987.

or have we been here before, with online services, CD-ROM, the fax and the telephone?

- What were the key information issues associated with its use?
- What happens when a supposedly accessible, comprehensive, powerful and freely available computerised information system is made available to end-users – many of them online novices?
- Would the Internet have sufficient weight and momentum to change information seeking behaviour and working practices irreversibly?

The more specific objectives of the project were to determine:

- The approximate level of Internet take-up in the media;
- Who uses the Internet. Is take-up dependent on nature and status of job and on the work environment? Were there differences between end-users and intermediaries?
- What Internet facilities were being used and for what purpose. Were information intermediaries using the Internet in different ways and to different extents?
- What users (and non-users) thought of the Internet. What were their expectations, attitudes and opinions regarding this much-hyped information tool? It was important to gather this data given that statistics about Internet use become so quickly out-of-date.
- Whether the potential for information overload that the Internet brings with it was a real worry to those at the information cutting edge. If so, what were the methods/strategies being used for dealing with this? Did information professionals have a new role to play here?
- Whether the alleged poor quality of data on the Internet was of real concern to users, and whether it featured significantly in their use/non-use of the system? In the rush for speed of delivery and total access, would traditional information quality and authority concerns take a back seat?
- What impact, if any, was the Internet having on the use of existing hard copy, online and CD-ROM information services – especially the traditional commercial online hosts who appear to be at most risk from the Internet's information-for-free characteristics and culture?
- Whether the role, status and prospects of the journalist and the intermediary would be changed or diminished as a result of Internet use – threat, opportunity or both?

Scope and coverage

With such a broad brief, what actually fell within the scope and remit of the research was crucially dependent on the working definitions adopted for the three key components of the study: the Internet, the media and information seeking.

The Internet

Despite the fact that there exist perfectly good, technically precise definitions of the Internet and its constituent parts – such as the World Wide Web (see Literature Review), none were adopted for the purposes of this study. This was because few people appear to know, or abide by, the technically correct definition. There is a huge problem or perception: terms such as 'cyberspace', 'the Internet', 'the Net', the 'information superhighway', the World Wide Web and even 'online' are all being used, apparently interchangeably, to describe the now vast network of computers interconnected via the telecommunications infrastructure. The Internet is seen by many, apart from the aficionados, as a label for any extensive, accessible and geographically wide computer network. The rise of the intranet – localised mini-Internets serving specific communities or organisations – is sure to compound the problem of recognition and definition. In fact these perceptions, and differences in them, were part of the research material of the project. Very early on in the investigation it became clear that journalists were no different from information consumers generally, in that the Internet was a word they all used but one which they defined or understood variously. It was a word suggesting infinite potential at one moment, daunting threat at another. The consequence of this was that their 'definition(s)' had to be our definitions; and that these 'definitions' became part of the study.

The Media

The Media was the focus for the study. Within the media it was largely the press that was investigated: tabloid and broadsheet national newspapers, English and Scottish, and regional newspapers were covered, as well as some news-based magazines. One paper, *The Guardian*, was investigated in some depth as a case study, to provide the project with a comprehensive and detailed insight into the situation at one site. The reasons for concentrating on the press were threefold: (1) to narrow the project down to manageable (and economic) proportions – something made especially important given that the prime means of investigation was the resource-intensive, face-to-face, depth interview; (2) the press is traditionally the biggest and most demanding information user and, as a consequence, had the libraries/librarians/online services on whom the impact of the Internet could be studied; (3) this was the area of the media with whom the research team had the best contacts – thus ensuring high levels of co-operation in an industry where co-operation and good will can be extremely difficult to obtain. Other sectors of the media were not neglected, however, for there was a need for comparative and contextual data, albeit on a somewhat smaller scale. In this connection data was obtained from broadcasting – largely, but not wholly, the BBC – and from the Internet-based news services – commonly referred to as the New Media labs, who, according to some commentators (Hunt, 1998) represent the future of news provision. Additionally, and for the same purpose, data regarding general Internet use was also collected.

Managers, journalists, online hosts, systems staff, information providers and information professionals practising in the media industry were the people questioned. All types of journalists were covered: those with management responsibilities, such as editors; feature writers; those with subject specialisms (foreign, medical correspondents etc.); general news reporters; freelancers; and trainee/ student journalists.

Finally, the views and actions of both users and non-users of the Internet were investigated. Not to do so would have prejudiced the study from the outset. Furthermore, there is no reason why non-users cannot express an opinion about the Internet (just as people can have views on cars but not drive). This was especially important as the study was as interested in perception and attitude as much as actual use; non-users might wish to search the Internet but not have the facilities to do so; and, even in the case of people who have rejected using it the reasons for doing so are of great interest. Just about everybody has a view on the Internet – and they are all valid.

Information seeking behaviour

The Internet is an all-singing, all-dancing information system. Its versatility, complexity and comprehensiveness means that there are many aspects of the Internet – and issues connected to it – that may merit investigation. For the purposes of this study it was only the information seeking behaviour connected with it that was of interest, although this term was interpreted to include communication behaviour as well. The issue of whether the Internet constitutes a possible alternative outlet for news production, while of great interest and concern for the industry as a whole, was outside the scope of this particular study. Similarly, its social and cultural significance was not investigated. The following were the information seeking and communication aspects and issues that were considered to be of significance:

1.   The extent of use.

2.   Distribution and pattern of use. Who were the users and non-users? How significant were factors like previous use of online, training, age, gender, job role, subject affiliation and nature of working environment in determining use? What was the end-user/intermediary split in use.

3.   The nature and purpose of use: kinds of searches conducted, commonly used Internet facilities and web sites.

4.   Searching characteristics, search strategies/engines/system preferences etc.

5.   Satisfaction/success or otherwise with searching.

6.   Information overload – existence and extent of problem, and strategies for dealing with it.

7.   Problems of validating data, assessing the quality/authority of data. Were they different from those encountered with other information sources?

8.   Extent to which other sources/systems/communication forms were being displaced by the Internet. The fate of the Library and traditional online systems were of particular interest, as well as changes in use of other information systems and sources, especially other online systems and oral communication.

9.   The role of intermediaries with regard to use of the Internet; extent and nature of delegation; training and research opportunities arising.

10.   Overall changes in information seeking behaviour – was there a greater reliance on electronic sources?

As the main research method was to be the in-depth, open-ended interview, data could not be gathered uniformly or systematically on all these topics. And neither was this intended. Within the broad boundaries set down by the interviewer – essentially the job, information seeking behaviour and the Internet – interviewees were largely responsible for what specific topics were discussed. Priority was given to what the interviewees considered to be important issues. More importantly, perhaps, in this way issues could be raised that the interviewer had not thought to be issues. One such unanticipated issue turned out to be of such general concern that it was added to the scope of the study: the 'dumbing down' of information seeking as a consequence of Internet use.

Chapter 2

Methods

Introduction

This was to be fundamentally an interview study, with 252 people in all being interviewed (Table 1). Questionnaires (79 returned) and observation (28 people observed in depth) were also employed, but on a limited scale and largely to buttress the interview data. Data was gathered from more than 50 media organisations (see Appendix 1 for the list) and around 350 people. Interviews were the preferred research instrument because they lent themselves so well to the investigation of the new, the changing, the controversial, and the ill-formed and ill-defined – the topic being investigated was all of these things. Inevitably, too, the choice of method was determined not just by the issue being studied, but also by whom it was being investigated. Thus, while there was little chance of getting very busy, preoccupied practitioners, like journalists, to subject themselves to the kind of examination that information researchers subject librarians, students and academics – such methods as diaries, questionnaires and talk-aloud techniques at the terminal – there was every chance of getting their agreement to be interviewed.

Sampling and sample

Obtaining a scientific and systematic sample was never a realistic – or required – goal, given the research aims, the principle research method adopted and the size and heterogeneity of the population investigated. We were interested not in numbers but in the quality and depth of the responses. Specifically, the following factors shaped the size and character of our sample:

1. The geographical spread of the population and the resource intensive data collection method adopted meant that there were limits to the number of people who could be interviewed. It was felt that 200–250 would provide a realistic – and numerically significant – sample.

2. There was a need to obtain a balance between journalists and librarians. A ratio of around 2:1 was thought suitable, taking into account (a) the greater number of journalists in the industry, (b)

the greater homogeneity of the librarians, and (c) the fact that librarians could provide us with not only a picture of their own Internet use, but also a broad picture of journalist use in their own organisation.

3. It was necessary to ensure that national and regional newspapers, newspapers and magazines, and traditional and Internet news providers were covered.

4. It was important to make sure that Internet users and non-users were represented in significant, if not equal, numbers. In the case of journalists, where sampling was especially needed because of the size of the population, it was simply not possible to draw up a sampling frame and then pick every nth person. This was because journalists are very busy and the unpredictability of their work makes them difficult to pin down. The intention, however, was to start by interviewing a cross section of journalists, picking up users and non-users of the Internet in *reasonably* representative numbers. In a very few organisations – *The Guardian* and Time Life for instance – a fairly systematic schedule of interviews was arranged, with subjects typically chosen on use or experience criteria. Often, and inevitably, though, it tended to be the journalists who were willing to be interviewed who were interviewed, and, not unexpectedly, it was Internet users and/or enthusiasts who were most willing to be interviewed. This would not have been such a problem but for the fact that Internet take-up proved to be generally much lower than expected. This problem was compounded by the fact that we were particularly interested in the 'early leaders' who might point to future patterns of use. General wisdom (Wallace, 1997; Cole, 1997) at the time put the figure for journalist Internet users at 7–10%, and we found that various factors did indeed restrict use to around these levels in some institutions. Interviewing at random, therefore, risked obtaining too small a sample of Internet users to make any meaningful analysis of how the new medium was being exploited. In the end, over 60% of our sample were Internet users. The danger of obtaining a self-selecting, biased sample was partly (and, admittedly, crudely) overcome by increasing the sample size and partly by employing questionnaires and observation to compensate for this. The published literature, which is in fact 'good' on huge samples, quantitative data etc. also helped in this regard.

Table 1
Methods employed and size and origin of sample

National newspapers/newspaper groups	Journalists			Librarians			New Media	Others[2]
	Interviews	Questionnaires	Observation[1]	Interviews	Questionnaires	Observation	Interviews	Interviews
National newspapers/newspaper groups								
Daily Telegraph	4	1	1	1				
Guardian	36	2	7	14	1	5	2	
Herald (Glasgow)	6			5	5		1	
Mirror	4			1		1		
News International	50[2]			15	10			
Observer	7		1					
Scottish Daily Record	1		1	4				
Others	3				4		1	
Regional and local newspapers								
Eastern Counties Network			1	1			2	
Newsquest Northeast	3		3	2	2	1	1	
Others*	27			1	7			
Specialist titles and freelancers								
Freelancers[4]	3						3	
Sunday Business	1							
Time-Life	4		2	2				
Others	4			1	2			
Broadcasting/wire service organisations								
Anglia TV					2			
BBC	7			17	4			
London Weekend Television	1			1	2			
VirginNet			4					3
Others	2			3	4		3	1
Other organisations								
City University							1	1
United States Embassy	1			1				
University of Central Lancashire		33[5]						
Grand totals	164	36	21	69	43	7	14	5

Notes

[1] Observation concerned Internet searches. General observation was also undertaken.
[2] Interview questions as part of general library interviews.
[3] Journalism students
[4] In addition, six other journalists from the national/regional and specialist press discussed their previous freelance experiences
[5] Inluding group interview with 24 trainee journalists from various local newspapers

Interviews

No research method is entirely free from problems, but interviewing must surely come closest. Interviews can probe for both qualitative and quantitative data. Furthermore, interviews have a habit of throwing up the unexpected, things that were not asked about (but with hindsight needed). With a good interview, the interviewee helps shape the scope and nature of the proceedings. And, of course, there is no real substitute for the method when it comes to studying non-use (and plainly we were interested in this), for, by definition, there are no beguiling numbers, transactional logs etc. to help here. Because the interview was felt to be so critical in obtaining the quality information required – and in that it did not let us down – we will dwell somewhat on its characteristics and performance in the field.

There are of course many types of interview – the very fashionable focus groups, telephone interviews, group interviews, and the one chosen for this research project, the face-to-face, open-ended depth interview. The specific attractions of this form of interview were that:

- Through the opportunities it provides to question, explain and reflect, a comprehensive exploration of complex issues like information seeking behaviour (and the Internet) can be conducted.

- It has proved to be a particularly successful research method with groups that we might call talking-heads – and we can include journalists in that description, because they generally have few qualms in telling researchers exactly what they think. Journalists are generally full of confidence and self-esteem and do not feel that they have to conform to the expectations of the interviewer (a big danger in user surveys involving technology), and they are also exceedingly good at expressing themselves, as the quotes we use in our results section hopefully demonstrate.

- Full and complete responses to questions are more easily obtained.

- Crucially for this project, data comes in the words of the interviewee. Too often, as in the case of questionnaires, users are shoe-horned into forms of words devised by the interviewer.

- The observational opportunities it provides when interviews take place in the workplace, as nearly all of ours did. You can double your information, treble your insight, the moment you step into someone's office or workspace – especially when that office/workspace is as open as a newsroom. Non-verbal communication can also be taken into account.

- The depth interview is especially powerful when the territory is unfamiliar – and in the case of the Internet both researcher and interviewee were undoubtedly entering unknown territory.

The open-ended depth interview in practice

Open-ended interviews are characterised by their open, wide-ranging questions and their loose, flexible and unstructured format. Topics are explored in depth on a one-to-one basis with the interviewer taking very much a back-seat. Interviewees are given the space to air their views in comfort. The ratio of interviewer to interviewee input should be 10:90 but possibly 20:80 in the case of retiring interviewees or non-users, where more prompting might be needed. What are being sought are attitudes, opinions and facts – and often in that order. The real gems to be quarried by the method are forms of words, expressions and quotes. Despite the wide-ranging and unstructured nature of the interviews, it was still important to be consistent in interview approach between our four interviewers, and across different interviewees. Guidelines were issued and an edited version is reproduced in Appendix 2.

Interviews were usually around 30 minutes long, but they could last an hour and a half if the interviewee was particular talkative, or was known to the interviewer. On the other hand, where a journalist's time or patience was limited, interviews were completed in fifteen minutes. Typically, for the reasons mentioned above, interviews were held in the newsroom, library or in a person's office. Opportunities to interview were grabbed as they arose – and it was far from uncommon for the interviewer to pass from one journalist to another without a break. Sometimes five or six journalists could be covered in this way in the space of a couple of hours. Space problems often meant that interviews could not be done in ideal conditions. At more than one location different chairs were occupied as people returned and others went to lunch, and many interviews were conducted with the interviewer standing. On one occasion an upturned litter bin was pressed into action to at least allow face-to-face interaction with a seated reporter. Interviews with librarians were easier to arrange (via the phone or by email) and manage. Co-operation was established with the Association of UK Media Librarians (AUKML) very early on, and this certainly made things easier. Most interviews with journalists were arranged through librarians resident in the media companies concerned. This worked to a mixed extent: those librarians who were closest to their users provided the most generous supply of interviewees. Anticipating some of the problems that we might encounter, we had a senior journalist, with wide industry contacts on the research team, who could be employed to overcome any pockets of interview resistance.

Getting people to talk long and hard about the Internet was generally not difficult. It is so topical that everyone wants to talk about it – even those who have never used it. In fact, by judicious (and crafty) questioning it is possible to use the Internet to explore a whole range of information phenomena that were once thought to be out of bounds in discussions with end-users. The Internet is the information equivalent of the Trojan horse. The opportunities for a comprehensive investigation of the entire communication system are there and can be readily grasped. This is just as well, for the Internet appears to be capable of impacting on every aspect of information provision and delivery.

It is sometimes claimed that there are no real rules to interviewing. This is not true; and such rules count if the interview is not to become stilted, boring, unproductive, uncomfortable etc. Because the researcher-interviewer is going into the fray with a small number of broad questions and relying on the dynamism of the interview process to reveal as much as possible, it is absolutely essential to capture, from the beginning, the person's interest and to make them relax. Small-talk usually helps. Curiosity, empathy and compliments certainly help too. There are other things that can make the interview a success:

1. The interviewer should never convey the impression that they are promoting the topic comodity (the Internet in our case) they are asking questions about. If they do – even unintentionally – they will be typecast, and the interviewee might want to please, or, in the case of non-users, either lie or shut-up completely. What should be done to overcome the problem is start by questioning the interviewee about their job, their work and, best of all, about the problems they experience when doing it. Virtually everything they say will have an information seeking (and Internet) connotation – you can then take each comment and mentally run with it through your analytical framework and tick it off. It is only through such an interaction between interviewee and interviewer that high quality data emerges – for thoughts on the Internet are seldom on the tip of the tongue or crafted with well honed prose. Through users recounting experiences – of a typical day perhaps – profitable lines of communication open out, and genuinely new and interesting data emerges. They will mention sources of information and systems as a natural part of the discussion – anecdotes, cases etc. alert the interviewer to a characteristic of information seeking behaviour. Any topics not covered can be swept up at the end, by which time the person is so immersed in talking about their job that they have lost their inhibitions and preconceptions.

Where, because of shortage of time or the demeanour of the interviewee, the normal preliminaries have to be dispensed with and the point has to be made very quickly, it is useful to pose a neutral, balloon-type question, such as, 'The Internet has been the subject of a lot of discussion recently; what do you think?' This has an obvious value of 'helping' those for whom the Internet plays little part in their information seeking behaviour to declare as much, while still permitting enthusiasts to put their case with relish. Once users find out the questions are about them and not you (or 'your' systems) they generally enjoy the experience. They find the questioning – and periods of reflection that go with it – intriguing and stimulating and sometimes come out of the interview feeling that they have been involved in an (information) counselling session. 'How did I do?' is a typical response. Wanting to talk about the interview afterwards is another common reaction. Indeed, when the pressure of being recorded and being 'formally' interviewed came to an end some interviewees suddenly opened up and talked at length, generally about the wider issues such as the sacrifice of quality journalism (and this was duly recorded).

2. Probing is an essential part of an open-ended interview. Its function is: (1) to encourage further communication, (2) to show interest, (3) to make a direct bid for more information. What is required from the interviewer is motivation and direction without giving signs that some responses are more acceptable than others (otherwise you are back to the pitfalls of questionnaires). Probing questions follow up an interviewee's responses; they are particularly important in getting to the depth and detail of information required, but must be asked sensitively to avoid discomforting the interviewee. Postural signs of interest and acceptance – like nodding of the head – have a big role to play, especially in noisy newsrooms. Brief assertions of understanding and interest: assenting comments like, 'I see', 'um-hm' play a part, in that they show that the answer is on the right lines, but has not been answered fully. You can go further and be rather more directional, though still retaining a neutrality: 'in what way were your needs not met' – a clarification probe. Silence can also be an effective, although sometimes disconcerting, probe, encouraging the interviewee to contribute more. Mirroring the thoughts of the interviewee can be useful too – through this process they can see what they said more clearly and can make modifications if their words were interpreted wrongly or if they were hurried into saying the wrong thing.

One should not come away with the impression that open-ended interviews are problem free and indeed some of the problems have already been alluded to, but the really big difficulty encountered is that it requires that the researcher step into a world outside their control, persuade and seek co-operation, ask (often personal) questions for which there are no stereotypical responses, and probe for data in unfamiliar territory. There are no prescribed or familiar lines of questioning – certainly not the sort that lend themselves to the satisfied/v. satisfied etc. so beloved of quantitative researchers. Open-ended interviews can be particularly challenging and unsettling for the novice interviewer, the challenge being to sustain a long conversation around a very general opening line and to keep the momentum going with the use of gentle prompts. By contrast, a structured interview with a long list of quite specific questions provides a high degree of security and confidence (a methodological comfort blanket). Recognising the problem and the dangers, all interviewers were issued with a list of broad topic areas which should ideally be explored (see Appendix 1). The main time that specific questioning was resorted to was when clarification was required or as a means of controlling an overexpansive/talkative interviewee.

There were other difficulties. Firstly, the presence of the researcher of necessity affects the work of the subjects of the research. In addition to actually being influenced by the interview process – and its possible artificiality – they may be affected in other ways. These may include being the subjects of a period of observation as well (see below), a changed routine caused by the temporary disengagement of close colleagues whose time is being taken up by an interviewer, or other similar reasons. Such factors may be enough to affect the quality and validity of the data gathered.

Secondly, establishing the necessary degree of informality in the interviewing process is easier said than done. The recording apparatus (see below), whether visible or not, mitigated against this, as did the fact that interviewers were aware of the general theme of the interview (and that being 'The Internet', this may have caused some anxieties for non-users). Another factor precluding, to an extent, a degree of informality, was the predictable constraint of a shortage of time. In part, a recognition of this fact by the researcher sometimes leads to an involuntary adoption of a more formal question-and-answer type formal interview in an attempt to avoid interviewees thinking the exercise was a mere 'chat' and, as such, something of a time waster. Unwanted formality crept in despite the researchers' best efforts. Thus it was noticeable that subjects seemed naturally to adopt the role of one required simply to respond to set questions, even when it was stressed that they were free to offer any observations and talk in general terms about their work, and that there was no schedule of questions. This may have been due to a variety of factors – time considerations, a knowledge of the interview topic, at least in its wider sense, or even to difficulties in being informal with an outsider in a work environment while undertaking professional duties. Apart from stating at the outset of interviews that the exercise was not to be regarded as an 'interview' as such, other tactics were adopted to make the subjects feel more at ease and able to talk a little more naturally. One of these was to undertake the interview at the Internet terminal. This involved sitting with librarians and reporters as they performed searches, noting relevant details (sites visited, search strategies etc.) and asking pertinent questions during the operation. The formal aspects of this are dealt with in the section on observation issues and problems. Here the concern is with the interview element in such fieldwork. One advantage in soliciting information during a search session is that the time constraint element of the face-to-face interview is removed – the 'interviewee' is actually undertaking work duties during the course of the conversation. Answering questions such as 'I see you went straight to the bookmark menu first – is that your general method of starting a search?' is easily undertaken while waiting for remote connections, reading hit-lists or even typing in query terms. It is arguable that even being able to concentrate on the screen rather than having to make eye contact with the interviewer (and attempt to ascertain some hidden meaning from his/her facial expression in the line of questioning) may assist in promoting both informality and candidness.

Thirdly, there is the problem of incomplete replies. As with any interview, participants were understandably unable to give complete accounts of their Internet use, or full arguments against it, or relate any issue exhaustively. Even at a very early stage in the data collection, it was noticeable how many respondents apologised for not remembering more information, as these quotes illustrate: 'I use the Internet much more than I've described ...'; 'I can't remember any examples ...'; 'I'm afraid I've got a poor short-term memory'. Participant observation compensated for this because the act of actually working with the Internet can bring out anecdotes of interesting past use, possibly not remembered in a conventional interview. In a hands-on session, comments like 'I use this site a lot ...'; 'I got a lot of material about X from here ...'; 'The last time I used InfoSeek I came across X document ...'; 'I didn't know X had a web site before ...' came quite naturally. Also, returning to each interviewee a full transcript of their interview provided much help with obtaining more complete or richer data from subjects. This was not always possible, but was undertaken as and when the opportunity arose.

Finally – and related to the above – privacy and confidentiality problems can arise. Thus discussing email (to whom? how often? why? etc.) may appear intrusive, as it would with 'conventional' mail.

Similarly, journalists are not noted for their openness with the material they are currently working with, and sometimes do not like discussing particular Internet sites they visit in order to acquire this material.

Recording

Open-ended interviews raise the problems of data collection: to use a notebook or tape recorder (or both)? The use of a tape recorder brings with it the problem of making the interviewee feel uncomfortable, perhaps stifling some of the more sensitive responses. And it can prove a distraction (especially when the tape needs changing). Interviews are intrusive anyway; taping them may make it seem doubly intrusive. One journalist was so wary of being taped he taped the interview too. There was also the problem that some of the interviews undertaken were done on the 'hoof' – and in those circumstances it is not easy, or advisable, to suddenly confront your newly-found interviewee with a tape recorder. In fact some people – especially non-users – might not respond at all if they know that every word they utter is being captured for further use. Non-users might feel that they have somehow failed – and do not want to 'broadcast' that fact. In addition the transcription times can be horrendous – something of real concern when several hundred interviews are being conducted. However, if the real data diamonds, the quotes, are to be captured then some interviews have to be taped. Also, if an interview session is being taped, then the interviewer is freer to think about the next question or interact with the interviewee. This is of particular benefit to novice researchers.

The big advantage of a notebook, as opposed to tape, is that it is not so obtrusive, you can take it out quickly (for the impromptu interview), you are much closer to your data and you are editing as you go along, so less typing is involved. And anyway, users are generally impressed by the fact that you are taking notes, that something they said is so important as to warrant the interviewer taking it down. Notes were even taken during taped interviews, both as a back-up in case of poor quality recording and to add a degree of authority to the respondents' answers.

It was not so much a choice of one or the other recording methods, more a case of horses for courses. Thus both methods were used extensively during the research. In the case of librarians, where professional connections oiled the wheels of the interview, to tape or not was not so much an issue – and as a result most were taped. One librarian did however refuse; his native (although slight) French accent might have worried him. Other subjects expressed concern after the interviews that they did not speak so articulately as might have been expected in 'normal' circumstances. Some apologised for 'umming and ahhring' and others claimed to not have given full answers. One member of the research team was a journalist, and he used his professional links similarly to obtain assent for recording.

To minimise the problems associated with tape recording the interviews, a pocket memo tape recorder, with a lapel mike which could also be detached and placed on a holder on a table, was purchased. This meant recording was rather more discrete. The tapes the pocket memo used were of the type that could be used by a professional audio-transcription system – something else the project purchased. The verbatim interviews were transcribed directly into a word processing package (Microsoft Word 6.0) by a qualified typist. The system worked well, the only problem being the audibility of some interviews conducted in busy places (e.g. public spaces, open-plan newsrooms).

It is perhaps as well to mention also the somewhat inhibiting effect of the microphone on the less experienced interviewers on the research team. This was because they were wary of revealing their interviewing inadequacies on tape, such as asking leading questions, being seen to identify too strongly with one type of response/outcome and offering their own opinions. Thus, novice interviewers, being particularly aware of the danger of data contamination by these means, might perhaps have been a little too careful and unadventurous in their questioning.

A total of 132 interviews were conducted on an open-ended, one-to-one basis and transcribed. While all of these were meant to explore the topic in-depth, this was dependent on the time interviewees made available. Probably a third of them explored the topic in genuine depth. Befitting its case study status, *The Guardian* accounted for around a third of all the depth interviews.

Other forms of interview used

Two other forms of interview were in fact undertaken. Both were intended to spread the research net in an economical and speedy way. Two discussion/focus groups were held with 24 trainee journalists from local newspapers in the north of England. They covered the same ground as the depth interviews and were run by the journalist on the team. These interviews were held with the intention of seeing the extent to which individual views conveyed to us at the depth interviews were shared by a broader body of journalists. The other type of interview was a closed question type that was held with 5 *Times* journalists. Journalists were interviewed about the Internet as part of a general library survey. The intention was really to obtain some quantitative data about Internet use in one particular location – something the project lacked at the time. The interviewer was briefed by the project team.

Size and character of total interview population

252 people were interviewed from more than two dozen organisations: 164 of them were journalists, 69 librarians and 14 systems editors/managers and 5 others.

Observation

The observation of journalists was an integral, if informal, aspect of the fieldwork. Observation was used in two ways. In the first instance it was used to prepare the ground for the interviews. There was a need to witness the whole information process in motion and in the round and then Internet use or non-use could be set against this information. Observation is particularly suited to studying communication in the office environment where lots of information is transmitted and received orally – and that is very much the case in newspapers. Thus it initially provided an understanding of the circumstances surrounding the Internet issues and processes being studied, and in so doing helped establish the credibility of the investigator and boosted interviewer confidence.

Observation cannot be divorced from the interview, because as a result of interviewing people in their offices or work places you can observe as well. Even when researchers set out with the prime intention of observing, interviewing opportunities were not forgotten. Thus, with many journalists searching the Internet in the library because of lack of facilities/support in their own working areas, it plainly made sense to observe proceedings in the library. At *The Guardian*, for example, librarians were watched as they answered journalists' queries on the Internet, and often gave a running commentary on their search procedure at the same time. On occasion journalists would enter the library, personally request information and then watch the information retrieval process. When this happened they would invariably be approached by the investigator to enlist their co-operation. Occasionally this would result in a long formal interview complete with recording apparatus. Generally, however, the librarian, journalist and researcher would converse informally during the course of the search, whereupon, armed with the required information, the journalist would retire to his or her place of work – a research activity no less rewarding in terms of data gathering. Indeed, on occasion more insight was possibly found by this hybrid form of observation. For example, during one such observation a journalist muttered 'I could have had a bunch of cuttings by now' whilst waiting for a hyperlink to open. Another, by contrast, waxed lyrical about the system when he was offered the history, street map and much tourist information on the French village of Camembert within literally seconds of his enquiry.

Through observation it was also possible to establish general levels of Internet use and establish where the Internet was being used. In *The Guardian* library, for example, the system was fully exploited – the terminal rarely remained unused for more than an hour. At the City desk, by contrast, it wasn't used once in three days observation, and interviewees claimed it was only employed 'about once a fortnight'. Similarly, the use of other information systems and their possible displacement could be studied simply by being where professionals access information – and observing what they used. Thus, to give an example, the heavy reliance (confirmed by interviewees) on both online databases and hard copy cuttings at News International was discovered.

Observation has its problems. There is the considerable amount of time it takes for seemingly little reward. Many hours were spent in *The Guardian* City office waiting for 'promised' Internet searches. However, journalists were otherwise engaged, either on the telephone, typing up stories or occupied in other pursuits from which little meaningful data could be extracted. Of course, that information is valuable in itself – although little solace to the observer at the time. It is also intrusive, and, as a consequence, a few journalists were unwilling to be observed. Finally, in the case of newspapers there is the physical lack of space in which to conduct the observation comfortably.

Observation was largely conducted near the Internet terminal in the library and on the newsroom floor. Most of the observation was conducted at *The Guardian*. General observation of the library was undertaken for a period of three weeks. Three half-days were spent with the City Desk; and one half-day each in the Pictures department, Features department, and Letters department. Observation was interspersed with informal chats and depth interviews. Observation was also undertaken at: *The Observer* (two half day sessions); *Sunday Business* (two half day sessions); the *Northern Echo* (afternoon session); and *The Herald* (two, two hour sessions).

Questionnaires

Questionnaires were used to a limited extent, although they were important in: reaching a wider audience than that allowed by interviewing; furnishing quantitative data to complement the qualitative results of the interviews, so putting the latter into a wider context; and, most importantly, discovering whether the strong, and possibly very individual views expressed by the journalists we spoke to, were shared by their colleagues and media information professionals. To these ends, two questionnaires were designed: one for librarians and the other for journalists. The questionnaires were very similar (see Appendix 3) and both were made available in hard copy form and placed in a machine readable form on the project's web site. The librarian questionnaire was divided into two parts. Part one asked questions about the availability of the Internet and it use. All but one of the seven questions were multiple choice, requiring simple alternatives such as yes/no etc. The first four questions concerned librarians' own use, and the others related to the access afforded to journalists at their news organisation. The single open question asked respondents to describe the kind of use they made of the Internet. 'The Internet' was not defined for this question – it was felt that each respondent would have a view on what they thought it was, and that this would be reflected in their response. Part two sought opinions and whether or not respondents subscribed to the view aired by journalists in their interviews. Twenty statements were taken from interview transcripts, with respondents asked to indicate their agreement on a four point semantic scale from 'strongly disagree' to 'strongly agree'. To reduce the risk of forcing opinions a fifth option, 'no opinion' was also offered.

The librarians' hard copy questionnaire was distributed to libraries on the AUKML mailing list, and others which, surprisingly, were not on the list – 19 (50%) responded. Most of the organisations were sent two questionnaires, although the really large ones, such as News International, were sent more (a dozen in their case). Forty three questionnaires were returned. Returns were made from 19 organisations. The journalists' questionnaire was constructed on very similar lines: part one was adjusted to ask just about personal experience and use, and part two was reproduced in its entirety. The hard copy version was distributed to student journalists at the Department of Journalism, University of Central Lancashire (33 were returned). Two questionnaires were sent to the Editor and an Assistant Editor of *The Guardian*, to enhance our case study data and a third was returned by a sports editor who returned a questionnaire intended for a librarian. That gave a total of 36 questionnaires.

The main problem encountered with the questionnaire was that the question about the kinds of use made of the Internet brought a very mixed bag of responses with some people answering with reference to specific sites, others to facilities (email, Web) and still others in terms of function (story ideas, background research etc.). Also taking journalists' comments out of context and putting them on a questionnaire may have led to ambiguous interpretation, but it is difficult to know whether this actually occurred. One question plainly came into this category: 'When journalists get 100% access, only 20% will refuse to use the Internet, but only 20% will use it as a force for good'. Half the respondents did not respond to this question. Some questions appeared to be difficult to answer using the options available. This question was a case in point: 'There will be a cataclysmic change ... in the way society works.' The general response to this question was to 'mildly agree' (15 respondents). Yet this appears to be a difficult concept to 'mildly agree' with. One explanation could be that respondents thought, rather, that the change itself would be milder than the 'cataclysmic' prediction by the original interviewee. Finally, there was a certain amount of overlap with the interviews – some respondents had also been interviewed, but that was acceptable because they had not been shown the quotes before nor had they been specifically asked for quantitative data

Having seen the relative success of some US online surveys – and feeling a moral pressure to practice what we preach, as it were, we also administered the questionnaire via the Web. HyperText Markup Language (HTML), which forms the basis of all documents on the World Wide Web, includes a facility to design and display forms which can be completed by anyone viewing the page. The browser (Netscape etc.) then transfers the contents of the completed form to a designated server in a standard format known as the Common Gateway Interface (CGI). A computer program stored on the server, known as a CGI script, can then be used to process the information passed by the browser. The Journalist and News Librarians questionnaires were each laid out as HTML documents using the 'forms' interface and stored on the City University server. CGI scripts were developed, using the Practical Extraction and Reporting Language (PERL), to process the completed forms and store the data, along with some information about the location of the sender, in a file. Before storing the data, to avoid hoax responses, the researcher script checks to see that the identification details have been completed and, if not, returns that part of the questionnaire to the sender for completion.

The response however was very disappointing – nobody had filled in the questionnaire by the completion of the project. Fortunately, not a lot rested on its success. It really was a methodological make weight. There are probably three reasons for this: journalists are too busy to fill in Internet surveys; many had already been canvassed by other means; and the 'army of journalists' surfing the Net looking for journalist sites is highly exaggerated (we had links to most of the important sites they might have been expected to visit).

Data Analysis

With so much interview data being amassed in a very unstructured form, analysing it was bound to be a big challenge (and headache). Software exists to analyse the very kinds of data that we were producing and a package called NU.DIST was evaluated to this end. However, the effort that was required to process the data seemed out of all proportion to the benefits gained. One of the reasons for this was that, with around 200 interviews it was still feasible to process the data through a word processing package, through simple cut and paste methods. Another reason was that we had a relatively narrow remit, by comparison with sociological/anthropological studies – the typical users of this software – and the same themes did crop up time and time again in our data. So with a relatively small canvas, which had visible patterns printed on it, the data could be handled and evaluated by largely manual methods.

The number of questionnaires returned did not merit computerised processing, although if the number of online responses had been higher there were plans to process these by the SPSS software package. The low numbers observed also meant that analysis of this data could also be undertaken by hand.

Chapter 3

Literature Review

There has been a great deal written about the Internet, although most of it is very light, repetitive or speculative in nature. And above all much of it is US originated. The Internet is its own best publicist and there are many web sites dedicated to chronicling every aspect of it. Online surveys abound and, indeed, journalists have featured in them. The press itself is also a good source of information on the Internet. This section takes the best and most current of the Internet reports and news items available, using them to set the scene for, and inform, the fieldwork described in the following chapters. It does this by:

1. Establishing some general characteristics – and statistics – about the Internet itself and its users. To fully understand the significance of what is occurring in the media in respect of the Internet it is necessary to establish what is happening globally. It is important to do this because it was the general reports, rumours and anecdotes of what was going on that fired our interest in investigating the Internet phenomenon in the first place – raising in our minds the possibility of all this leading to an information big bang in the media. Also, it was necessary to clothe our largely qualitative data with quantitative data – and the literature seems at times wholly absorbed with statistics, so it was a good source

2. Reviewing what has been already discovered about the use of the Internet by the media. While the present study constitutes the first major scholarly investigation of the use of the Internet in the British media, a number of reports have emerged from the US on the topic. These reports – many obtained via the Internet – provide interesting material: partly because the US leads in the introduction of Internet, and partly because the US situation appears to be unique (in respect of the public availability of government information, for instance). Such discussions as have occurred in the UK press are also evaluated.

3. Placing the current study in the context of previous online research undertaken in the media. The Internet is, after all, an online system of sorts, albeit on a giant scale. It has a long pedigree – if not a long life, and what has been learnt about the use of commercial online systems, like FT Profile, by journalists, can

assist us in our understanding of the Internet too. This is especially so in the case of end-use and its significance to the information profession. New Media journalists in particular are guilty of losing sight of the media's online pedigree; and they do this to their cost.

The size and growth of the Internet

Two of the most interesting (and hyped) aspects of the Internet are its alleged size (enormous) and growth (phenomenal) – and here we are talking about both its physical size and usage. It is the rate of growth perhaps, more than its physical size, or number of users, that causes the alarm, panic, and the soul-searching seen so frequently in the popular and professional press. The trouble is, that while these characteristics of the Internet are beguiling to journalists and the general public alike, the waters are easily muddied. This would not matter so much if it was not for the fact that it is the scale of growth that drives many organisations and individuals into investing heavily in the Internet. Of course, there is the real fear of being left behind by its progress. The figures seem to be growing exponentially and appear to be out of control. The main Internet driver seems to be growth itself: the Internet is a massive self-feeding mechanism.

If the numerous reports in the media are to be believed then the use of the Internet is growing at a spectacular rate, and will continue to do so, even faster in the near future (*The Guardian*, 1997). Pundits proclaim that, with this enormous growth, will come 'dramatic changes ... to contemporary society' (Batty & Barr, 1994). However, even before you can begin to contemplate what these 'dramatic changes' might be, there is a need to examine more closely the figures that are bandied about. This is not easy because the picture is rapidly changing, with data being recalculated, redefined and reappraised seemingly daily. The first problem is defining what precisely it is that is being measured (the term 'Internet' is not used in any standard way) and the second is sorting out which method of calculation is being used – or should be used (there are a large variety). Given (a) that there are differences of opinion on both counts, and (b) that we are talking – whatever the definition and method of calculation – about something that is happening globally, then there are bound to be huge differences in the figures. Take the problem of definition first: terms such as 'cyberspace', 'the Internet', 'the Net', the 'Information superhighway' and even the World Wide Web are all being used, apparently synonymously, to describe the now vast network of computers interconnected via the telecommunications infrastructure. Even the word 'online' has been redefined (stolen perhaps) to incorporate the Internet. As a result, the original online services – the online commercial hosts – have been re-badged as 'oldline'. The rise of the Intranet – localised mini-Internets serving specific communities or organisations – is sure to compound the problem of definition. Although there is now an 'official' definition of the Internet one suspects that it will continue to be used as a label for any extensive, publicly accessible and geographically wide computer network.

For the purposes of establishing size and growth statistics the Internet will be regarded as the computer network that is linked by a 'globally unique address space based on the Internet Protocol (IP)', is able 'to support communications using the Transmission Control Protocol/ Internet Protocol (TCP/IP)' and to 'provide … services layered on [this] communications and related infrastructure' (Leiner et al, 1997). The conformity, at least in statistics relating to the historical growth of the Internet, suggests that there is some agreement as to what commentators, if not the general public, consider to be 'the Internet'. There is a third problem, though: data collection methods, sampling frames and samples leave much to be desired. This is partly a problem of the newness of the Internet, but also partly to do with the fact that some of the parties have a vested interest in talking up the size and growth figures – often for advertising purposes. This has an impact on the quality of use/user surveys that will be referred to in the following sections.

Number of hosts

Determining the size of the Internet in terms of the number of hosts connected to it is fraught with difficulties. The simplest and most straightforward measure is to count the number of 'hosts' connected to the Internet (Batty & Barr, 1994), although even here there are the problems of establishing what precisely a 'host' is, and what we mean by 'connected'. Gray (1996) raises the issues of 'hosts' versus 'host names' and 'web sites' versus 'web pages'. His definition of a host, as an IP address, appears to have general support (despite the fact that one computer may have more than one of these), for his host estimates are supported by Huizer (1997), Hobbes (1996) and Lynch (1997). Gray also distinguishes between being 'on the Internet', as in having a host name and IP address on a name server, and having all these characteristics and responding to a 'ping' sent to determine if the computer is actually functioning on the network at any given moment. The latter requirement would exclude both computers behind security firewalls and those turned off when the signal was sent. Huizer (1997) also makes this distinction. Using definition one – all IP addressed machines – the following figures are arrived at: they show a remarkable consistency across the different sources consulted (Hobbes, 1996; Gray, 1996; and Huizer, 1997).

Date	Hosts (millions)
1993	1.3
1994	2.2
1995	4.9
1996	9.5
1997	16.1 (Huizer only)

The picture is clearly one of spectacular expansion – almost doubling every year. The Internet has grown from just four networked computers of the Advanced Research Project Agency Net (ARPANET) at the University of California to an estimated 16.1 million hosts worldwide by January 1997 (Huizer, 1997). Despite this dramatic increase, Hilgemeire (1996) claims that 'the growth has [only] just begun' and is due to 'get its full speed' in 'the second half of the 1990's'. Such statements should not be discounted as simply hype, as, to date, the rate of expansion has already exceeded all previous predictions. Thus Batty and Barr (1994), in an admittedly early study, used 1993 figures to forecast that capacity and address scheme restrictions would limit the number of hosts to 6.25 million at the current level of technology. This limit was, in fact, surpassed as early as July 1995, just two years after their paper was published. The authors also speculated that, if the aforementioned limits were set aside and their data extrapolated, by March 2005 the number of hosts would exceed the current population of the planet – something that was said about the growth in the number of journal titles in the 1970s, and, no doubt, about book publishing before that. They join Hilgemeier (1996) in turning to an S shaped growth curve to make a more rational prediction of future connectivity, although, unlike Hilgemeier, they did not put a date on when the levelling off would begin. Hilgemeirer gives the year 2007. This particular discussion is best ended with Gilster's (1997) graphic and dramatic assertion that a new network connects to the Internet every 10 minutes. By the time that this report is read there will be many, many more connections.

In an interesting exercise Batty and Barr (1994) produced information on the geographical spread of the hosts and related this to national populations, ending up with a calculation based on the number of hosts per 1,000 people. In these terms, Northern Europe and Switzerland showed the greatest connectivity. High figures for Norway, Iceland and the Scandinavian countries lead the authors to generalise high levels of Internet growth as 'a phenomenon of small isolated countries.' This hypothesis is also advanced later in the case of Internet usage. Victor Keegan (1997), of *The Guardian*, notes another feature of the geographical spread of hosts (sites, for him) – its inequality: 96% of them are located 'within the rich 27-nation OECD area'.

More recently the number of pages on the World Wide Web has been used as an index of Internet size (*The Guardian*, 1997). It is claimed that there are now 30 million pages on the World Wide Web; just four years ago (1993) there were only 130,000 (Keegan, 1997). With the 'new network every ten minutes' comment of Gilster in mind, these estimates must surely be millions out by now.

Number of users

All kinds of methods have been used to obtain user figures: telephone and face-to-face interviews, mailed and web questionnaires and subscriber lists have all been turned to. Despite, possibly because of, this, calculating the number of Internet users is even more problematic than counting hosts. The first problem is that computers are often equated with people or users. Batty and Barr (1994) point out that a PC may (though not necessarily) have the same status as a mainframe supercomputer if IP addresses are counted 'one for one', but the number of users will differ enormously between the two machines. Plainly a connection does not mean use and, on the other hand, one connection might involve many users. For this reason modem ownership figures – it is said, for instance, that the total number of adults owning a modem is around in 15% in the UK – have to be treated with a high degree of caution (*The Times* Interface, 1997). *IT Link* (1996) claims that even 'reputable sources' range in their estimates of global Internet users by a factor of four, from 15 to 60 million. *The Guardian* plumps for a figure somewhere between the two, claiming a current population of 40 million (Keegan, 1997); a figure that gets broad support from Gilster (1997), the popular Internet writer. Nua Internet Surveys (1997) gives the number at 45 million. However, any given figure is dependent upon the definition with which you start – and especially whether you are counting home or business users or both (industry commentators are very bad at stating which); and this really matters, for it is forecasted that that there will be more than twice as many home users as business users by the end of the century (Oldfield, 1997).

Turning more closely to the situation in the UK, using data from (unreferenced) surveys by NOP, Dataquest and Romtec, *IT Link* puts a figure of two million for the number of British users. Nua, however, cite an NOP Research Survey claiming a UK population of 4.5 million (Nua Internet Surveys, 1997). The thorny problem of what constitutes 'use' and, consequently, 'users', was not broached. Lawson (1996) approaches the topic from a different perspective, suggesting that by the middle of 1996 8% of the population had accessed the Internet at least once and that would rise to 10% by the end of the year. If you take the relatively hard – but narrow – measure of the number of registered dial-up users with commercial providers, you arrive at a figure of just 792,000. One of the most recent polls (NOP, 1997) introduces the very slippery term 'access' to the discussion. According to NOP one in 25 households (another interesting variable) have 'access' to the Net. This figure is a big increase on the last survey (1996), when it was more like one in 50. The same survey gives a British population of three million Web users.

The international comparisons made by *IT Link* are interesting. In Germany two million people had work access to the Internet and in France the figure was one million with access from work (and a hundred thousand from home) and Italy ('less again'). Figures from the USA are estimated to be between 15 and 28 million, although this huge figure is forecast to be exceeded by Japan, which will reach 30 million users by the year 2000. Batty and Barr (1994) point out that patterns of both connectivity and usage are consistent with the structure of the world economy, with Western Europe and the USA predominant. They disagree with *IT Link*, however, over the position of Japan, claiming that Japan shows surprisingly low usage, and describe the country as 'a third world power' in network terms. Strict telecommunications regulations are cited as being a major factor in this apparent anomaly. Growth rates produced by CommerceNet (1996), show use in the USA and Canada, rising by 50% in a six month period, from August 1995 to March 1996, meaning that nearly a quarter of the adult population now use the Internet – a figure which places UK growth in context. Owen (1997) puts all these figures into (true) perspective by noting that even in Californian households that 'are comprehensively wired up, right down "to the cat", only 8% currently have an Internet connection'. Behind all the country comparisons lies the issue of language. English is very much the language of the World Wide Web and this must exert an influence on use, but this is not really raised as a factor in most country analyses.

Volume of use

Perhaps measuring use rather than counting users is more rewarding – and hopefully less prone to huge margins of error. After all, you can have many registered users who make very little use of the system and vice versa. Calculating the number of visits to sites rather than the number of visitors appears an attractive solution – and that is the measure favoured by most hosts when they come to assessing (and publicising) the popularity and success of their sites. This data is even more spectacular. But even here there is the problem that a visit might entail nothing more than a stop on the way to somewhere else, or worse, an unwanted visit (an irrelevant link). What significance is there in that? Also, if a number of features in the site are utilised during a visit by one person this may be counted as a number of visits – inflating use figures significantly. This is best illustrated by some figures IBM released regarding 'use' of the site set up for Garry Kasparov's confrontation with their Deep Blue computer: according to IBM they received 3.5 million visits, but these visits resulted in 65 million hits or search operations (Keegan, 1997). Plainly this example refers to home or personal use – and all the most popular sites appear to be those aimed at the consumer (something that will be returned to later); but even academic/business sites exhibit high levels of use and growth. Thus, Agriculture Online, a US service offering farm news, such as commodity prices, obtains five million hits in a month. Two years ago that figure was less than a fiftieth of that.

Where sites require a user to register, another type of use data can be obtained. Possibly this subscriber or membership data is rather harder than some of the other use indicators that have been already reviewed, because there is a solid expression of a longer term interest in the case of people who take the time to register – a wish to come back again. Figures again can be impressive, with *The Times* Internet edition now boasting more than a million registered users. It would seem that many of these users are from abroad (and sports fanatics); but whether they are personal or office users is unknown (Clements, 1997). The *Daily Telegraph* claims 800,000 subscribers, with 38,000 readers visiting its site every day (Drayton, 1997). Most of these readers are young professionals. The *Times* and *Telegraph* sites are free, but even in the case of sites that charge, figures can be quite impressive. *The Wall Street Journal* exceeded 100,000 paying customers for its web edition in April 1997, just one year after it started charging (Nua Internet Surveys, 1997).

Finally, in the rush to demonstrate the march of the Internet, some researchers have chosen awareness as a measure. Of course, awareness is a vague word – and it can be a long, long way from use. One such study claimed that 'almost every adult in Europe, the Americas and the Far East has heard of the Internet' (*The Times* Interface, 1997). According to this criteria the Swedes (97% aware) lead the world, although the US, the birthplace of the Internet, was just a percentage point behind. The biggest increases in awareness since the 1996 study have taken place in Germany, Spain, Cyprus and Britain. On the same theme, a Motorola (1997) report claims that 91% have heard of the

Internet. On the indicator scale, heard of must count below awareness – you might, for instance, have read about the Internet. More interestingly the same report claims that 63% of those who have heard about the Internet have no interest in it.

Patterns of use and user characteristics

Because of the volatility and rapidly changing nature of the data only the most recent studies – those published in 1996 and 1998 – have been used here. Also, because of the very different situations in the two countries, US and UK studies are carefully distinguished in the text.

General purpose of use

The Internet is unusual in that it is a genuinely popular information system, a system used as much, if not more, for personal use than work use. But it is not easy to determine the scale of personal use. Home and personal use are often confused. While much home use is personal or leisure use, people do work from home – and the Internet actually facilitates this. Also, people who use the Internet at work use it for personal and recreational purposes. In some professions, like journalism, there is a very blurred line separating personal and work Internet use. The distinction would be very difficult to make in the case of sports and features reporters.

High consumer use is a main feature of the Internet: Pitkow and Kehoe (1996), in a study that appears to based on global data, found that 63.6% of all respondents 'primarily' accessed the Web from home. The figure was somewhat lower in the case of European users – just 36.7%. The more recent NOP survey (1997) is broadly in line with this finding, claiming that 34% of people use the Internet from home. Home use is said to be growing faster than office use – partly because it starts from a much smaller base (businesses entered the arena first), and partly because of the huge size of the potential population (everyone is a consumer). In the UK, home use of the Internet rose 150% in 1996 (Lawson, 1996). Future growth is likely to be even more spectacular if plans to link televisions to the Internet come about. As Keegan (1997) pointed out, 'fewer than two million people in Britain have PCs (not all with modems), compared with 22 million households with television sets'. By the end of the century it is forecast there will be 32 million home users as compared to 14 million business users (Oldfield, 1997). Comparative data from the US shows that in the USA home use was stabilising at around 10.3 million (Rackiewicz, 1996).

As mentioned previously, home use is not the same thing as personal use. Thus the INTECO study reported by Rackiewicz (1996) notes that although home use was not increasing in the US, 'more adults were accessing the Internet at work to get personal information.... Users at work generally have higher bandwidth available to them and they can write off Internet/online subscriptions as a work related expense, rather than having to pay for it personally'. Of course, it is easy to become mesmerised with figures and it is salutary to note that even in the wired United States 70% of personal computer-owning house-holds do not use the Internet or online services.

Evidence from site usage also points to high volumes of home/ personal use. The most popular sites are those of large consumer appeal. Thus the Queen's Internet web site was accessed 6.25 million times in one month (Knight, 1997). And a relatively unknown (by UK users anyway) 'alternative' consumer health site – the Ask Dr Weil site – attracted more than 2 million visits in April 1997 alone (Driscoll, 1997). Even if the number of users is somewhat lower than the number of accesses, because of people visiting the site more than once, we are talking about phenomenal levels of use – of what was, not so long ago, regarded as too difficult a system for mass use (CD-ROMs were largely introduced because of the alleged difficulties with remote online systems).

Work/Business use

There is general agreement regarding the extent of Internet use at work, with studies on both sides of the Atlantic showing a substantial increase; for example, from 17.4 to 24 million (32%) in the six months from May to September 1996 in the case of the US (Rackiewicz, 1996). The same study also claimed business to business transactions were increasing through the appearance of 'intranets' while Brennan (1997), using unreferenced data from *The Wall Street Journal* (28 March 1997) to describe this increase as 'skyrocketing'. In the UK Jameson et al's NOP (1997) survey indicated that shopping on the World Wide Web doubled between June and December 1996, with 22% of current (December 1996) users saying that they intended to use the network for this purpose. In the US The Internet Informer (1997) claimed that subscribers to consumer services increased by 51% in 1996. Also noted by the NOP (19997) was the possibly surprising finding that usage figures were geographically uniform – London and the South East had, predictably, dominated in previous studies but this was no longer the case. The UK study added the interesting point that the number of users doubled in firms employing fewer than 50 staff. A study of small business use of the Web (Oldfield, 1997) partly confirmed this finding. British small businesses' Internet use was above the European average, with 40% of them having email facilities

(European average 32%) and 32% using the Net for information (European average 24%). But in terms of business use of the Web, it is again the smaller countries – Malta, Switzerland and Finland – that lead the rest of Europe in terms of Internet and email use.

Companies may be worried about trading on the Internet, but they do not seem worried about being connected to it: Durlacher's Quarterly Internet Report (cited in Nua Internet Surveys, 1997) claims that 85% of large UK corporates have some form of Internet access, and by the end of the year the figure was likely to be 92%. The travel and automobile trade were tipped to be the biggest growth sectors on the Internet.

Gender

There is broad agreement amongst international commentators on the impact of gender on Internet use. Men were by far the biggest users, although women were rapidly catching them up. Surveys conducted in 1994 and 1996, using global figures, show that female use of the Web rose from just 5% in January 1994 to 31% in November 1996 (Pitkow and Kehoe, 1996). This latter figure is broadly in line with those of Lawson (1996), and NOP (1997) – 33% and 35% respectively. However, the CommerceNet study (Rackiewicz, 1996) gave a higher figure – 40% of the population. The difference might possibly be explained by the US origins of the CommerceNet study. Pitkow and Kehoe (1996) found a higher representation of women amongst US Internet users. By contrast, European users were predominantly male, with only 19.8% of searchers being female. The shrinking of the gender gap is put down to the fact that: 'men having been using it [the Internet] in the office and bringing technology into the home ... once people [presumably women] find out about the Net they are hooked' (*The Times* Interface, 1997).

A further shrinking of the gap is forecast. By comparing 'long term' with 'newcomer' users, the CommerceNet study was able to highlight a trend towards greater female use, although whether this will reach, or even surpass, 50% is not clear. A 1995 NOP report showed female use at just 25%. They note that 'current' (December 1996) 'use now reflects the approximate proportion of female to male PC users in Britain – i.e. one third to two thirds'. The 1997 NOP survey indicated that in fact it might have surpassed that: 'the number of women as a proportion of the overall Internet user base is continuing to increase, representing approximately two in five of all current users'. There is some evidence to suggest that women and men use the Internet in different ways, with men seeming to enjoy browsing and showing a high tolerance of its imperfections, whereas women appear relatively disorientated and disenchanted with the Internet (Ford and Miller,

1996). Women also tend to use it for work purposes, while men often search for items of personal interest.

Age

Piktow and Kehoe (1996) are also in a very good position to throw light on age trends, as their World Wide Web survey results now draw on a bank of data collected every six months over a period of three years. Their studies are valuable also for their sample size – reaching 15,000 online respondents for their sixth survey. Their longitudinal analysis indicates that, although the average Web user is – as expected – relatively young, the average age of users is steadily increasing, reaching 34.9 years from the latest returns available. This figure is broadly in line with that reported in *The Times* Interface (1997): 'most web users are in the 35-to-45 age range'. NOP (1997) claim to see the strongest growth in the 25-34 age. What then of children's use of the Internet? According to Consumer Technology Index of Computer Intelligence (1997) there are 1.5 million child users of the Internet in the US alone (1996 figures). Already 'more than' 50% of US households with children now have PCs. With increased government initiatives and pressure aimed at wiring public schools for Internet access, Jupiter Communications predict that the growth in number of children with access to the World Wide Web will grow to 20.2 million by the year 2002 (Digital Kids, 1997)

Occupation

More than half of those aged 19 to 25 are in education. The value of the Internet for educational purposes is also highlighted by NOP (1997), which shows growth in the educational area to be the greatest – increasing by 48% in the past year – while those older than this were more likely to be in computer related professions (Digital Kids, 1997). This fits well with the CommerceNet results if one assumes older users were also 'long time' users. European users were more likely to be in computers or education than their US counterparts.

Other characteristics

The CommerceNet study alerts us to many other characteristics of Internet users, and it seems to be that the face of the typical Internet user is changing. Fewer Internet users now (September 1996) consider themselves to be 'computer professionals' (11% newcomers, to 23% long time users); fewer newcomers have worked with computers for the past five years (59% from 70%); fewer have a college degree (72% from 88%) and fewer live in households with an income of $80,000 or more (17% from 27%). Usage among newcomers was lighter than with long term users, suggesting that as users become familiar with the

Internet their overall use of it increases, with the World Wide Web capturing an ever greater share of online time. The investigators final conclusions are worth quoting at length: 'New users differ significantly from previous users. While still upscale, they now cover a broader spectrum of educational backgrounds, less likely to be computer professional or any other managerial or professional occupation, and live in lower income households. They are lighter users and are more likely to be using the Internet for personal reasons ... Much of these changes are likely the result of increases in penetration of Online Services and Internet Service Providers, the steps taken to facilitate World Wide Web access, exposure in the mainstream media and rapid increase in penetration to a point where a large proportion of the population at least knows someone who has access to the Internet' (CommerceNet, 1996).

Through the Piktow and Kehoe study we also know something about the political affiliation of Internet users: 'centrists' were the largest group of Web users, followed by 'left liberals' and then 'libertarians'); and their marital status (45.7% were married). You could not imagine users of Dialog or Blaise-Line being asked these questions! It shows how things have changed, how use of this information system is seen as something different and more important.

To summarise, the absolute size and growth figures we have on the Internet are probably unreliable and the data are best regarded as indicators, relative measures of growth.

The special case of journalists

Journalists have always been in the information front-line: after all, information is the commodity with which they work. They have had a succession of computerised systems thrown at them – and in that respect the Internet is nothing new. But they cannot really ignore – though they may reject – the Internet, for it has so much potential to change their working lives; not only in terms of the way they gather information and communicate, but also in regard to where they practice their craft (on hard copy or electronic newspapers). The use of online commercial hosts by journalists pre-dated the arrival of the Internet by some 12 years and we know quite a lot about how they were received. This data is valuable in gaining an understanding of how the Internet is being, and is likely to be, received.

Use of commercial online hosts

Computers have been changing the way journalists do their jobs 'ever since newspaper newsrooms threw out their Royal typewriters and switched to cold type production systems and television newsrooms went from tape splicing to digital editing' (Paul, 1996). Although computers have been used in the US for reporting for several decades, dating back to their use in covering presidential elections in the early fifties (Garrison, 1997b), they have only been in use in the UK for last 15 years or so. Their use for editorial information seeking purposes in the UK can be dated to the arrival of FT Profile (then World Reporter) in the libraries and newsrooms in the mid-eighties (Nicholas et al, 1987; 1988). FT Profile proved the dominant host, but NEXIS, Dialog, Reuters TEXTLINE and Business Briefing later found niches for themselves. Take-up amongst journalists was always patchy, with some broadsheet journalists (at *The Guardian, The Times/Sunday Times* and *The Financial Times* for instance) taking to the new retrieval medium with enthusiasm and tabloid journalists (at the Mirror group, *The Mail,* and *The Express*) preferring to stick with their hard copy cuttings. Even at the broadsheet newspapers less than a quarter of all the journalists chose to use online, the rest either delegated the search, were ignorant of online's presence, or felt that online had nothing to offer them (Nicholas, 1996). Even those who chose to search themselves – several times a day in some cases – also delegated some of their searching, usually the more difficult searches or those that had to be conducted on unfamiliar hosts. Things were complicated by the fact that the arrival of computerised information systems into newspapers gave rise to a debate (still unresolved in some quarters of the industry) over ownership and territory. A number of librarians, like those at *The Independent* and the Mirror Group, argued that FT Profile and the like were a library resource and their efficient use – because of their high cost – demanded that this should be the case. Broadcasters were even more adamant about the (alleged) inefficiencies of end-use and, until very recently, online at the BBC and Independent Television remained firmly in the hands of the library staff.

Online was used for a wide variety of purposes, although fact-finding and browsing for ideas were the main ones. The searches of journalists were typically short – the majority took less than 10 minutes – and simple: few words or commands were used. The characteristics of the online users were: they tended to be male, have an interest in computers and work in certain departments – City and Foreign for instance. The introduction of online searching did herald the decline (the death in the case of the Mirror Group) of the cuttings collection. The labour intensiveness of the operation ensured this; but it did not lead to the demise of the library. Indeed, end-use seemed to have a stimulative effect leading to higher volumes of delegation; although it did require a change in staffing requirements – computer proficiency became a premium. In general though, commercial online systems were introduced slowly into newspapers, without any fundamental changes taking place in the ways that newspapers were organised or reporters worked. Probably library staff benefited the most (there was a rise in status for some) and saw the greatest changes (a huge shift towards computerisation).

A variant form of end-use has more recently taken hold – and that is the end-use of internal databases, containing the company's own newspapers, and sometimes also the titles of other newspapers obtained in swap arrangements with other media companies. Most of the internal databases were put in place in the mid 1990s. The net impact has seen end-use trickling down even into newspapers that had for so long fought shy of end-use – *The Mirror* for instance. The principal reason for this being that searching is now perceived to be 'free' – something internal databases have in common with the Internet. Even in the case of newspapers that have commercial online arrangements, internal databases have had their impact – commercial online searching has fallen. Searching internal databases is a relatively new phenomenon and its impact is still being felt. Many a journalist will still be wrestling with the problems of searching these systems, thus possibly delaying or masking the impact the Internet will have.

Computer-aided journalism

In the USA the rise of online commercial host searching and the parallel development of public records becoming widely available in a digitised form – all of which could be evaluated by powerful statistical and relational database programmes – gave birth to 'Computer Assisted Journalism/Reporting' (known interchangeably as CAJ or CAR.). According to Paul (1996), one of the early pioneers, although the change to computer assisted production 'dramatically' altered the way news is delivered (on both sides of the Atlantic), the impact it has had on news-gathering has been more subtle, but 'no less dramatic'. CAJ has developed into 'a two pronged approach to news gathering ... online based news gathering that uses specialised commercial services and Internet based services such as the World Wide Web, and database oriented analysis using existing and originally created databases from both the public and private sectors' (Garrison, 1997b). CAJ had grown to such an extent that by the mid nineteen nineties 'leading daily newspapers [in the USA] had developed not only a routine approach to investigative projects that included CAR when appropriate, but a growing number had begun to integrate CAR tools and strategies into daily reporting by design' (Garrison, 1997b).

CAJ has spawned a number of specialisms, of which Computer Assisted Reference, is probably the key one. It concerns the use of online resources such as 'dictionaries, encyclopaedias, gazetteers, almanacs and glossaries', some of which may now be found on the Internet and be accessed by journalists or media librarians. In another contribution Paul (1996) provides the URLs and a brief outline of the contents of a number of locations relating to all of these categories, together with some prudent advice, including a warning to beware of incomplete or unauthenticated compilations by 'hobbyists'. 'Computer Assisted Research' is another specialism. It entails working with secondary material. In terms of electronic information this may include databases of reports and articles that may be accessed online and interrogated, online news releases and, these days, World Wide Web home pages of important people or organisations. Having the facility to access primary news sources, however, in the form of using hyperlinks to personalities' email addresses, receiving messages sent by newsmakers to bulletin boards, and undertaking other interactive activities on the Internet blurs both the divisions between types and statuses of sources but also, consequently, between the relative roles of the information officer and reporter. Semonche (1993) provides an interesting example of the nature and potential of computer assisted research. She describes how the *News & Observer* acquired and indexed 3000 US state government databases on magnetic tape form, and shows how access to these helped reveal, for example, that a chicken processing plant destroyed by fire hadn't been inspected once by Health and Safety officials in its 12 years of existence.

What Paul terms Computer Assisted Rendezvous is possibly the most exciting and potentially fruitful prospect in journalism's exploitation of the Internet. She equates her definition of the word 'rendezvous' (a place to which people customarily come in number), with the 'virtual communities' of the 'wired world'. These are the thousands of news-groups, bulletin boards and listservs the Internet is spawning that link people with the same interests, ideals or professions in electronic discussion groups. Rheingold (1993) describes this aspect of the Internet as being 'like a giant coffee house with a thousand rooms; it is also a worldwide digital version of the speaker's corner in Hyde Park ... it is a mass medium because any piece of information put onto the Net has a potential worldwide reach of millions'.

What computer assisted journalism in general – and the Internet in particular – appears to have done in the US is to have blurred – or redrawn – the lines between librarians and reporters. News librarians now have access to primary/raw news, once the monopoly of the reporter (Garrison, 1996a and 1997a; Semonche, 1993). Of course, the Internet also gives the general public similar access to the same primary sources (Nicholas and Frossling, 1996). Online commercial hosts did break one journalist monopoly before that, which has largely gone unnoticed – and that was regarding direct access to the wire services, but they never offered this in real-time. So they never encroached quite so much as the Internet does, in theory, on the journalists' information patch. Indeed, in regard to commercial online services it really was more a case of giving the journalist the tools of the librarian. The tables have been turned with the Internet. What the Internet has achieved is the blurring of distinctions between primary and secondary source material. Primary material – personal conversation, witness accounts, letters etc. were never the domain of the information system. Now they are. Accounts of the Internet being used to broadcast news by actual participants serve to illustrate the point. Bacard (1993), for example, describes how dissident Chinese students used 'computer networks' to communicate directly with the outside world when other media were being routinely censored by the authorities, and Press (1991) reproduces a startling email message from Moscow sent during the attempted coup in 1991. It includes the lines 'I've seen tanks with my own eyes', 'They stopped CNN an hour ago' and 'We are sitting at home distributing all the information we have ... Thank Heaven [the KGB] don't consider us mass media!' Other similar reports relating primary news sources, in the form of statements or accounts by participants and eyewitnesses at major events, are far from rare (see, for example, Long (1994) regarding Sarajevo).

The implication of these developments and possibilities for news librarians and journalists is, of course, enormous. The question of access to primary (and, potentially, far more current) literature emanating from politicians, personalities etc. and others involved in the news is not a mere academic one, for it possibly changes the information environment, affecting the activities of librarians, journalists and other professionals – and not only those in the media. Whereas, for example, it has been the traditional role of the investigative reporter to find news creators, interview them, observe, and build up banks of primary data, the Internet has created a situation in which librarians themselves and, indeed, the general public, have direct access to these sources. For Nicholas and Frossling (1996), developments such as these question 'even the fundamental premise of professional journalism itself'. The reporter's world is said to have fundamentally changed by suffering the loss of exclusivity over the news and monopoly over news production, and a weakening of the media's role as news arbitrators. They point out that whereas at one time journalists dominated and controlled the flow of news information, nowadays 'anyone with a PC and modem can access wire services, news broadcasts and electronic clippings services'. They can access newsgroups too: 'when earthquakes or other catastrophes occur, cyberspace conferences are immediately set up to relay information, pinpoint locations (and) notify distant relatives'. Even traditional news channels can no longer be the property of the media – the wire services newspapers rely on to cover the world are now available in real time to the general public too. Thus the Internet has given the individual 'an engaged role in the movement of information and opinion'. In short, 'for the first time in history, the general public has the ability to determine what it finds important, and furthermore, individuals can express themselves fully in an unedited and uncensored form.'

What we have been describing in this section is largely the American vision and experience. A rather more conventional attitude towards media librarianship, a more sceptical attitude towards machine-readable data, greater demarcation lines between the work of journalists and librarians and the great dearth of publicly available data in the UK has meant that CAR has failed to take root in the UK to the same extent. There are some notable exceptions – *Panorama* and *The Guardian*, for instance. And even when it is practised in the UK nobody talks about it as being anything special – 'Oh, computer aided journalism, we have been doing that all the time' is a typical response.

Use of the Internet

As can be seen from the above discussion and the literature that has informed it, there can be little doubt that the *potential* for the exploitation of this new mass medium – the Internet – by both professions is enormous. It is therefore surprising that there has been a dearth of detailed, formal research into how the Internet has impacted on the information seeking practices of journalists and media librarians. Yes, lots of people speculate in print on what might or could happen but rarely is any hard data produced. The closest we get to this is the now ubiquitous Internet-delivered questionnaire surveys. Apart from their inherent bias towards users of the Internet these surveys are limited in that they tend to be concerned only with quantifying the increase, although not nature, of computer use in the media. Questions exploring the profound implications for the information environment remain, as yet, unaddressed. Furthermore these surveys are exclusively US in their coverage.

Typical of the research carried out to date is that by Ross and Middleberg (1997) who conduct an annual postal questionnaire survey of 'The Media in Cyberspace', the latest one – the fourth – being carried out between September and November 1997. According to the authors, the surveys 'provide by far the largest body of data on journalists' use of cyberspace', with 2,000 US magazines randomly sampled, except those prominently concerned with computing issues, which were deliberately under-represented. US national daily and Sunday papers are also surveyed. As the questions – and answers – have changed a number of the annual surveys have been sourced. The latest survey saw 2,500 journalists responding – the majority coming from publications that are already online. Just 9% had no Internet access or failed to indicate that they had access. In 1995 that figure was 37%: enormous changes, then, here. Of those that had access, 45% claimed that their colleagues went online every day. Another 29% went online weekly. Both figures are up by approximately one-third on the previous year's (1996) survey. Despite this seemingly dramatic change in information seeking behaviour of US journalists, the study makes plain that 'for all the hype about online technology changing the way journalists do business, most journalists get story ideas the old fashioned way. This is described as getting a pitch, consisting of finding sources and leads. Few journalists troll the Internet in a relentless search for stories.' Thus in the 1997 study none of the Internet sources – listservs, email, the World Wide Web and newsgroups – were cited by more than 4% as their primary source of stories – this figure was to double in the 1997 survey, however. Plainly, the Internet is still an information sideshow, albeit increasingly less so. The 1997 study indicates where things might be changing. It appears that journalists now rank the Internet as their second most important sources – after a live source – in the case of a breaking story.

Journalists use the Internet for a wide variety of purposes – 20% of respondents cited more than ten purposes. There is an inevitable overlap between categories. Article research and reference – a catch-all category if there ever was one – has been the chief purpose for a number of years, named by two-thirds of the journalists. But in 1997 it was eclipsed by personal email. Email appears to be the big growth area, having risen in three years from 58% to 70%. However, use for emailing sources dropped for the second year to 37%. It appears that: the practice of making journalists email addresses public is becoming less popular, journalists are less likely to respond to email; and journalists are less interested in keeping in close email touch with their readers. The novelty appears to be wearing off in the face of the email barrage. The other main purposes to which the Internet was being put were: downloading (45%); finding new sources/experts (42%); reading publications online (38%), interestingly, something which is declining in popularity; press releases (39%); accepting story ideas (30%); newsgroups (26%); and images (21%).

As in previous years' findings, when journalists did venture onto the Internet they were 'more likely to use free information services provided online by non-profit or public interest groups than corporations'. This was thought to result from a wariness of business interests leading to sins of omission in companies' information provision – nevertheless financial information is usually what they are looking for. Nothing really special or innovative about that. With regard to web site preferences, Ross and Middleberg note the current tendency of site creators 'to go overboard with fancy web site videos and audio feeds', but found that journalists did not tend to be interested in these facilities – journalists, processors and packagers themselves, are very wary of anybody else doing it on their behalf. What they wanted was a fast-loading home page with a journalists' track. Fewer than half the journalists bothered to respond to questions about multimedia. Not one respondent in 1996 cited video as an important reason to access a web site, and under 4% mentioned audio. 1997 saw the numbers creep up to 10. Photo images were, however, valued, although even here only 16% indicated that they would be an important attribute of a site. Journalists' web site requirements are for *just the facts, please, and throw in a few photos.*

Returning to the relative unpopularity of email – especially in the light of the rapidity with which email has taken hold in many sectors of society – especially in academe – and journalists' preference for personal contact, surprisingly, only 6% of journalists rated an email feedback mechanism incorporated into a web site as important. This finding – and many of the others previously reported – certainly does call into question the impact that computer-aided journalism is really having on US journalists. Telephone contact was still the preferred medium for direct and personal contact. Interestingly, there are marked differences between newspaper and magazine journalists. For the former, face-to-face contact is the overwhelming favourite (74%), followed by telephones (19%) and email a distant equal third – with fax – (4%). By contrast, magazine reporters rate email second among these three options (at 26%), with the telephone top with 45% and face-to-face contact at 27%. This may be explained by the urgency with which newspaper reporters have to gather data – they simply do not have time to wait for an email reply delivered at the convenience of the respondent. It may be that face-to-face and telephone contact will remain the preferences for these journalists for the foreseeable future, simply on the basis of the instant, interactive and familiar communication they afford. Magazine writers, on the other hand, have a more flexible time span in which to make their enquiries, and a delay of one or even two days for an email to generate a response may be quite acceptable in their particular information seeking environment A need for an understanding of the data and issues also helps explain all journalists preference for personal communication forms, whether they be face-to-face, telephone or email.

The 'Media in Cyberspace' study first began asking questions about search engine preferences in 1996. The authors note the various problems associated with eliciting information of this kind, such as that some engines are free standing web sites but can appear in other sites too (such as AltaVista, which can be found on a Yahoo page); that some services offer multiple searches simultaneously by combining search engines; and that changes are made 'every day' to search engines. Results, therefore, need to be interpreted with caution, and the fact that Yahoo was ranked first (by 43% of respondents), AltaVista second (19%), Netscape's site third (16%), and that 15% did not answer suggests that there is some confusion in the respondents mind. What this shows more than anything else is probably the futility of asking such questions; far better to ask journalists to describe how and why they search as they do – something perhaps you can only do in an interview (hence the attraction of the interview to us). Of more interest and validity was the finding that 'considerably less than half' the number of participating journalists could undertake a Boolean search (something that Web search engines are alleged to be rapidly making obsolete). However, even this statistic, portrayed as something negative, is an improvement on the proportion of journalists who could perform Boolean searches on FT Profile (Nicholas, 1996). Yahoo was considered 'easy to use' for non-Boolean trained users and their preferred search engine, while Netscape's popularity was explained by the fact that the Netscape Navigator 'browser is set to use the Netscape site as the home page'. The lack of popularity of Lycos surprised the authors because it 'seems to have the largest number of web pages catalogued' (but then when has size alone ever been an important characteristic in the end-use of an information service?). Of course, Lycos has disadvantages: 'the search display can be very confusing … the database is not purged for a while … there is no indication of what [search term match] options mean' (Liu 1996), though there is no real evidence to indicate that journalists are aware of this.

There were two other interesting pieces of information contained in the Cyberspace study: (1) that a high proportion of journalists access the Internet from home (38%); (2) that access to both the Internet from home (up by 9% in two years) and work (up by 18%) has been increasing, but work has been increasing at a faster rate.

Since 1994 Garrison (1997a) has also conducted a similar study to that of Middleberg/Ross. This study is somewhat smaller in size (about 200 respondents) and rather broader in scope (all online services are included). It attempts to discover: how many newspapers used online services, their frequency of use, the most popular resources and who actually conducted online searches. The study was broad in scope though and looked at commercial online hosts as well as the Internet. It showed that there has been considerable growth in use of online tools in news gathering in the past three years, described elsewhere by the author (1996b) as newsrooms 'flocking' to the Net. What gave rise to this vivid description was the finding that 81% of papers said they used online services in 1996, as compared to only 57% in 1994. This figure has since risen to 89% (1998). The frequency of online searching, perhaps not surprisingly, also rose, with daily, weekly and monthly searching patterns all increasing over 1994 and 1995 levels. 52% of respondents now search online daily or more frequently. As to the place of the Internet in all this, the survey makes the claim that 'the World Wide Web has become 'the online resource of choice at US daily newspapers'. In support of this statement, the author points out that the Web was used by only 25% of papers in 1994, but by 67% in 1996 and by a giant 92% in 1997. By contrast traditional online host searching is on the (slight) decline, with NEXIS-LEXIS dropping by 3% over the four year survey period.

Regarding the very important question of who conducts online news-room research, Garrison explained that 'at one time, [this] was exclusively the province of news researchers in the news department library'. Plainly, more and more non-librarians have begun to handle online research, with the survey showing that 48% of journalists did their own online research in 1997 – a rise of 24% over the last three years of the survey. If these figures mean – and it is not quite clear – that fewer librarians are conducting searches on behalf of journalists, then it would be interesting to know if that was because of the intro-duction of the Internet because the trend in the UK has been more than not for commercial end-user online searching to stimulate the delega-tion process. Other important survey revelations were these: that it is largely valid, accurate information that makes a web site worth visit-ing (ease of access is a distant second); the favourite web sites are largely governmental; and verification was the biggest problem asso-ciated with using the Web. Of course all these facts are related. In a companion study Garrison (1997b) provides further information on the use to which the widely reported and truly spectacular increased online activity is put. Online proved most useful for gathering back-ground information for news stories: 19.7% of respondents indicated that this was the case in 1996, compared with only 8.4% a year earlier. Online appears to be still used as a replacement for the cuttings files. However, 'the most stunning change' pertains to the role of online in accessing governmental information: 15.5% cited this role in 1996, but only 1.7% in 1995, reflecting, for Garrison, increased access to online governmental information 'at all levels'. (This must relate directly to the Internet and it would have been useful if the author had distinguished between commercial and Internet sources). Finding people and story sources, including expert sources, was another 'widespread' use of online services – again, journalists must largely have had the Internet in mind when asking this question. This type of use also showed an increase, albeit smaller than in the other examples, between surveys (combining results to include story and expert sources gave 7.7% in 1995 and 9% in 1996). Checking other newspapers' stories was also undertaken online by 5% of respondents in 1996 (3.5% in 1995).

The existing data – albeit exclusively US in character – *appears* to point to a redefining of both the roles of journalists and librarians taking place. But it is a pity that Garrison, and other researchers have not progressed much beyond their – sometimes ambiguous – raw questionnaire data in their investigations for we need a lot more qualitative data before we can truly assess the situation.

Little research appears to have been undertaken into the nature of the stories and articles generated by either the Internet specifically or from online sources generally, although there is some literature on the added value that electronic databases can bring to stories, and it might be supposed that some stories arising out of computer aided investigative journalism may not have surfaced had the data retrieved online not been available or easily accessible in another form. Regarding the value that electronic information can add, Garrison (1995) describes how the principally anecdotal information reporters deal with can now be supplemented by database figures showing trends so that individual testimony turns into statistical evidence. He gives the example of how a drink driving story that once might have been a simple account of an accident can now be written as illustrative of an increasing incidence of such cases in a particular local area, with such claims backed up by figures obtained online. Indeed, the story may not even, in itself, be considered 'newsworthy' enough to run but for the other evidence unearthed. In fact, British journalists have been doing this since the mid-eighties under the general name of online research – see the case of *The Guardian* City journalist looking to inject a bit of interest into a boring and repetitive annual company report in Nicholas et al (1987).

In an ongoing national (USA) research project focusing on the development and use of CAR, Garrison (1997b) attempted to establish how recent technological changes had affected the nature of both investigative and daily news reporting, and decided that an analysis of the basic subjects of the stories reported would go some way in providing an answer. His study posed three research questions:

- What are the leading daily stories and special projects that use general CAR tools and techniques?
- What are the leading daily stories and special projects that use online CAR tools and techniques?
- What are the purposes for using online CAR for these daily stories and special projects?

To answer these questions, Garrison sent questionnaires to all US daily and Sunday papers with circulations of at least 20,000. Tick box questions covered various aspects of Computer Assisted Reporting and open-ended queries sought information about 'the top three recent stories and projects' used in both 'general' and 'online' CAR. Data, available from the 1995 and 1996 rounds of the survey, revealed that there was a remarkable range in responses 'for both years for both measures' (i.e. general CAR techniques and specifically online use). The study found that even the top cited subject, education, was represented by less than 7% of the overall number of stories produced with the general help of CAR journalism, a figure that, as Garrison pointed out, indicated the overall diversity of responses. The education stories incorporating computer techniques included performance analyses of both subjects, such as student test scores and administration, in the form of budgetary and other matters. The extent to which information of this nature would be in the public domain at all in this country is debatable, and it would appear unlikely that student test results would reside in web or other Internet server directories, at least not individual and identifiable details. A similar observation could be made regarding certain budgetary information, such as staff salaries, mentioned in the study.

Elections, political campaign contributions and other political subjects ranked second. All the main UK political parties had web sites for the UK election of 1997. Again, however, the data obtainable was likely to be less than that obtainable in America – there is no obligation here, for instance, to publicly reveal sources of political funding. The third most common story category from CAR was local government spending policies, which included obtaining and analysing information on city budgets or other finance or tax issues. Articles about murder/rape, and stories discussing courts and sentencing come fourth and fifth respectively. These were the only subject categories in 1996 to take up more than 2% of CAR inspired writing. In 1995 the same subjects, plus general crime statistics analysis, mortgage loan analysis and information derived from the Department of Motor Vehicles also represented more than 2% of CAR stories each. The most frequently listed story subject resulting from specifically online research was business and finance (5.2% citing this in 1996; 4.9% in

1995). 4.9% mentioned using online sources for stories about 'the Internet or, specifically, the World Wide Web', and 'crime and courts' stories were also occasionally named (3.5%) subjects for online research in 1995. These subjects 'were not measured in 1996'. It is not clear whether this implies that no respondent listed them.

Garrison summarises these stories and story sources as generally public in nature, such as crime, courts, the Internet, elections, and education. He concludes that 'because organisations in the public sector were among the first to have digitised their data and make them available to the public, they were more often in use and more often used for investigative stories and projects. Other subject areas, such as local crime data, may not be as readily available and fewer stories were being produced'. Plainly, CAR can only thrive in an environment where information is liberally and generously placed in the electronic public domain. This is a long way from happening in the UK – and this very fact could explain why CAR has failed to take hold in this country. With improved lines of communication and more journalists sourcing their stories in the public domain duplicate stories are inevitably going to appear – and this was what Garrison noted: 'email, distribution lists, fax and the World Wide Web has facilitated the spread of story ideas and thus explains some of this duplication'.

Perceived reporting strengths of the Internet

With the information needs of the British journalist very much in mind, Nicholas and Martin (1997) highlighted a number of factors which suggested that the Internet could meet some real needs:

- Journalists often feed off the unexpected and 'it could be argued that computerised information systems (through their prodigious cross-referencing) increase the opportunities here.' And with the World Wide Web and its hypertext links a more prodigious cross-referencer you could not get.

- A high proportion of information handled by journalists is not sought, so that 'much information seeking is undertaken to provide explanation and context to this.' The Web, again, with its huge information reach could provide much of this background.

- Journalists require up-to-the minute information, and the various news wire services that feed 'real time' news stories get information to journalists more or less 'as it happens'. The Internet also offers much in the way of live relays of information. The problem with the Internet is not so much the currency of the data it offers but ascertaining its date of origin (and provenance).

- Despite long and increasing investment by newspapers in information technology of all sorts there are still problems in getting needed information. This is because many organisations – including the government, business and commerce – are 'not in the business of communication'. In theory, the Internet, through its many alternative sites should be able to help here.

- A big obstacle for journalists in meeting their information needs is the sheer volume of information they have to deal with. With a huge daily diet of phone calls, email, faxes, wire services, and 24 hour television news, this is hardly surprising: inevitably information gets in the way of information. One more communication/retrieval form of the proportions of the Internet might be expected to break the camel's back – and the Internet certainly has the propensity to do this. However, with the possibility of all information being channelled through one system – the Internet – and with the filtering tools available on the Internet (baskets and the like) it is possible to view the Internet not as a source of information overload, but as a solution to it.

- Newspapers need information from around the globe – and this inevitably stretches the resources of most newspapers. Thus *The Guardian* has only two correspondents covering the whole of Russia. Coverage has traditionally been obtained by subscribing to wire services. The enormous international – and local – reach of the Internet must offer huge opportunities here. Sometimes the opportunities have unexpected (and unwelcome) outcomes. Thus, before the Internet, foreign correspondents would report to their editors what they considered to be 'the big story' in their area. Now newsdesks search the Internet and decide from 'home' what the story is, and, in an exact reversal of past practice, instruct the foreign correspondent on what to cover. This represents a small but significant change in the information seeking environment.

Perceived reporting weaknesses of the Internet

With all the euphoria that surrounds the Internet it is not easy to criticise the resource without appearing to be old-fashioned, a Luddite, unduly negative etc. However, weaknesses there inevitably are. Coy et al (1996) point to several general problems associated with Internet use. These are that it is slow (the Web is described as the World Wide Wait), security is poor, support for multimedia is weak, and 'good stuff' is hard to find. Anecdotal evidence provided by Garrison (1996a) indicates that for journalists one of the major disincentives could be, however, the inaccurate and poor quality of the information available – the authority of the data question. He cites one commentator (Feola, 1994) as lamenting the 'misinformation explosion', and relates evidence offered to him by personal communication. Examples include missing vehicle registration numbers, obtained later by personal enquiry, and reporters' names truncated. Naturally enough, given this evidence, one editor is quoted as counselling younger reporters against relying too much on online data.

In the above examples, the accuracy of the information could be checked via other channels, as the databases cited were from identifiable public sources (such as the Department of Motor Vehicles). Looking specifically at the Internet, Garrison considers the major failing to be that of verifiability. Even much of the 'official' information available 'must be double checked', as the federal government takes no responsibility for any mistakes transmitted. Surprisingly, errors attributable to unreliable, incomplete or (possibly, on the Internet) disreputable sources are not discussed. Journalists are always in a hurry and speed of information delivery is a key characteristic of their information needs – and the Internet has a reputation for being very slow at certain times of the day. Indeed, surveys show that speed is 'the number one problem of Web users', with 69.9% of respondents complaining of this problem (Pitcow and Kehoe, 1996). Nevertheless, this represented a reduction from the 80.9% who complained in a similar survey six months earlier. But it is not just response time that we are considering here – finding something can take an age when every search seemingly produces 70,000 hits. Furner (1997) quotes the 'common aphorism' that characterises the Internet as a library, 'where the shelves keep moving, where there is no catalogue, and where an extra lorry load of books is dumped in the entrance hall every five minutes.' The continuing lack of expertise shown by news reporters with online searches has already been noted, and despite the supposedly 'user friendly' nature of Internet search engines and their employment by untrained end-users, the sheer volume of material available is likely to discourage journalists who are not short of information anyway (Nicholas and Martin, 1997). Pitkow and Kehoe (1996) even report a significant number of users (13.4%) complaining about the problem of finding sites already 'visited'.

Interestingly, few commentators mention another weakness of the Internet – the relative youth of its archives. In many cases you would be lucky to find information more than a few years old. Real-time data is not everything to journalists for they need to place currently breaking stories in a historical, social, economic etc. context. According to Nicholas and Martin's (1997) study, a considerable amount of 'old' information was also required by reporters. As many as 50% of all *Guardian* journalists, for example, 'regularly' required information that was more than two years old. Many interviewees wanted searches to delve 'as far back as [FT Profile] goes', and one even suggested, with perhaps a touch of journalistic exaggeration, searches 'to the beginning of time'. The need for historical or archival data will not so much inhibit Internet use by journalists, more likely it will make them less likely to relinquish the commercial online services. Intuitively one would certainly think that the Internet is perceived as a breeding ground for new, immediate ephemeral information, rather than as a graveyard for ageing data. Certainly Internet user studies (e.g. Gray, 1996) show a declining use of FTP and gopher searches that would access more historical records, if only by emphasising the growing fascination with the World Wide Web.

Even before the Internet arrived on the scene editors had been expressing their worries about journalists being marooned at their desks by the incoming tidal wave of information, that comes to them via the post, phone, fax, wire, television and computer. Always short of time, the pressure is for the journalist to stay in the office read the mail, take the phone calls etc. It has been argued that this can lead to journalists (and their readers) obtaining a far too institutional view-point on events. Take the case of a paper's education correspondent. 'They would get about a metre and a half of post a day. Masses will be coming from educational institutions, from pressure groups, trade unions. It is all institutional, its all about providing education – little of it is consumer oriented. It is not about what is going on in the class-rooms, it's not about what parents are wanting etc. To get that information you must leave the office. But that takes a tremendous act of will' (Nicholas and Martin, 1997). Now, whether the Internet adds to this problem really depends on the extent that consumer groups and members of the public avail themselves of the two-way opportu-nities provided by the Internet. In the US there is plenty of evidence to suggest this is happening – take the recent flurry of stories on State militias, but even in the UK things are slowly changing, with *The Guardian's* New Media Lab reporting a tremendous response to its electronic European Cup initiatives (Hunt, 1997).

Perhaps the most damning criticism of the Internet – and all it stands for, was made by the well-known *Times* journalist (and former *Times* editor), Simon Jenkins (1997). Talking about the impact of the Internet on society as a whole – but based on his own personal experience as a journalist – he says that the effect of the Internet will be both minimal and short-lived: 'the Internet will strut an hour upon the stage, and then take its place in the ranks of the lesser media' (Ceefax/Prestel, touch screen, CD-ROM). For him the really significant event was the invention of the book and he presents a long list if its merits vis-a-vis the Internet – compact, portable, independent, easy on the eye, cheap and virus-free. The Internet's (short-term) popularity is put down to the fact that it is heavily subsidised by the computer industry and government. The value of the Internet as an *aid* to information retrieval and dissemination is admitted – indeed Jenkins uses it this capacity, but even here it is a distant second to the book: 'With both the Internet and books at my disposal I make vastly more use of the latter'. Jenkins sees red over the much-lauded two-way communication characteristics of the Internet and the accompanying view that the 'closed' book (read any printed publication) is dead. To those who claim 'the advent of digital hypertext will liberate the reader from the "tyranny of the writer"' he retorts that this is 'freedom of the brain-dead'.

Conclusions

Despite considerable doubts about the quality and origin of much of the data used to chart the Internet's size and growth it is clear that we have a computer service of awesome size and growth and that it is very popular with certain sections of the population. The most recent data indicates that the Internet has become a mass market. It is esti-mated that in the twelve months to June 1998 six million adults in Britain used the Internet, and by June 1999 it will be 9 million (NOP, 1997). The fact that the number of people subscribing to *The Times* Internet site has exceeded the number buying the hard copy newspa-per is something that also warrants reflection. The Internet would appear to be passing some important milestones: the number of users exceed the readership of *The Sun*: it has a far higher user population than commercial online ever achieved, and it is now busy overhauling CD-ROM. Its influence appears to be incalculably greater than any of these information icons. It is much talked about, everybody has a view on it and its truly international character means that many in the communication business are attracted to its global presence. There is much growth in the pipeline – it is early days in the life of the Internet – but whether it can continue growing on such a scale is open to doubt, although not by the Web TV advocates. As the Internet settles in, its user profile is changing from a largely masculine academic/techno-logical one to a profile that resembles much more closely the general population of library users, book buyers and newspaper readers.

Things are much further advanced in the US. There the Internet is making even bigger in-roads. Studies point to 89% of journalists with access to the Internet having used it, and 45% making use of the Internet on a daily basis (Middleberg and Ross, 1997). As we have said, this data is likely to have painted a too rosy picture because of the methodological bias inherent in many of the studies. There are also some distinctly national factors at work. Internet use is being driven-up by free local telephone calls; the free and widespread availability of local and central Government data; the large number of 'beat' reporters employed by large local newspapers – all with a narrow, local brief; and, in the case of newspapers, by the fact that journalists are not slaves to a particular style of newspaper reporting, as they are in the UK. But even in the States – pockets of CAR activity aside – the Internet has some way to go before it displaces traditional journalistic methods. It is still nothing more than an adjunct to existing systems of communicating and gathering information. Thus the biggest survey of US journalists found that none of the Internet sources – listservs, email, the World Wide Web and newsgroups – were cited by more than 9% as their primary source of stories (Middleberg and Ross, 1997). But this study also shows that things might now be changing. Also disciples of CAR, like Garrison, have had to admit that even in the favourable climate of the US CAR has a marginal impact on newspaper reports. Possibly the most interesting finding to come out of the US is that online in general and the Internet in particular are leading to growing end-use and diminishing intermediary use. The explanation could lie in the growing use in the US media of personal researchers, working alongside journalists.

Chapter 4

Internet use and users

Internet take-up

The media was chosen for study because it was felt that journalists, as information seekers and packagers *par excellence*, should be in the advance guard of Internet users and setting a hot pace. All the indications from the United States were that this was very much the case, with more than 90% of respondents in one study indicating that they used the Internet – daily for 45% of them (Ross and Middleberg, 1997). Very early on in the project it became clear that the situation in the UK would be very different – and despite what appeared to be considerable and direct benefits for them in using the Internet (itemised in the previous section). Best estimates and straw poles (Wallace, 1998; Cole, 1997) suggested that probably fewer than one in five national journalists used the Internet, and that the proportion was much less for regional journalists – maybe fewer than one in ten in their case. These figures were inevitably rough and ready, based largely on personal experience and observation, albeit from experienced industry watchers. The likely reasons put forward for this allegedly low take-up amongst UK journalists were very interesting and are taken up more fully later on. Briefly, though, they were said to be: (1) few journalists had easy or convenient access to the Net; (2) journalists had more than enough sources and systems to get along with; (3) they did not believe the Internet was all it was cracked up to be – poor currency, poor quality and a 'dumbing down' of information were the big weaknesses for them; (4) time was their major concern and they were not at all convinced that the Internet would save them any time; (5) it was still early days. Many of the journalists were waiting for the arrival of desktop networked PCs before they tested the waters. And, according to the New Media journalists, the most enthusiastic proponents of the Internet, we are just five years into a revolution that, if the usual technological uptake pattern is followed, will take forty years to work its way through.

The project made no concerted attempt to gather quantitative data, partly because it was not a quantitative study in the first place but partly also because there was always going to be a problem with determining numbers of users in a fast changing situation. In fact 78% of the people we interviewed were indeed Internet users (see Table 2) but not too much store should be set by this for, as we mentioned in the methods section, the way journalists were recruited for interview, meant a heavy bias towards Internet users. However, on piecing together what quantitative data we did obtain, there was general agreement with the personal observations mentioned above: that use was generally low and patchy in the UK. Thus:

- A closed question interview survey of 50 randomly selected *Times* journalists showed that over two-thirds of them did not use the Internet.

- A group interview with 24 trainee journalists from various local and regional newspapers showed that here too use was patchy and low – just four (17%) used the system.

- Although 24 (56%) of the 43 people interviewed at *The Guardian/ Observer* (excluding New Media journalists) were Internet users, this in fact represents about a tenth of all journalists at the paper, and there was a strong bias towards Internet users amongst our sample. Comments from those we interviewed and the results of our own observation bear this out.

Table 2
Use of the Internet: depth interview data

	National and regional newspapers		Specialist publications & freelancers		New Media		All journalists		Librarians		Total	
	No.	%	No.	%	No.	%	No.	%	No.	%	No.	%
Users	34	60	9	82	13	93	56	68	47	94	103	78
Non-users	23	40	2	18	1	7	26	32	3	6	29	22
Sample	57	100	11	100	14	100	82	100	50	100	132	100

Use at *The Times*

Probably the questionnaire survey of 50 randomly selected *Times* journalists provides the most statistically representative picture of Internet use. This survey showed that, while over two-thirds of journalists did not use the Internet, 12% used it daily or more frequently (see Table 3), quite a polarisation, which can largely be attributed to ease of access. Thus, the few *Times* journalists who had desktop access to PCs equipped with Internet access – some working in the newsroom and those on the Interface section – were amongst the biggest users of the Internet.

Table 3
Use of the Internet by *Times* journalists

Frequency of use	No.	%
Several times a day	2	4
Once a day	4	8
Several times a week	4	8
Once a week	3	6
Once a fortnight	2	4
Variable	3	6
Didn't use	32	64
Total	50	100

Regional newspaper use

A good picture of the poverty of regional journalist Internet use emerged from group interviews that were conducted with 24 trainee journalists from various local and regional newspapers. The picture is almost universally one of patchy and low use and poor provision. The most active paper amongst them was the *Yorkshire Evening Post* where access was provided at three terminals, two for reporters, one for pictures but even then 'most reporters don't use the Net at all'. On the *Harrogate Weekly* paper, two screens were in operation but both were used by freelancers who were setting up the paper's web site: 'Reporters don't use them at all'. The *Lancashire Evening Post* (Preston) had a terminal in the newsroom, with one or two people who used it. Use is far more restricted elsewhere. It is just the supplements editor at the *Blackpool Gazette* who uses the Internet to research stories. Again it was said that 'reporters don't use the net'. Limited access and use was also reported at *Spenborough Weekly* where 'there is one computer where you can access the net, and that is in the feature writer's office. So you have to go in there from the news room, when it is not being used. I wouldn't say the reporters use it at all'; and at the *Harrogate Advertiser* where the one terminal is in the marketing office: 'reporters don't really use it'. And at the *Lancashire Evening Post* (Preston) it was a case of 'some access, but nobody uses it'.

For four newspapers there was no access whatsoever. In two cases journalists were forced to search elsewhere. At the *Yellow Advertiser* (Basildon), a keen journalist had to search from home, while at the *Ashton Weekly* a journalist went to a cybercafe to do a piece on

Africa. In the cases of the *Lancaster Guardian* and the *Chorley Guardian* not only were there no terminals, but also the Internet was 'never mentioned'.

Use at *The Guardian/Observer*

Because so many journalists were interviewed at *The Guardian* it is worth looking at these figures in detail. Of the 52 people interviewed at *The Guardian/Observer* 68% were Internet users. To this statistic we can add that 44 journalists have attended library training sessions. On first hearing, this sounds as though the Internet is widely used amongst journalists there, but comments from those we interviewed and our own observation suggest otherwise, and that we are getting a misleading picture from the interview data. It looks like a few journalists – most of the ones that we interviewed – make heavy use of the system and that most of the others do not use it at all. These are the comments of a few of our interviewees on the use of the Internet by colleagues in their own departments: 'The Internet is used in a very limited way by a very small number of people [on *The Guardian* City desk]'; I was surprised [when I arrived on the staff] how little it was used'; 'I came over to talk to you because I am the only one on that desk [in Features] who uses it habitually and there are probably eight people on my desk, none of whom use it for either work or pleasure'; 'There has been a huge reluctance [to use the Internet]'; and finally, 'Very little use generally at the foreign desk'. (However, *The Observer* foreign desk uses it a lot).

Heavy users

There were, however, three groups of people who patently used the Internet quite extensively: student journalists, media librarians, who were obviously taking up the slack in journalists' use of the Internet and, unsurprisingly, the New Media lab journalists.

Student journalists

Student journalists, however, searched the Internet with some alacrity (see Table 4). Benefiting, no doubt, from academe's generous Internet provision, students showed, not surprisingly, far higher levels of Internet use, with 97% of them having used the Internet and 58% claiming to use it very frequently (several times a day). What remains to be seen is whether they will maintain that level of use when they enter the workplace – and a workplace still lacking in desktop Internet access.

Table 4
Use of the Internet by student journalists

At work	No.	%	At home	No.	%
Very frequently	19	58	Very frequently	1	3
Sometimes	8	24	Sometimes	1	3
Occasionally	5	15	Occasionally	6	18
Never	1	3	Never	25	76
Total	33	100	Total	33	100

Librarians
While a good proportion of journalists still have to make up their mind – or have their minds made up for them – regarding the journalistic value of the Internet, their librarian colleagues had no such doubts: 94% of those interviewed used the Internet – very much a case of information professions leading from the front (Table 2). This was supported by the questionnaire returned by 43 media librarians, which provided some quantitative data about library Internet use and provision. 93% of the librarians canvassed said they had Internet access at their newspaper and 74% used the facility. Of the users one third used 'it all the time'; 28% 'used it heavily some of the time' and the rest (39%) 'used it occasionally'.

New Media journalists
Plying their trade, as it were, on the Internet, it is not surprising that 93% of the New Media journalists we interviewed fully utilised its information retrieval and communication properties.

Factors influencing use

A large number of factors have been commonly attributed to Internet use – ease of access, age and gender amongst the most notable. These factors – and other less common ones, like training, online experience and seniority – were looked at in an attempt to understand use and non-use of the Internet.

Access

Ease of access and use of the Internet – as of the use of any information system – go hand-in-hand, as some of the regional trainee journalists quoted earlier only too well demonstrated. Lack of Internet access appeared to be the major explanation for the low and uneven take-up amongst journalists. Taking into account both interviews and questionnaire returns, nearly a third of journalists had no desktop access to the Internet. The poor provision, certainly in the case of the national newspapers, was largely due to the fact that the editorial systems on which journalists do all their work – and, in some cases access, online systems like FT Profile – cannot access the Internet. Even where there was access, via stand-alone PCs, it was generally remote – with journalists having to walk to the far end of a large office, or even go to another floor, to find a terminal. The situation was sometimes made worse by the lack of provision of a printer. And some reporters were reduced to using library terminals. One interviewee, speaking for many, summed up the situation at their own newspaper: 'We have problems of access because we can't get into the Internet through our desktop terminals. There is one terminal on each floor [of a very large office] which you can use but if anybody else is using it – and searches can be quite long – you can just be wasting working time just trying to get at it'.

Over half of all non-users indicated that they would use the Internet if access was improved. And certainly those with easy access – senior reporters on national newspapers, those working for some specialist publications (who tended to work in networked PC offices), news librarians and freelancers, who had invested in home Internet terminals – were all heavy users. This can come as no coincidence or surprise. This is best illustrated by the case of one young reporter at *The Guardian*. She is lucky enough to work very close to the only terminal on her floor, giving her easy and convenient access. Her brief is wide, and entails a large amount of desk research. As the compiler of the daily Jackdaw column she was charged with finding interesting stories from the press around the world. For her the Internet has been a godsend. She no longer has to contact foreign correspondents and ask them to fax material to the office or wait for hard copy newspapers to arrive. The loss of the terminal, removed for repair during the course of the project, 'made me realise how much I rely on it'.

Having home access plainly increases the opportunities to search the Internet. It tended to be the older/more senior journalists that searched from home. Although home use of computers was not particularly widespread amongst mainstream journalists – around a quarter had home facilities – those who made extensive use of the Internet at work and had home facilities also tended to use the Internet a lot at home. Indeed, in some cases their home facilities outstripped those they had at work: 'I have an arrangement which I negotiated to work one day a week from home but recently I haven't been doing that because I have got a brand new computer with Windows 95 which is absolutely terrific but unfortunately the office software is very outdated and doesn't work properly on it'.

Age/seniority

If this relatively poor Internet take up in the workplace was unexpected, another surprise was the chief characteristics of those who have actually taken the Internet route. Far from being the stereotypical young, most (66%) were experienced journalists in their thirties/forties, which runs counter to all that we have been led to believe (see Table 5). Young, IT literate post-PC graduates were supposed to flood the workplace, expecting to use the Internet as a matter of course. However, young journalists were not the big users or even the strong proponents expected, although the survey of current journalism students indicates that this might change in the near future. Even including New Media workers, just 21% of Internet users were in their twenties. Data from surveys of Internet use also reflect Internet take up by older age groups. The annual Graphic, Visualisation, & Usability Center's survey of Web use (Kehoe et al, 1997), involving over 10,000 respondents, consistently finds the average age of users to be in the mid thirties, with the latest survey giving a figure of 35.7 years, the highest of all their eight surveys and continuing an upward (older) trend. Despite European respondents being younger on average (at 30.2 years), the figures are remarkable given the high number of young users taking advantage of university access who skew the average age down.[2] Internet user profile study results also challenge the young male stereotype. Researchers found that 'the Internet seems to be attracting more ... older (35–54 years) users'. Thus it is reasonable to speculate that what is happening in the newsroom may be a fair reflection of Internet adoption throughout the workplace generally.

The age profile of users is partly explained by the age profile of journalists in the sample (see Table 6) and workplace, partly explained by the fact that it is the 'older hands' who saw the introduction of online ten to twelve years ago and assimilated it into their journalistic practices and are now viewing the Internet in much the same light. But probably the real reason is that age and seniority go hand in hand. Thus the greatest interest in using the Internet came from senior managers and editors, and not the rank and file journalists. The middle-aged, having emerged successfully from the scramble to get established in their early careers, can now both experiment at

---

[2]Kehoe et al (1997) give the figure for 'school' access at 12.70% for the 19–25 year age group. However, the figure is probably much higher for the 18–21 band.

work (certainly it was mainly those in authority who had desktop access) and have the resources and wit to use home PCs with Internet access. In many cases seniority gives the reporter the luxury of more flexible work practices, more autonomy and more job security. These were found to be ideal conditions to instil interest in the Internet. Victor Keegan (50 to 60 age band) at *The Guardian* is a good example of this. As Assistant Editor, he writes many of the editorial comment columns. Although, of course, the majority of these are reflections on some aspect of current news stories, often when space affords it the 'third leader' is humorous or offbeat. Keegan has some autonomy in the choice of these subjects, and can change the emphasis or even the subject depending on the information he manages to unearth. During his interview he flicked through a scrapbook of editorials he had written, pointing out the many that had been researched from the Internet. These included pieces about car fatigue, the Fourth Earl of Sandwich ('Did you know there's an Internet site dedicated to sandwiches?') and, ironically from the Internet, information overload.

Contrast this situation with young general reporters in the regional press. They don't have the autonomy or time to experiment with the Internet, which may well not satisfy their particular information needs anyway. Interviews in the tabloid press revealed a high degree of job uncertainty and anxiety, with junior staff employed on short term contracts with extremely heavy workloads. Marr (1997) even reports cases of reporters being employed on a piecemeal basis, paid by each column inch of their material published(!).

Table 5
Internet use by age[1]

Age	National and regional newspapers		Specialist publications & freelancers		New Media		All journalists		Librarians		Total	
	No.	%	No.	%	No.	%	No.	%	No.	%	No.	%
Up to 29	6	18	0	–	5	38	11	21	15	33	26	26
30–39	5	15	5	71	5	38	15	28	19	41	34	34
40–49	16	48	2	29	2	16	20	38	12	26	32	32
50–59	6	18	0	–	1	8	7	13	–	2	7	7
60 & over	–	–	–	–	–		–	–	–	–	–	–
Total	33	100	7	100	13	100	53	100	46	100	99	100
Unknown	1		2				3		1		4	

[1]Those who had personally used the Internet on more than one occasion.

Table 6
Age profile of interview sample

Age	National and regional newspapers		Specialist publications & freelancers		New Media		All journalists		Librarians		Total	
	No.	%	No.	%	No.	%	No.	%	No.	%	No.	%
Up to 29	7	13	1	11	5	36	13	17	15	31	28	22
30–39	12	22	5	55	6	43	23	30	19	45	42	34
40–49	21	38	3	34	2	14	26	33	15	31	41	32
50–59	11	20	0	–	1	7	12	15	–	–	12	9
60 & over	4	7	0	–	0	–	4	5	0	–	4	3
Total	55	100	9	100	14	100	78	100	49	100	127	100
Unknown	2		2				4		1		5	

Table 7
Journalists non-users by age profile

Age	Proponents[1]		Indifferent or hostile[2]		Total	
	No.	%	No.	%	No.	%
Up to 29	1	8	1	6	2	7
30–39	2	17	6	38	8	29
40–49	4	33	5	30	9	32
50–59	3	25	2	13	5	18
60 & over	2	17	2	13	4	14
Total	12	100	16	100	28	100

[1]Those who expressed interest or enthusiasm about the Internet, but who had not yet used it personally
[2]Non-users showing no interest or with negative views about it.

Experience of online searching

Young Internet-using reporters start from a disadvantage because they were not around when electronic information providers, like FT Profile, first hit the newsroom ten years ago. They have not had time to acclimatise themselves or immerse themselves in the 'new' online technology. A decade of online experience would seem to more than compensate for the higher general computer literacy of the new journalist intake. Commercial online systems were generally greeted very positively by a minority of journalists – interestingly, editors again lead from the front. The only criticisms related to (surprisingly) poor currency and limited range of sources, rather than to the system or the concept of electronic databases.[3] With a decade of online access and experience now accrued, it may be only natural that the journalists who have ridden this wave, now in their late thirties and older, would accept the Internet with equal openness.

Gender

Perhaps not so surprisingly men still greatly outnumber women when it comes to Internet use: 66% of the journalists who used the Internet were men (see Table 8). In the specific case of *The Times* sample all but one of the Internet users were male, although the difference was not so pronounced at *The Guardian*. But this might partly be due to the inherent gender bias in journalism itself. Thus the interview sample itself was weighted 70:30 towards men. In places of high Internet use, such as in the offices of specialist publications, women were more likely to use the Net, but not to the same extent as men, except in media libraries, where more women are employed. However, the stereotypical (young) males are dominating the 'New Media labs', like *The Guardian*'s, VirginNet's and News International's LineOne. 94% of Internet users in the New Media labs were male. What remains to be seen is whether they constitute the future face of the media industry. The data from the admittedly small student sample suggests otherwise, as there was no discernible gender difference in use there.

Table 8
Internet use by gender

	National and regional titles		Specialist publications & freelancers		New Media		Librarians		Total	
	%	No.	%	No.	%	No.	%	No.	%	No.
Sample – male	78	47	55	6	55	13	93	26	70	92
Sample – female	22	10	45	5	45	1	7	24	30	40
Total	100	57	100	11	100	14	100	50	100	132
Users – male	62	26	44	4	44	12	94	24	64	66
Users – female	38	8	56	5	56	1	6	23	36	37
Total	100	34	100	9	100	13	100	47	100	103

[3] It should be said that journalists from the tabloid press, not afforded such luxuries as research time, and more interested in entertainment rather than hard news, were less positive. One news editor said he didn't use Datasolve because 'I have enough problems already'.

Training

Even today journalism courses only pay lip service to the existence of online services – despite the evident interest of their students (Cole, 1997). It was even suggested during one interview that at a particular school of journalism many of the lecturers were refugees from 'the first round of automation' (in the mid eighties) who felt they could not adapt to the new medium. A study by Scott (1995) found that technology was generally very inadequately taught even on US journalism courses. Surprisingly, even the Pawley report (Pawley, 1996) on the future of broadcast journalism training, published in the USA where computer aided research is common in the newsroom, barely mentions electronic information. Newly qualified graduates simply do not come into the profession with the same information seeking skills as their older colleagues who acquired them during the early days of the IT revolution.

With greater usage in schools, however, and the ever expanding home market, there is evidence that current students are going to be quite heavy Internet users – if they are provided with that all-important access. The questionnaire distributed to students at The University of Central Lancashire Department of Journalism showed near universal and extensive personal use (predominantly at university – there were few home PC owners), and over two thirds of respondents considered that their job as a journalist would change over the next five years as a result of the Internet.

Training

Logic would suggest that training would be a major determinant in the use of the Internet but this is only partially true. Non-users, who were not ideologically or otherwise against the Internet, invariably lamented the fact they did not have time to attend training sessions (such as those held at *The Guardian*) or that they had no time to learn: 'Of course, I would use the Internet if I knew what I was doing – but I don't have time to attend what I know are excellent training sessions'. A lack of in-service training (though not, it seems, training provision) appears to have inhibited use among some older journalists who have not taken up the Internet. Many journalists who reported that they happily used online services (from their own desktops) felt that they needed training on the Internet, even though it is supposedly the ultimate in end-user friendliness: 'I think it is sold to people on the idea that it makes things simple, but that is as much a con as telling everybody they can learn a foreign language in seven days by buying cassettes'.

Big users, however, were not necessarily those who had been trained. Rarely was training mentioned in the interviews, and almost never as a formal ongoing process. Many users were entirely self-taught: 'Very much the best way of finding out about it is to try it out yourself. There are sites that actually that introduce you to various features of the web. There was a really good one which was specifically for social science researchers. The one that explained about all the different data sets and access to them. There was a kind of process you could use to find your way around various sites'. It is tempting to believe that this has a lot to do with the innate user-friendliness of the World Wide Web, but this was also true about FT Profile – few journalists were trained to use Profile, but a lot still used it, but rarely in any sophisticated sense (Nicholas et al, 1987). Plainly this is partly to do with journalists' natural independence and partly to with a lack of time, but sometimes other factors – some surprising – were involved. One interviewee learned to use the Internet to avoid imposing on librarians' time, never considering for a moment that they were there to offer training: 'I am fairly impatient and I found if I asked for something that the library staff, through no fault of their own, couldn't get it to me for 4 or 5 hours. So I thought, if they are too busy to do it, it can't be that difficult, I will do it myself. It is very straightforward. The hardest thing to start with was just remembering our user passwords to actually get into the system to get onto the Net'.

Despite the rather downbeat remarks about journalists and training, around 35 journalists did find the time to attend *The Guardian* training sessions. Typically these people were shown very briefly how to use a Web browser to enter search terms, and took it from there: 'I think I was started in a sense that I was basically shown how to get into it and how to start up a search engine and then after they had shown me that I played around until I came up with something'.

Categorising Internet users

From the data that we have accumulated there were notable patterns and it is possible to discern seven categories of 'user'. Going from heavy user to non-users they are: Net worshippers; the economically driven; pragmatists; occasional dippers; enthusiastic novices; non-believers; resentful dinosaurs.

Type 1 – Net worshippers

These are the young 'computer generation' IT whiz kids who have embraced every aspect of the Internet, and are culturally committed to it. They often work in new media or earn their money as freelancers. They see the Internet as a means for introducing a form of democracy to the news business – current management structures are far too top down for their liking. Although only a small minority of the sample, their views were very strongly held and, to an extent, signpost at least a possible future, so it is worth discussing their characteristics in some detail.

Firstly, the New Media journalists are not generally seen to be in the mainstream of newspaper production. Apart from physical factors that often distance the journalists in New Media labs from their mainstream colleagues – at *The Guardian*, for instance, they are located away from the main site in a separate building, their personal make-up is very different too. They are typically far younger than their paper colleagues: most seem to be in their twenties/early thirties. Almost inevitably too, they are culturally and educationally different. They talk easily about the nature and direction of journalism – they are convinced they are at the beginning of a revolution; they do not find it strange or boring talking about the information retrieval side of journalism, for that is what empowers them, gives their work its flavour, and gives them the edge (over their print colleagues). Techniques such as Selective Dissemination of Information (but of course not called that in the brave new world of information retrieval – 'baskets' is the preferred term) are talked about naturally – and in glowing terms (in their case as a cure for information overload). This makes the job of the information professional easier – they speak the same language (albeit in somewhat more dated terms) and they share the same (information) concerns. Perhaps where they differ from the information professionals is in their apparent naiveté (or unbridled enthusiasm). It is almost impossible to get them to say anything 'bad' about the Internet – overload, authority, cost and displacement are swept aside as being either not a problem or inconsequential.

Type 2 – The economically-driven

These people work in small newspapers with no library (e.g. *Sunday Business*), and are attracted to the Internet for the wealth of free information it provides for what they regard as little time expenditure. Although a minority of the overall sample, they are the predominant group working for publications of this type. Desktop Internet access is the norm at a majority of these locations, *Sunday Business* and *Microscope* magazines being examples. Their Internet skills are high, and they are adept at using the system to access information that would otherwise be expensive to obtain. As reported in the case study, journalists at *Sunday Business* managed to find a tremendous amount of financial information from the Internet. There was little evidence of searching for the obscure or offbeat information the Internet is known to provide.

Many of the economically driven are at the top of the profession. Senior managers and editors want to save money and see the Internet as a way of doing so. These people are also the most enthusiastic about exploiting the Web for disseminating their product – indeed, they are wary of not doing so, for fear of being left behind. Bob Jeffreys, editor of *The Herald*, says that it is not desirable to chop forests down to produce copy every day and sees the Internet, in the form of Web publishing, as a way to cut raw material and distribution costs. He is also mindful of the decline in newspaper readership (see Greenslade, 1997, for some up to date figures) and is casting an eye at the future of the market when a new generation of children, educated 'on screen' become news consumers. Also, his evaluation of the Internet as a 'great research tool' has not been formulated simply on the basis of the quantity and quality of the information available in its vast databanks and open access files, but also on the cost that would be incurred by obtaining this information from other sources. He gives the example of one of his colleagues researching a particular Kansas judge and the cases he presided over, and how an enormous amount of information was retrieved from the World Wide Web that would have 'cost much more time, trouble and a lot of money' from anywhere else.

This group also incorporates a body of freelancers who have invested in Internet technology for use in researching stories from home. Not having access to expensive online services or huge cuttings files, for them the Internet is a godsend, with its almost endless supply of foreign newspaper files and free Web news services (BBC 'News 24' being a good example). Because of the cost, freelancers are cut-off from commercial online hosts. This group are also heavy and expert users, partly by necessity, but also as a result of easy and constant access.

Type 3 – The pragmatists

This group incorporate the Internet into their array of general information sources. They do not regard it as heralding a fundamental shift in society, or, less spectacularly, as an excellent way to reduce company bills, but they do appreciate the convenience, the power and extended information reach of the Internet. The great majority of information professionals and librarians fall into this category, particularly those on national newspapers where the information units are generally well served with Internet connections. Journalists in the national and regional press who have desktop or otherwise easy access to the Internet also tend to fall into this category.

Pragmatists look at each enquiry and make a professional decision as to whether they will be researched from online services, cuttings, hard copy books, CD-ROM, the Internet, or a combination of these sources. Sometimes this decision is based on knowledge of sites bookmarked – a particular archaeological question was answered at *The Guardian* from the Internet, for example, because a member of staff was interested in this subject and had bookmarked appropriate sites. On other occasions information required is considered to be off the beaten track as far as online services go, and so the Net is employed. A majority of librarians cited 'ephemeral', 'weird' or 'unofficial' information as that best sought from this The Internet, although journalists tend to stick to trusted, 'official' sites. Specialist publications staff with fewer financial constraints than those mentioned above, working at papers employing information professionals, have also developed the pragmatic approach.

Interestingly, pragmatists are not necessarily heavy or very frequent Internet users. The pragmatism of information professionals at News International, for example, is practised with an enormous bank of various sources to decide from. News International simply has far more information sources than any rival. Guardian librarians put the Internet in context: 'We don't look for gossip on the Net – we get that from NEXIS – we want hard facts'. Thus, there is little replacement of other sources by this group. Also, most Internet users are accomplished users of all the available sources and systems. Amongst pragmatists, heavy Internet users are simply heavy information users. Indeed, there is evidence that, already, some practitioners are so used to working with the Internet alongside other sources that they have already stopped seeing it as anything special or spectacular: 'to me it's just natural'.

Type 4 – The occasional dipper

This group includes a large number of journalists who use the Internet only when other sources do not solve their information problems. The majority of Internet end-users in the national and local press fall into this category, but only a small minority of librarians. Generally their low use is not through any dislike of the Internet – in many cases they would use it more if they had either better access or training: 'If it were possible to access it from my keyboard at my desk rather than having to go somewhere else and find an Internet terminal I would use it more. The problem is, it is one of those things where you can go for an hour being trained up and knowing how to use it but unless you use it regularly you forget again'. In this way they are similar to the enthusiastic novices, described below. In another way, however, they are very different – they have tested the waters, and know only too well, even if only in a general sense, what the Internet can do for them.

Interestingly, however, they do not have access at home, and offer a variety of reasons for this (slow CompuServe accounts; systems incompatible with work environment; expense etc.). There was little evidence of journalists frustrated by their lack of workplace access spending time at home undertaking their Internet enquiries.

Type 5 – Enthusiastic novices

These are journalists who don't know exactly what the Internet offers, but are intrigued by what they have heard, and express interest in using the system themselves once given a demonstration. The bulk of this group is formed, interestingly, by both older (50+) and younger journalists (under 30). They generally blame time constraints for not mastering the system. None of them claimed that their age was a barrier or that, nearing retirement (some interviewees were in their late fifties) it wasn't worth the effort of learning: 'People older than me on the paper use the Net – it's just that I haven't got around to attending one of … the training sessions'. Some trainee journalists are in this group, usually after exposure at university; or by having a general computer literacy gained at school or through friends in higher education who enthuse about the Net. For the younger journalist job security – or lack of it – is often a factor in their lack of Internet use, particularly on the tabloid press. New recruits these days are often contracted for three to six months, work long hours, receive no encouragement to get to know the history or ethos of the paper and, unsurprisingly, have no time or status to indulge in pioneering activities like searching the World Wide Web for stories. Many are so busy they don't even have time to communicate with the library, let alone attend Internet training sessions. Looking through the glass panel separating the library from the features section of one national newspaper, the information manager ruefully remarked that the young men and women frantically working just a few yards from him probably didn't even know where the library was (no longer marked by rows of cuttings files), let alone have an idea what information facilities were available. For this reason, many new journalists simply roll over and turn into non-believers, the next category type.

Type 6 – The non-believers

This group comprises those who are basically not interested in the Internet. They have a variety of practical reasons for their abstinence, and would be unlikely to adopt the system even if they had desktop access. Apart from problems of time constraints and job status, the biggest problem for this group is that of authenticating data. A third of non-users cited this as a factor: 'I wouldn't trust any information I got from the Net without consulting other sources'. For others information overload was the issue: '[to find] something which would take ten minutes to look up with a standard series of reference works [you retrieve] 30,000 hits on the Internet – it's hopeless'. A minority of interviewees – but a very large body of journalists, according to many librarians – also continue to enthuse about hard copy. One interviewee happened to have a pile on her desk: 'Look at these: from just scanning them the size, fonts, format etc. I know what kind of story they are without having to read them. I know the tabloids from the broadsheets, I know the popular article from the specialist one etc. etc. That is faster than anything the Internet can do. On the Internet it all looks the same'. A final reason for the predominance of this group is that, in general, journalists have more than enough sources and systems to get along with – there really is no information impoverishment or gap to be filled. When such gaps are identified they invariably summon information staff, who then may or may not use the Internet on their behalf.

Type 7 – Resentful dinosaurs

This group represent the polar opposite of the 'Net worshippers'. The two groups encounter each other often with daggers drawn. They see the Internet as a threat to their privileged access to information, and are not in the least interested in empowerment or democratising the news. The whole ethos of the Internet as a conduit for the free exchange and sharing of information is anathema to them. Such journalists jealously guard their information sources and are even suspicious of revealing their information needs ('Sometimes we can't tell what information they want – they're scared of telling us. They don't really want us to know what we are researching' – a *Guardian* librarian). They are irritated by the fact that anyone with a PC and modem can reach a potential audience of millions by posting material on the Web: 'Where previously you had to have your little John Bull outfit to print anything, suddenly you can circulate 30 million copies of some drivel'. They are particularly worried about the prospect of electronic delivery of newspapers and the effect on their jobs, with rolling deadlines, interactivity and links to original documents so the public can check the accuracy of the reporting.

This group constituted a small minority of those surveyed, mainly because the majority of subjects were users or enthusiasts. However, there is much literature around expressing these views (see, for example, Jenkins, 1995) and the very lack of take up strongly suggests widespread negativity of this sort. The same group was encountered back in the eighties when the impact of full-text systems was being evaluated: they have not changed their attitudes despite seeing many of their colleagues searching online systems for a dozen years or so.

Use of the World Wide Web

It may seem as if there are as many uses for the Internet as there are Internet sites or Internet users. Amongst a seemingly endless list of activities, project interviewees variously claimed to have indulged in real-time chat with Czech dissident students; accessed OECD statistics; bought government reports; checked the latest information about computer viruses; downloaded free software; kept abreast of current events; and monitored the activities of a religious cult. Internet practice in the newsroom could be split into three distinct categories: information retrieval, communication, and technical support. Information retrieval concerns the consultation of the vast Internet file archives, with the World Wide Web being the area primarily exploited. Communication refers to the use of email, litservs, newsgroups, bulletin boards or IRC (Internet relay chat) facilities. Technical support includes the downloading of shareware or freeware, and using the Internet to seek technical assistance or increase expertise in using IT, rather than for story or background research. The divisions are not, of course, mutually exclusive – a reporter might email an expert in a certain field to obtain facts. Similarly, technical support from the Internet may come in the form of consulting a computer newsgroup.

Information retrieval

The journalist who lamented the fact that, as he saw it, 'the Internet is still controlled by the baseball-cap-turned-backwards anorak brigade tossing puerile jokes into the ether' was clearly unaware of the uses to which the system is put by those for whom it is a legitimate and valuable means of acquiring information. Use was found to be dominated, at least where journalists were concerned, by accessing: (1) 'official sites' – sites of government and other quasi-government institutions such as universities, research institutes etc.; (2) online newspapers and news services in general (see Table 8). Almost all journalists who mentioned specific sites or site types included at least one of these types of site. By far the most popular locations were online newspapers, mentioned by over three quarters of journalists, and consulted by all journalist user groups equally heavily. Librarians appeared to rely on these sites less heavily, possibly because they had better access to alternative online sources like FT Profile, although there is some evidence, particularly in broadcasting, of these sites being exploited as an online cost-saving exercise.

Government web sites were mentioned by 33 percent of those naming specific sites, although others mentioned press releases, and seeking information from 'institutions' generally, so it can be fairly safely

Table 9
Web use: sites and site types used

	National and regional journalists		Specialist publications and freelancers		New media journalists		All journalists		Librarians		Total	
	No.	%	No.	%	No.	%	No.	%	No.	%	No.	%
Directory (i.e. for addresses, spellings)	3	14	2	29	0	0	5	12	10	29	15	20
Entertainment/sport	6	27	1	14	3	25	10	24	16	46	26	34
Financial/company	8	36	4	57	1	8	13	32	3	9	16	21
Government	9	41	3	43	4	33	16	39	9	26	25	33
Graphics/pictures	3	14	0	0	1	8	4	10	3	9	7	9
'Institutions' (includes universities)	11	50	5	71	2	17	18	44	11	31	29	38
News services	5	23	5	71	1	8	11	27	2	6	13	17
Newspapers/magazines	17	77	4	57	6	50	27	66	13	37	40	53
'Obscure information'	4	16	1	14	0	0	5	12	25	71	30	39
'Official sites'*	17	77	6	86	3	25	26	63	14	40	40	53
Press releases	6	27	3	43	1	8	10	24	2	6	12	16
Science/environment /geography	9	41	4	57	3	25	16	39	9	26	25	33
SDI	2	9	1	14	4	33	7	17	1	3	8	11
Total specifying sites/areas	22	100	7	100	12	100	41	100	35	100	76	100

*Including those naming specific official sites, such as government.

assumed that these sites were accessed by an even higher percentage of journalists. Interestingly, however, the biggest attraction for librarians, cited by nearly half of those mentioning specific sites, was entertainment sites such as BBC television pages, film company promotions and pop star home pages. These kinds of sites were referred to by only 24% of the journalists. Librarians were also more enthusiastic users of what may be generically labelled 'obscure' sites – those containing exotic, bizarre or alternative information or views, or where information is unobtainable from other sources. An example that fits all of these categories would be the full text of the self-styled 'Unabomber' manifesto.

Sites offering financial information, whether paid for or free, were less popular, despite evidence from other quarters (MORI, 1997) that City journalists were beginning to use the Web to acquire data. Nevertheless, using these sites and company home pages (mentioned by a third of respondents) was more common than exploring the Internet backwaters for the offbeat information that librarians obviously enjoyed (and an activity often ascribed to journalists). Fewer than a quarter of journalists ventured into these Web waters – with even less enthusiasm from specialist journalists. Similarly, journalists were far more likely to be verifying facts or researching specific information on an individual or organisation than surfing the Net speculatively for possible stories, an activity undertaken by only a tiny minority of national or regional journalists (although they did use newspaper sites for ideas and leads). There were differences between user groups, and freelancers and New Media people did, indeed, use the Internet in this way.

Table 10 shows that the Internet was used, like online and cuttings, largely to check facts (42%) or get background information (34%) – plainly related exercises – in a hurry. In the words of a managing editor at the Press Association: 'It is most useful for getting factual background information on immediate stories. We are always in a hurry. PA is judged by its speed in getting the story out – we have to be accurate of course, but we have to be first. We were first with Princess Diana's death for example. The recent landspeed record, we used the internet to check out the history, previous records, detail of the current attempts. Very useful for topics like that'.

There were quite large – and unsurprising – differences between librarians' and journalists' use of the Web: librarians were more likely to use the Web for fact checking than journalists, and journalists more likely to use it for browsing for story ideas.

Table 10
Purpose of Web visit

	National and regional newspapers		Specialist publications & freelancers		New Media		All journalists		Librarians		Total	
	No.	%	No.	%	No.	%	No.	%	No.	%	No.	%
Background information	8	62	2	33	3	50	13	28	9	47	22	34
Ordering books	0	0	0	0	0	0	0	0	1	5	1	2
Browsing/ surfing for story ideas	4	31	6	100	3	50	13	28	2	11	15	23
Technical support	1	8	2	33	5	83	8	17	2	11	10	15
Checking facts	6	46	4	67	2	33	12	26	15	79	27	42
Total specifying purpose	13	100	6	100	6	100	25	100	19	100	65	100

Notes
1. Some subjects used the Web for more than one purpose.
2. Low numbers are due to the fact that reporters did not mention a specific use.

Specific uses

Web newspaper sites

The extensive use of the Internet to consult other news publications might have been expected given the highly incestuous – and competitive – nature of the newspaper business, and is a natural extension of the journalists predilection for researching from cuttings or online databases of newspaper archives such as FT Profile. Victor Keegan's online use was typical of many. The assistant editor of The Guardian explained, '[I] rely very heavily on searching through the Net and the newspaper databases – World Reporter – I use them both. I'm using them both as part of the same thing at once'. The Guardian Editor, Alan Rusbridger, would even like an FT Profile equivalent search engine for Web papers: 'The [Internet] search engines are so ropey at the moment. If you had a search engine as on Profile coupled with the Internet that would be awesome.'

Newspapers of every description were mentioned with, not surprisingly, the foreign press appearing to be particularly popular online targets. Of those who named specific newspapers, types of papers or geographic targets, over 50% (including questionnaire respondents) named US titles or the US press generally. Not surprisingly,

The Washington Post was the paper mentioned most frequently. Slate, the Microsoft US news digest that only appears online (and has, since the fieldwork, become a paid-for service) was also mentioned.

Librarians used newspaper sites less than journalists – about 50% fewer interviewees mentioned such sites specifically, and only 16% of questionnaire respondents did so in answering the open question asking about uses of the Internet. There may be several reasons for this. Firstly, as information professionals, they are skilled in and happy with online services that provide access to newspapers, such as FT Profile. Secondly, there is a large amount of data-swapping between newspapers, a large number of which (all the nationals except *The Express*, *The Guardian/Observer*, *Herald* and *Scotsman*) exchange the electronic text of each day's edition, saving online bills and obviating the need to access those titles' Web versions. Data suggests that librarians avail themselves of this in-house database more than journalists. Thirdly, there isn't the pressure to be one hundred percent abreast of 'the news' (although there is a caveat here too, with Information Managers stressing the need for their staff to anticipate the needs of their end-users). Finally, of course, librarians do not write stories and have no need, therefore, to search for news leads by electronic or any other means.

The broadcasting industry tends not to have agreements with national newspapers. This is possibly the reason why the financial benefits of searching Web, as opposed to online, papers were most vociferously expressed from this quarter, where financial constraints seem to dominate conversations about information retrieval: 'librarians have never been financially naive and were quick to recognise a good thing when they saw it'.

While many interviewees mentioned newspaper sites as one of a list of different Internet locations accessed, without much elaboration, those who did describe how they took advantage of this resource indicated a range of uses. Indeed, their list was as wide as may be expected with the hard copy cuttings file – researching for specific information or to fill in the history or background to a current issue; keeping abreast of the news in other countries or searching for stories the wires may have missed. An excellent example of searching papers for specific information was given by ITN Online editor John West. A journalist friend in Jerusalem had an appointment to interview a Palestinian Minister about corruption. She had no information about him except that he had been implicated in a report on the problem (which she had not been able to get hold of), but hoped to gather information on the ground in the city. However, a suicide bomb incident occurred and all the news switched to that, making it impossible for her to obtain the required information on the other story. She phoned West in London and he found six articles about the report from the Internet, including extracts from newspapers such as *The Irish Post, The Palestinian Times* and others. He was able to tell her by phone of four cars the Minister had taken for his own use, missing funds and other relevant facts – all while she was waiting outside his office on the West Bank.

Journalists at (the original) *Sunday Business* used paid systems on the Internet to search newspapers[4]. Because of the cost, this was generally for specific information or background details to stories, rather than to browse publications looking for starting points: 'You get access to everybody. Using the Profound database across the Internet ... you hit with all these papers and all these publications'. UK Plus, the Associated Newspapers web site, was also used: '[it] is excellent for undertaking primary research as it incorporates a search engine'. As with Internet accessible databases such as Profound, some services are not necessarily free – although prices are rock bottom compared to charges for online services.

Interestingly, few interviewees mentioned the fact that newspaper sites often boast their own archives and in-house databases. Researching the extensive archives of *The Washington Post* and *The Times*, and *The Guardian*'s database of the House of Commons Members' interests were all mentioned by individual journalists, although librarians, who in overall terms appeared to use newspaper sites less, were more aware of these facilities, and, perhaps not surprisingly, more aware of the cost savings that could be achieved by using them. One magazine librarian, for example, enthused about *The Wall Street Journal* archive being accessible over the Internet for only US$48 per annum.

As to the hyperlinks facilities provided from newspaper sites, this also does not seem to have been exploited fully – comments being limited to one respondent who made use of *The Daily Telegraph*'s link to the University of Keele's database on past election results, and another who, interviewed as he undertook a search, showed all the extensive navigational skills of one who had a terminal at home – which he had. As with other aspects of the research, findings here clearly show that even Internet enthusiasts often do not exploit the system to its full potential, and, indeed, may even be unaware of the various sub-layers available for enhancing information retrieval.

Thirty two percent of respondents stating specifically that they

---

[4]*Sunday Business* was re-launched too late for the fieldwork to include an examination of any changes in working practices in the new paper.

accessed newspaper sites did so for general background information and/or to browse online titles, often with the intention of looking at stories that have escaped the attentions of the wire services. The editor of *The Guardian Weekly* (a digest of the daily paper sold principally overseas), Patrick Ensor's use is illustrative: 'The *Washington Post* is a particular case in point. *The Washington Post* puts the whole of its paper onto the web site and we find that particularly useful because it is a major source for us. It is a cheap source of *Washington Post* news (it is available on FT Profile) but it is also a very good way of retrieving stories that we will want to use ourselves because not all *The Washington Post* stories that are sent into various syndication services which we access contain the whole of *The Washington Post*. So when we want to pick and choose stories that have not necessarily been sent out to the syndication service, we are quite often alerted to those by *The International Herald Tribune* which is, of course, a part of *The Washington Post*, and they quite often print stories which don't appear on the wire services. At that point we can then go in to the Internet site of *The Washington Post* and retrieve those stories. It is a very good site and it is quite good for researching as well. So quite often if we have problems with American stories or Martin Walker's left us with a funny name, for instance, I will go *The Washington Post* site and do a search.'

Some reporters are charged with the task of reading the world's press for interesting and unusual stories to go into their digests of world news (*The Herald*'s Diary, and *The Guardian*'s Jackdaw, for example). For such journalists browsing newspapers and magazines is an essential activity, and those interviewed indicated that this task has been made a lot easier by the Internet: 'I look at online magazines pretty regularly. Probably more so than most people because of doing the Jackdaw column. I use it on a daily basis. Sometimes readers send in and say you might want to look at this or I might be reading another magazine which will mention something else, or I just click on and have a look around. I also use it every Friday because there is another column I do which is in Saturday's paper, which is looking at foreign newspapers, and it is great for that because basically I just go in and get all the interesting paragraphs from foreign newspapers.'

Many specialist or subject journalists access online newspapers for this purpose. A sports editor, for example, described how one of his staff trawls sites of Australasian newspapers to keep abreast of rugby developments in the Southern Hemisphere, and the Foreign Editor of *The Observer* uses the Internet to see what other newspapers are doing in their coverage of overseas events, describing this as 'basically a fishing expedition'. Some journalists have narrower briefs. One searched every day for stories from Russia. For her the Internet is a godsend – she can now access titles it would otherwise either be difficult to get hold of or out of date by the time they arrived. She also keeps up to date with international news generally by reading European newspapers online – she regards the US media as being too insular to give her the coverage she wants.

More than a third of the journalists naming sites or site types on the Web used news services over the Internet to keep abreast of current events. The majority were journalists working for specialist publications, as freelancers or in New Media environments. This is hardly surprising. Most national and regional newspapers have access to 'traditional' online wire services. Freelancers, on the other hand, do not have such access – they are inhibited from subscribing to paid services by the high cost. Many have networked PCs at home, however, and find the Internet a good substitute. Some freelancers spent an hour or more every day consulting all the various (free) news services that they could access on the Internet, as well as all the day's online papers, which one interviewee claimed 'saves me a fortune'.

The more specific, tailor-made approach to current awareness – SDI (selective dissemination of information) – was generally not adopted, although the possibilities afforded by the Internet for these were enthused about by the New Media camp. On the rare occasions the subject came up, respondents indicated either that their brief was too wide, indefinable or changing according to current stories. One very enthusiastic science reporter, however, regularly checks The American Association for the Advancement of Science, which, 'has organised a site called Eureka Alert which is actually where university press officers, research institutions and laboratories put all their press releases in one place you can go to. God, if British and French universities did the same that would be brilliant. But I can also get into the web site of maybe 30 or 40 universities research institutions and see what is going on'.

Accessing specialist magazines specifically for current awareness in a particular subject field was mentioned by only one interviewee, a science specialist reporter on the staff of *New Scientist*. He regularly accessed magazines like *Nature*, *Scientific American* and others to inform himself of scientific developments.

No librarians indicated that they used the Internet for current awareness purposes, possibly because their job role does not require them to be aware of developments in a particular subject area (although use is made of listservs to keep informed of their own professional interests in information work). Rather more surprising was the fact that only one indicated the possible use of the Internet in this way on behalf of their end-user clients.

Despite the heavy consultation of online newspapers and other current news sources, often for finding story ideas, the suggestion that journalists spend much time surfing the nether reaches of the Internet for this purpose was laughed at heartily by one journalist, and dismissed out of hand by others. Nevertheless, this is what many journalists are in effect doing when they scan the US or other foreign press. Freelancers and New Media journalists do, however, openly admit to surfing. For the former the Internet is regarded as something of a treasure chest of potential stories, leads, ideas and inspirations. Although only a small number of freelance or ex-freelance journalists were interviewed, all but one (who planned to go online 'after the next big job') had access to and used the Internet, all 'browsed', 'searched' or 'scanned' the Web for stories and mentioned colleagues who did the same. Considering the constraints mentioned earlier on their information seeking, possibly commanding less attention from potential contacts by not having big name publications behind them, and – not least – tending to have desktop and therefore constant and easy access to the Internet, their exploitation of it in this way is not surprising. Only one journalist from a national paper specifically mentioned (or rather, was observed) 'surfing' for stories, and only two librarians gave instances of journalists doing so.

Official sites consulted
Of course, online newspapers, magazines and news or current affairs services represent just a tiny – but very popular – fraction of what is available over the World Wide Web, and, apart from just two respondents who indicated that newspapers were the only attraction for them, they invariably formed just part of a vast selection of sources exploited in the newsroom. Over half of journalist users said they used 'official' sites generally or named specific institutions from which they obtained data. Government was, predictably, the most heavily accessed institution, with the majority of those citing 'official' sites indicating that they take material from the various H.M. Government departments, local councils or, from one Time Life journalist, sites of overseas governments, in her case East European. This same interviewee uses the Internet to research the activities of opposition parties – last year doing so in her coverage of the Serbian elections. A journalism student on work placement at *The Herald* in Glasgow, on the other hand, searched the Net to discover what local councils were doing in tackling environmental problems ('Cheshire County Council have got fantastic recycling facilities!'). Others sought press releases, reports, statistics or simply any general government information relating to whatever story was being researched (such as advanced passenger train safety regulations, for example).

University and research sites were nearly as popular as government ones, particularly with specialist and freelance workers for whom it saved the time and effort required to 'telephone round, find out who you need to speak to, not catch the person in – or ask for research papers that never arrive'. All four science reporters interviewed emphasised their use of academic sites – one explaining that 'It's no surprise that science scores better on the Internet than the arts. Science invented the Internet. The World Wide web is actually a creation of a laboratory in Switzerland called CERN and it's no accident that this is the case because the Internet is built up of academic networks'. A good example of research undertaken from university and other academic sites was this one given to us: 'If there was an earthquake I would know what to do ... I would go straight to the USGS site at the University of California. I would go straight to the Global Seismology Unit in Edinburgh ... there is a virtual earthquake site ... a map of all recent earthquakes ... etc.'. Although this interviewee was enamoured with the Internet and used it by choice where he could have opted for other information sources, he claimed that in one sense it was becoming a necessity – the Internet was becoming the only medium by which he could obtain some of the material. This is particularly true with regard to scientific or academic institutions. 'The perfect example is NASA. NASA does not issue anything on paper at all. If you are not on email or on the Internet – tough.'

Librarians were also big users of such sites. The Guardian library's Internet bookmark file includes a whole range of folders of sites grouped under titles such as Health, Science and Technology, Social Sciences etc., and librarians were observed making considerable use of these in their searches. Evidence from questionnaire returns also indicated extensive use of these sites. Interestingly, in the in-depth interviews given, this group generally put more emphasis on using the Net to find 'unofficial' or 'offbeat' information.

Obscure, offbeat, unofficial sites
Over two-thirds of librarians, as opposed to only a very small minority of journalists (12%), said they used the Internet to find 'obscure', 'unofficial', 'offbeat' or similarly described information. This description included material that was impossible, or very difficult, to acquire by other means, cult information or strange and unusual facts: 'the sort of "oh gosh" information tabloid papers love'; 'I suppose you could say it was ephemeral stuff in a way....' Examples included unusual facts about the history of Middlesborough in the FA Cup (in preparation for the Final in 1997), the Heaven's Gate Web site ('It was quite spooky knowing that the people that had designed it were all dead.'), the full text of the Unabomber's manifesto, and the history of the racquet game Petanque.

One example of information professionals accessing information normally unavailable from traditional information sources involved a Guardian librarian who found the Web site of the Tupac Amaru revolutionary movement. The search was conducted on behalf of foreign correspondent John Hooper, who was in Lima covering the group's hostage-taking at the Japanese Embassy. Worried about being faxed sensitive material, he phoned the paper's office in London, and took notes from web site information read out to him. The information from the site was more current than the information directly outside of the Embassy. When told this story later, another *Guardian* journalist was rather sceptical of this explanation, claiming that all communiqués by the group would have been carried anyway by recognised news agency wire services, a claim quickly denied by the library: 'There is no way John could have got that information from any other source'.

How is this difference in information-seeking between librarians and end-users accounted for? As already mentioned, the majority of journalists specifically target what many describe as 'official' sites, such as governments, universities and other institutions, by doing so thus circumventing any quality problems associated with Internet data. Librarians also consulted these sites, in almost equal proportions – 20% of librarian users specifically mentioned organisations such as universities or research institutes (25% of journalist users did so) and 17% mentioned government sites, similar to the 15% for journalists. However, there appears to be more Internet take up by librarians who tend to be heavier users. It is natural that this greater experience (stemming, of course, from better access and training – in information retrieval if not specifically on the Internet) has lead to more experimentation, greater breadth of sources consulted and a wider variety of information types retrieved. Secondly, librarians are intermediaries – they extract the information requested of them by their journalist colleagues. It is no surprise that journalists were happy to give librarians the more difficult or obscure queries. One *Guardian* correspondent had tried all morning to get through on the telephone to the headquarters of the British Petanque Society, finally recruiting the Information Manager to find out about the sport for him (she found the information needed on the Internet in a matter of seconds). Thirdly, after ten years of online access in the newsroom, many journalists undertake their own searching on FT Profile. Indeed, there were many complaints about the restrictions placed on this by the strict limit on passwords available. Queries not satisfied by Profile, which may be of the rather obscure, 'offbeat' type, are passed to the information staff. Finally, journalists would be expected to be familiar with bodies and institutions appropriate to their particular subject area, and more likely, therefore, to consult the World Health Organisation or the Central Intelligence Agency themselves.

Entertainment sites

As searching the Net for obscure and unusual information is practised more by librarians than journalists, so too is using it to find information about or provided by the entertainment industry: nearly half the librarians interviewed described using such site types, as against only one tenth of journalists. This type of search was also the second commonest mentioned in questionnaire returns from librarians. It is, however, possible that journalists use of such information was underestimated, because only six features journalists (and not one film or music correspondent) were interviewed. Of these, half did, in fact, search for entertainment news and information, so the assumption that librarians tend to procure this type of information more than journalists may not be well founded.

The BBC TV web site was the most commonly mentioned entertainment site, and searching the Internet for film and pop music information was mentioned by a majority of librarians. Biographies or the latest activities of famous actors, soap opera plot lines and rock band concert dates are all easily found on the Internet. Many entertainment queries are, of course, of the simple fact seeking kind, such as requests for film dates/stars/full titles etc., although this is not always the case. An example of in-depth research in this area undertaken by librarians on the Internet is provided by the Information Manager of Newsquest North East. The film *101 Dalmatians Live* caused a controversy in the United States because of the question of cruelty to animals in its production. As the picture was released in the US first, the library at Newsquest used the Internet to get US reviews, comment, reaction and information about how the animals were treated in preparing for an article written to coincide with the UK release: 'The paper would have paid a lot for this kind of information online and would not have been able to gather nearly as much material'.

Commercial sites

Company sites are used by some organisations heavily – the Press association is a good example, but usually only for factual data. 'We use airline web sites a lot. Whenever there is an incident we can get straight to a lot of material through the web sites. We use business and commercial sites a lot. Basic data.'

The Web as a giant directory

Another use of the Internet was, as one respondent said, 'as a glorified telephone directory' and many librarians used the Web in this way.

Questionnaire returns gave this as the most popular use: typical examples were consulting online Yellow Pages, using expert finding services (such as 'Profnet') and confirming of overseas telephone numbers etc. Using the Internet in this way possibly reflected the predominance of straightforward factual questions put to librarians by journalists. Very few journalists admitted to using the Internet themselves for this purpose, possibly because this type of use is more difficult because you need to know individual sources in the first place. In order to try and reduce the number of such trivial enquiries received, librarians at News International and The Guardian are incorporating Yellow Pages hyperlinks, contact (and other) details of newsmaking people in the intranets they are constructing.

Although several librarians themselves surfed the Internet, this was for personal ends, such as for travel information. Only a couple mentioned this activity in relation to story ideas. Both of these had stronger ties to the field of journalism than other information colleagues who did not regard it as part of their role to hunt for stories in order to pass them on to reporters. One was a BBC researcher who described herself as half librarian and half journalist; and the other was a librarian who, according to a senior colleague, has 'pretensions to being a reporter'.

Technical support from the Web
This was a very minor use of the Web and those that availed themselves of it were the more computer literate of the journalists. Naturally enough, the practice was widespread amongst New Media workers (and IT correspondents), who have both the general IT and specific Internet skills to exploit the Web: 'We use the internet to access software sites and download. For instance, we have just bought this machine and loaded all the software and [one of the programmes] didn't work, so we spent ten minutes basically accessing that manufacturer's site on the Internet and essentially found out that we needed to download some extra software, which we did. I thought that was a prime example of sorting something out in an hour which prior to using the Net would have taken three weeks to get sorted by the distributor channels and speaking to the sales people.'

Another journalist illustrated how they used it for this purpose: 'I have also used it to download shareware programmes and freeware programmes which are useful to me, which are put on my desk top. I use a version of post-it notes for my desk top as a reminder of things to do and things that are coming up – messages and so on. There is a useful conversation facility for things like blood alcohol units and miles per hour and kilometres per hour – things like that – which I saw on shareware or freeware pages and had a look and thought, "Yes, that looks good, I'll have that, download it."'

Those not so adept at computing, however, did not see any advantages in being able to access shareware or freeware. The recognition that these facilities are available over the Internet is, as yet, very limited. Even with the few who did realise there was this possibility, there was concern about problems where the use of specialist software is a prerequisite for downloading certain documents. They find the necessity to add 'plug-ins' or other extensions difficult and time-consuming: 'There was an OECD publication came out which listed the most recent papers and I know they have got a web site and I know that they have got a lot of these things on their web site, so I went to look for it and then discovered that we need an acrobat reader in order to download it [but] people here don't use it very much. I think I could have done it – but I didn't want to spend half an hour on the only office terminal sorting it out so I didn't bother with it.'

Communication

Email

It is no surprise that communication is a major function of the Internet – after all that was why it was constructed in the first place (Tseng et al, 1996). The use of email has become widespread in universities. However, the newsroom is a very different environment. Two factors make this so: its information culture and the information battering it receives. First, the culture, unlike academia, where the culture is one of information sharing, is often one of secrecy (Nicholas and Martin, 1997). If this is only to be expected between newspapers, maybe it is surprising to find that it applies even between staff in the same organisation. The second factor is the information bombardment the newsroom already receives from the post room, fax machine, wire services and telephone – much of it unsolicited communication, of little value, that nevertheless requires attention, so that the valuable material can be extracted. How then does (or will) email fare in this very different environment?

Before answering the question, a note first on the fieldwork. As part of a general effort to avoid 'shoe-horning' people, it was left to respondents to define 'The Internet'; 'The Web' or any other related term. The meaning attributed to these words by the interviewees themselves was as enlightening as other comments made about the system. With the term 'email', many respondents were unsure whether to include in this internal messaging systems. Some thought this facility was part of the Internet, even when not having a gateway out of the office, and others, conversely, were not aware that external mailing was indeed a facet of the Internet. Although more concerned with the latter activity, comments about how internal emailing was impacting on work practices generally were nevertheless accepted, and relevant comments are included here.

What we discovered was that the use of email was far from common and that it broadly mirrored use of other Internet facilities, both with respect to organisations and individuals.

Where email was used
The greatest use of email was in the New Media labs, where, like the Web, the system was used voraciously and for many purposes. Specialist publications, where Internet access generally was also often better than in national newsrooms, were also big users. Often, as in the case of scientific or financial publications, their contacts and information providers also had email facilities – the former with universities and research institutes, and the latter with large companies and financial centres. Email was used in nearly all national newspapers, with only *The Mirror* an exception, but there were many complaints both that the people needed to be contacted did not have access and that the system used was 'clumsy' or inadequate. In some cases, for example, attachments were not accepted – nor long email messages. The regional press seems to have even less access, with the information units (as at *Northern Echo*) or New Media labs (as at Eastern Counties Network) being the only places with email facilities. In the broadcasting media there appears to be very varied availability. At the BBC this is true even within different sectors – all news employees had access to external email, while at BBC Westminster only producers and editors had access. At LWT only the library had email facilities.

Who uses email?
In an admittedly subjective classification of both Web users (or those employing the Internet for information retrieval), and email users into 'non', 'light' and 'heavy', there is a high correlation between an individual's use and/or attitude towards the World Wide Web, and use and/or attitude towards email (in other words, heavy users of the Web tended to also use email extensively). To take an example, a *Guardian* personal finance reporter enthuses about Net searching: 'Type in the word and you will find the most up to date information on it ... and also it is anything and everything. You name [a topic] and it will be there'. About email he declares 'I think email is brilliant', giving plenty of reasons to support this view. Conversely, low- or non-Web users are similarly restrictive in their use of email. A

Table 11
Use of Email/newsgroups

	National and regional journalists		Specialist publications and freelancers		New media journalists		All journalists		Librarians		Total	
	No.	%	No.	%	No.	%	No.	%	No.	%	No.	%
Email uses												
For keeping in contact with journalists	7	21	1	9	0	0	8	13	1	3	9	9
For overseas contacts	13	38	7	64	9	64	29	48	16	47	45	47
For communicating with contacts	6	18	6	55	8	52	20	33	2	6	22	23
For communicating with readers (receiving mail only)	8	24	2		5	36	15	25	4	12	19	20
For communicating with readers (interactivity – both receiving and replying)	0	0	1	9	4	29	5	8	0	0	5	5
For contacting Web authors	0	0	1	9	2	14	3	5	7	21	10	11
Other uses	5	15	3	27	1	7	9	15	3	9	12	13
Email attractions/problems												
Attractions: overcoming time differences	8	24	5	45	8	57	21	34	12	35	33	35
Attractions: masks disabilities/inequality	0	0	0	0	2	14	2	3	0	0	2	2

Attractions: cost	5	15	4	36	0	0	9	15	3	9	12	13
Attractions: facilitates document transfer	1	3	2	18	0	0	3	5	2	6	5	5
Attractions: convenience	5	15	1	9	3	21	9	15	5	15	14	15
Problems: no screening process	5	15	2	18	0	0	7	11	0	0	7	7
Problems: fate of message unknown	5	15	0	0	0	0	5	8	2	6	7	7
Problems: lack of face-to-face spontaneity	10	29	2	18	0	0	12	20	3	9	15	16
Problems: system failure/incompatibility	8	24	0	0	0	0	8	13	0	0	8	8
Total number using email	34	100	11	100	14	100	61	100	34	100	95	100
Listservs												
Total number using listservs	1	3	3	27	5	31	9	15	8	24	17	18
Newsgroups												
Purpose – story ideas	1	3	3	27	2	14	6	10	0	0	6	26
Purpose – finding contacts/experts/eyewitnesses	4	12	1	9	5	36	10	16	2	6	12	52
Purpose – gauge opinion	2	6	0	0	2	14	4	7	1	3	5	22
Purpose – technical support	0	0	1	9	5	36	6	10	0	0	6	26
Total number using newsgroups	6	18	4	36	7	44	17	28	6	18	23	24

journalist from *The Observer* said of the Web, 'I think a lot of things in it wouldn't be really relevant to what I did and it could be easier to look in World Reporter'. Of email his opinion was: 'I sometimes worry that people in the office ... send messages instead of ... having a proper conversation which you can actually do more quickly ... I prefer the telephone'. In a modern communications environment the following remark by a journalist is perhaps surprising: 'I know a lot of journalists who are absolutely paralysed by people even using email. They don't understand how email works, they don't understand how to retrieve files [from the Web]'.

Thus, with heavy Web users also using email extensively, it is no surprise to find that the biggest email users are the New Media specialists. This group appear to use the function as much as, or even more so, than those in the academic world. Indeed, they virtually live online – and are very proud of the fact. Freelancers and specialists are also big users, and librarians use email heavily where they have access – far more, in fact, than mainstream national or regional journalists. With greater Internet access in most newspaper libraries it may be that, for information staff, email is easier or quicker to use. Younger librarians are also more likely to have had experience of email in their professional education. As with journalists, their greater use of email is also directly related to the degree of their use of the Internet generally.

In some ways the high correlation of Internet searching with email communication is hardly surprising – heavy information users employ all means to obtain their information, yet in other ways it could be seen to be surprising. After all the two activities are very different, even if the overall aim may sometimes be similar – the speedy acquisition of vital information. Despite the reservations expressed by a minority of interviewees, email can be considered to be extremely intuitive at the basic level of sending and receiving messages (leaving aside the rather more complicated possibilities involved in electronic filing, constructing folders etc.). Web searching, on the other hand, involves at the least a knowledge of what a search engine is, how to formulate queries, evaluate hit lists, use hypertext etc. Secondly, the access problems alluded to earlier with regard to the Web do not apply to the same extent with email. At *The Guardian*, for example, every reporter can enjoy (albeit rather archaic) email facilities from Atex desktop terminals, although Web access was not available on these machines, leaving large numbers of journalists relying on one terminal often many yards from their desks, and sometimes not even in the same department. Finally, email use would be expected to be higher than Web searching among reporters simply because they cannot ask intermediaries to send their emails.

Uses of email
Email has a number of attractions for journalists: it is invaluable for overseas communication; it is a convenient way of keeping in touch with each other; it is a means of obtaining information from contacts; and it provides for better contact with readers.

Overseas communication
One predominant and specific use of email was for overseas communication. Over half of email users mentioned email in this connection. For journalists on national newspapers, where extensive foreign coverage requires international communication, it is common. The cited advantages of using email included speed, price and convenience in bypassing time zone problems. One features writer had a lot of contacts in the United States and actually asked for a direct external email facility to be able to contact these respondents with greater ease. She was not alone in saying that this was email's only function. Obtaining news information via email was far less common, even for foreign correspondents. One foreign correspondent mentioned that he had received information from contacts about Afghanistan and Albania, but said that 'those were definitely the only cases I can remember where it was definitely email'. However, in the future he expects the medium to 'increasingly push fax out'.

Journalists based overseas also used email, partly because of the advantages mentioned earlier, but also because they felt more in touch with the office. Interestingly this is because of the problems they encountered in phoning in. An editor explains, 'They had a story, they would come on [ring up] at a time when everybody was stupendously busy, the desk didn't want to get involved in a conversation … because it was wasting valuable time.… They used to come back [to *The Guardian* office in London] and say "Why does no-one ever talk to us?"'. Now they feel more in touch.

Communicating with contacts
As already mentioned using email to communicate with contacts was far less common (23% of respondents admitted to this), for reasons that are outlined later. More common in certain quarters of the specialist press and by freelancers and New Media people, only a small minority of those in national or regional papers appear to make extensive use of email for this purpose. Those who did, emphasised the advantages of email over the telephone (if not over personal contact), saying, 'You can end up having quite chatty relationships with people that might only ever have had the time to talk to you for a few seconds on the phone'. This can lead to more face-to-face contact rather than less: 'I find myself going out of my way to try and arrange to actually

meet people that I have built up this strange electronic relationship with. As time goes by you realise you have not only never seen these people, you have never heard their voice.'

New Media workers used email extensively to keep in touch with contacts. One VirginNet journalist describes the 'tremendous benefits' of interviewing people by email: 'You can do it over a long period and always go back to them to check something out'. This was always difficult with the telephone or letter. This group saw no problems at all associated with using email for this purpose.

Communicating with readers and listservs
The possibilities of reader communication via email were raised, although there was strong aversion to this in some quarters of the more traditional press because of the fear of being overwhelmed by junk mail. The proponents of reader interaction by email, like the editor of *The Guardian Weekly*, cited its immediacy and geographical reach as the principal attractions and a high computer ownership as a guarantee for its success: 'I think the email has made an enormous difference to a lot of people's lives and it has certainly affected my life because with the high computer and modem ownership among readers I find letters to the editor now come to me via email rather than on paper. Whereas a year ago I would have said that one out of ten letters was an email, now I would say we have got parity between email and written letters. I think also journalists are going to have to become a bit more directly accessible to readers who want to email them with their views and tell them what they think or give them some information.' This editor though does see the downside: 'This is probably a mixed blessing for journalists because they will be glad of a tip-off but they won't be too glad to have to spend half their day answering people's email requests for very low grade information.'

Obviously journalists who work on columns which rely on readers submitting material are amongst the first to see the benefits of email: 'For Jackdaw (a *Guardian* column) I use it because people send stuff in and there is an email address at the bottom of the column and quite a lot of readers send things they have seen on the Internet ... so they mail me with various things they have seen. Again, we do a debate ... we get two people to argue an issue through a series of letters and now they can just email me the letter so that means it is already in our computer system, it doesn't have to be typed in.' The last point is an economically important one, of course.

The letters editor of *The Guardian* confirmed that more and more letters were coming in from readers in email form. Although at one time their quality was measurably below that received by other means, now they are of equal standard, if not higher. Interestingly, by already being in digital form and therefore uploaded onto the page without ever passing through a hard copy stage, such letters escape the generally required final approval by the editor who only sees paper correspondence. Although the press is rather lukewarm in regard to readers email, the broadcasting media has no such qualms. The BBC's Today programme encourages them so that live reaction can be obtained to items broadcast. One BBC librarian said, 'I don't know how I managed without email for so long', citing as one advantage that information users found it easier to formulate and edit their enquiries on screen.

Journalists working for specialist publications and New Media workers were the only (non information profession) people to use listservs. (Two *Guardian* journalists did experiment with them but quickly withdrew when their mailboxes became too full for them to read.) One New Media editor employs someone to trawl through various listservs – and newsgroups, as is described later – to find interesting material for his site, citing the practical, problem solving nature of much of the material on these listservs. Bill Thompson, a freelancer contributing to Radio 5's The Big Byte, ITN's online editor and others also used listservs, mainly for computer related discussions. Listservs were employed far more by librarians than journalists. Apart from the very active LIS-Link, the Library and Information Services discussion group, there is also a mailing list specifically for media librarians, run by the AUKML (Association of UK Media Librarians) and used by information professionals working across the press and broadcasting industries. The list is, in part, to share ideas, seek information and provide current awareness generally. It may not be a surprise that librarians have taken more to this form of communication. As one interviewee put it 'journalists are in the communication business, but they aren't in the business of communication'. They simply do not share ideas and findings the way other professional groups, notably academics, do. Indeed, so secretive are they that librarians have complained to us that they sometimes find it difficult to meet their users' information needs because they are so evasive about what they actually are.

An email function that appears to be used almost exclusively by librarians is contacting people responsible for constructing or maintaining web sites, an activity that appears fairly common among this group. It is mainly to seek further information, clarify a point or to help determine the authenticity of the site or the information therein. One librarian gave the example of a task she had been given of checking out rumours about the possible release of a new Hammer

House of Horror production. They found an official Web site and were able to communicate via email with the producer himself, who was happy to spend time answering her questions. 'Fanzine' sites were also mentioned by *Guardian* librarians as good sources of information that included contact email addresses. Interestingly, not one reporter mentioned following up email addresses on Web sites in this way.

Keeping journalists in touch with each other

An important use of email in the national and regional press appears to be to keep reporters in touch with their newsroom and vice versa, rather than to communicate with contacts. One national newspaper's sports editor, for example, estimates that nearly 50% of his staff (excluding the subs) are out of the building at any one time. They use email extensively to stay in contact with the office and to file stories – their role as sports reporters naturally demanding their presence at external locations. The advent of email has lead to a reduced presence in the building. In fact, the sports correspondents appear to be the one group at the paper (apart from those working in the New Media area) whose working practices have been directly affected by the Internet. Interestingly, the sports editor himself does not like 'the to-ing and fro-ing' of messages, and prefers to use 'one quick phone call to sort everything out'. Nevertheless, he does see the advantage of email over fax, which is discouraged as it has to be converted into digital form. The editor of *The Guardian Weekly*, expanded on this point: 'I see the email as being a huge advantage for newspapers. Anything that comes to you via email does not have to be re-keyed in before it appears in a newspaper. Faxes I think are increasingly out of date for newspapers because it means if someone sends their column in by fax someone has got to re-key it in with scanning technology which is far from perfect. So I welcome email and I am always encouraging people to use email to send in their columns.'

The extensive use by New Media journalists of email was based as much on cultural reasons as on practical considerations, such as cost or overcoming time zone differences. One such journalist, at VirginNet, simply couldn't understand the low take-up amongst conventional journalists. For him it created a community ('Surely all journalists would want that ...?'), and a very effective way of keeping in touch. Another New Media specialist went even further, and waxed lyrical at the new communication opportunities afforded especially for the 'disenfranchised', making colour, weight and good looks all immaterial to the communication process. Another emphasised the democratic qualities of email: email took you straight to the person you wanted to speak to, be it a company executive or the newest trainee recruit: 'with email, everyone is equal'. Hierarchy barriers were broken down as much as race or class barriers.

Miscellaneous uses

Other stated uses of email were rather idiosyncratic. One obviously time-conscious journalist said that the facility was good to use as messages could be sent to one person whilst simultaneously talking to someone else on the telephone. A similarly novel use was outlined by a personal finance reporter who, having Internet access at home, emails himself between house and office with reminders and daily task lists. Some personal use was also reported, the most systematic being a subscription to the mailing list created to serve members of the pressure group Families Need Fathers. This particular journalist actually works with email all the time, being one of the letters editors and so reading 'about 30' emailed correspondences to *The Guardian* daily.

Finally there was the (increasingly important) use of the email network to deliver the news itself. The editor of *The Guardian Weekly* explained: 'We launched an email service for our readers in December 1996. Two out of three of our readers are subscribers and we are obviously concerned that we will lose a large revenue base if we were to give the paper away on the Internet. However, we do recognise ... that the distribution of *The Weekly* is obviously going to be fraught and dependent on mail services, which are far from perfect. There are inevitably going to be parts of the world where you may only get the paper [after] ten days, weeks in some cases. I even had a complaint from someone in the Pacific saying why did it take five or six weeks to reach him. So the news value of the paper that takes five or six weeks to reach you is really quite limited.... We also discovered in a readers' survey taken about eighteen months to two years ago that 70% of our readers have access to or use a computer and of those half were able to receive email messages. So for 1996 we were putting forward ideas of trying to get an email edition of the paper out and we have now succeeded in doing that. But to protect our subscriber base we are currently giving it away free but only to postal subscribers of the newspaper. This service is produced after the edition goes to bed which is on Tuesday lunchtime. So on late Tuesday afternoon, depending where in the world you live, you will have access to [nearly] all the files which have appeared in *The Guardian Weekly*. People can subscribe to whole sections or they can pick and choose from the index and then order stories automatically from a server in London.... We now have 2,000 people who receive the email service every week.'

The often enthusiastic – and inventive – use of email fully described above was not reflected by the average reporter in the national and regional press. There appear to be many doubters and plenty of reasons why journalists have not embraced this communication channel. The discussion now turns to an examination of these reasons.

Reasons for low take up of email amongst journalists
As many as seven separate reasons were given why email found little favour amongst journalists (one couldn't imagine any being cited in an academic environment): it would overload them with junk information; it was too faceless and so not a good investigative medium; it could leave incriminating evidence; not enough people were connected; the systems themselves were not user friendly; it would lead to a deterioration in internal communication; and there was no guarantee of obtaining an immediate response.

Overload
Fear of receiving junk email in large quantities represented the most widespread reason why respondents failed to take to email, and accounted for about one third of all complaints about the medium. Overload is dealt with at length in the next chapter but its worth saying here that it was only really in the context of email that it was though to be a serious problem. Unless some very sophisticated but intuitive automatic filtering system becomes available in the future it seems unlikely that electronic communication will gain in popularity among the doubters. Even in the United States, where journalists have been brought up in a culture of Computer Assisted Reporting, studies (such as that by Ross and Middleberg, 1997) show a marked disinclination by journalists to embrace this medium. Remarks included, 'I get enough crap coming through the post without having to clear out my [email] message queue every day' and, similarly, 'The problem with email is that there is no screening process – the crap comes straight in and I have to deal with it'. Even Internet enthusiasts such as *The Guardian's* assistant editor Victor Keegan were wary of email. He enthusiastically subscribed to several listservs when his desktop PC was first networked, and then spent weeks trying to extricate himself after being swamped by a volume of communication that he couldn't hope to address under the time constraints imposed by his job. Months after unsubscribing he was still receiving unwanted mail.

Not a very effective way of dealing with contacts
There were several problems associated with using email for dealing with contacts. These problems, largely similar in nature, constituted around a third of the reasons given for not using email. Principally, email messaging was said to lack the spontaneity and flexibility of face-to-face contact. It did not enable the journalists to employ all their investigative skills. The ill-considered, off the cuff 'one liner' remarks,

so often immediately regretted, were the stuff of good stories as well as being a constant source of considerable embarrassment to government ministers, among others. It is not surprising, therefore, that journalists did not rate email highly as a one-to-one communication channel between themselves and potential story-makers. The potential, in face-to-face or even telephone contact, to ask 'on the spot' questions was highly prized. There is also tradition of course: 'As journalists we are still very conditioned to ringing a human being and asking it and hearing it'. Other comments included the failure of email to allow journalists to get to know their respondents or to 'get a feel for what is going on'.

Provides incriminating evidence
Another problem in using email for contacts was that, as with other forms of the written word, electronic messages could end up as incriminating evidence. This was voiced strongly by one journalist. Not surprisingly, the person also avoided facsimile or other written communication, and was even reluctant to use the telephone, beyond making contact arrangements or for exchanging pleasantries. This was because, as a financial correspondent, they dealt in sensitive information, often receiving confidential material and sometimes even being in possession of facts prohibited to him by insider dealing regulations or even criminal law. In this situation information and communications technology had led to more personal contact with informers rather than less. A direct result of new technology was greater surveillance and monitoring powers over phone, fax and computer traffic (regardless of the legality of such activities) the natural consequence of which was more of the traditional face-to-face on neutral ground meetings. At least at one media organisation, Reuters Financial Television, journalists' use of email was tightly controlled because of security risks with information flowing out of, not into, the newsroom.

Not enough people are contactable via email
A very small minority of respondents said they would use it more if their contacts could receive it: 'an awful lot of people I deal with are not geared to using external email at all'. The same journalist described situations she sometimes finds herself in when needing to forward mail: 'I sometimes end up having to print out emails and send them as faxes, which is crazy'. Another journalist at the same paper has the very opposite problem. As an economics correspondent, she was often in touch with university academics who, of course, have email facilities. However, she failed to avail herself fully of these contacts partly because the system she worked with 'is tricky to use', and also because it does not accept document attachments. For her,

then, it is more of a case that the contacts cannot mail her rather than vice versa.

Antiquated email facilities
Even internal emailing/messaging systems were regarded in a dim light by some journalists. This was principally due to the antiquated nature of the systems themselves. No less than a quarter of *Guardian* journalists who spoke about email listed various shortcomings with the system – and not always accurately, according to the paper's information manager. Their chief complaints were that the system: did not support attachments; did not include subject headers; and could not easily be used to send external mail.

Negative impact on internal communication
The adverse effect of email on face-to-face office interaction was mentioned by a number of journalists. One interviewee recalls that when *The Guardian* first had internal email a colleague with whom he worked very closely began sending him messages. 'I used to say, "Why don't you speak to me?" and he'd say, "You look so busy"'. The same journalist goes on to confirm that 'a lot of things which used to be done by getting up and walking around are now done by messages', and concludes that this is bad because it breaks contacts and diminishes the exchange of ideas, whereas, 'When you start a conversation you go on to talk about other things – all that is very valuable'. A small number of library staff also lamented what they saw as a gradual disengagement from their journalist colleagues because of electronic messaging. Describing the time before the advent of email, one *Herald* information professional says: 'They would come in and ask us [for hard copy cuttings]. Vary rarely with a phone. They phone now and we send things by email, everything is sent by email more or less, or if they can't access it, we print it out and leave it in a tray so we don't see the staff. But when it was a hard copy they'd come in and say, "What have you got on such and such" and we got the cuttings out and gave them a packet or looked for the stuff ourselves and handed it to them and they would come and sit within the library and use it so there was really a daily contact with staff. We knew everybody. Now we don't know a soul.'

No guarantee of obtaining a response
The advantages of using email for international communication were generally recognised, but for communication within the UK, these advantages did not appear to apply. There was much talk of email being sent 'into the wide blue yonder', of unanswered communication and of the whole uncertainty of whether recipients had actually read their mail or would reply, and when. Emphasis on the advantages of

the telephone testify to the need of journalists for real dialogue, and spontaneous responses. New Media professionals, however, did not appear to suffer – or admit to suffering – from this problem. Unlike many in the national and regional press, New Media journalists tended to praise email users for promptly replying to their messages. Claims were made that a custom was being built up whereby one always responds quickly to email messages. In the experience of one young multimedia company director, emails were responded to more urgently than faxes. Certainly, staff at VirginNet adopted an (alleged) policy of immediate response, and lengthy interviews and observation in the workplace give the distinct impression that New Media people regard themselves as a pioneering community, failing to understand any reservations about email.

Information professionals
None of the problems cited by journalists regarding email were mentioned by information professionals. At *The Guardian* the library emails journalists all the time. There were very few complaints about email from this group. Some concern was expressed (though only by three respondents) that journalists failed to check their email frequently enough for the librarians to make effective use of it as a means of passing on information or replies to queries. One librarian even resorted to telephoning any reporter she communicated externally with by email to make sure they were aware a message awaited them! Other librarians simply did not even attempt to use email with journalist colleagues. Pat Baird, information manager at Mirror Group newspapers sums up what appears to be a general situation in newspapers: '[Email] is a very important aspect of communication within the company but it is always the services that are involved in communicating with one another – the IT department, the editorial support people, the other media departments, the directorate. I am in constant touch with them. But I don't think I've ever emailed a journalist.'

Newsgroups

Paul (1997) is one of a number of commentators reporting or recommending extensive use of bulletin boards and newsgroup discussion lists in the United States, both for consultation and research by journalists, and for inclusion on newspaper Web sites. Paul claims they are indispensable in, for example, finding people involved in some way in newsworthy situations. Others (Outing, 1997) emphasise the interactive nature of the medium in outlining possibilities for readers to become active agents in the news process. The present study, being more concerned with information research and retrieval by journalists, sought views on the use of newsgroups in this regard. Did they, for instance, represent an opportunity for acquiring hitherto unobtainable information, or were they – as some critics claimed – trivial, low grade and unworthy of a serious journalist's attention?

One of the most striking results obtained from our research was that there appears to be very little take-up of any newsgroup facilities on this side of the Atlantic. The majority (over three quarters) of respondents either never mentioned this aspect of the Internet or, when asked about it, stated simply that it was not used. A few were frank enough to admit they did not know how to access groups, and others – even some Internet users – did not appear to know what they were. Only a tiny fraction of the sample stated reasons for their non use, when doing so claiming that the communication is banal, repetitive and of poor quality or, more commonly, being unaware of the service.

Users and advocates of newsgroups were primarily the New Media journalists who, of course, championed all aspects of the Internet. Half of this group specifically mentioned newsgroup use. Specialist and freelance journalists were also users – about a third of those that used the Internet indicated some use. However, barely a sixth of users who work in the national and regional press mentioned newsgroups – and much of this was accounts of other people's efforts – and personal efforts as in this case: 'Nick in the office here was looking for [some information] for his daughter and he put a query out [on a newsgroup] and he got back quite a lot'. This low use has to be set against the fact that there were – as of November 1997 – nine such discussion groups specifically for practising journalists. Take up – and interest – amongst librarians was equally low. There appears to be some recognition of the potential within the Internet using community, but so far this potential remains unrealised.

Within the very small newsgroup user community, three (possible) uses were put forward for using them. The most common use being to generate story ideas. Other uses were to seek out experts, contacts or eyewitnesses, gauge opinion about a particular issue from the general content of messages, and seeking technical support.

Finding stories
'Surfing' newsgroups for story ideas was most popular with specialists and freelancers. The popularity was no doubt partly due to financial factors – surfing the Web was often a lot cheaper – and possibly easier – than virtually any other method of finding some stories. Examples of such use were given by two specialist journalists who scanned computer virus newsgroups for stories. The first concerned a company called Firewall One which maintains the firewall for Microsoft. The source code for the firewall programme was 'allegedly'

posted on a newsgroup, Newsnet News. This was found and a story published about it in a leading computer magazine. The magazine was nearly sued, although they were careful to say that the problem had 'allegedly' happened. Similarly, somebody alleged in a newsgroup that a new Pentium chip had a bug in it. Others read this and also found the bug. Pentium, meanwhile were forced to insist its product was free of problems. Eventually scientists and journalists discovered the debate and joined in. Pentium were eventually forced to recall 2.4 billion dollars worth of chips.

Another journalist made the point that you have to be careful with newsgroups (quite apart from questions regarding the authority of the information) because people do not think their messages are going to be used by journalists. They say things in a newsgroup which they would not if they knew this would happen, and do not really want to be quoted.

Despite the possibilities illustrated by these (rare) examples, there was some derision amongst journalists on national titles that they would have time to 'surf the Net' for story ideas, and their low take up of this opportunity through newsgroups reflects this attitude. Indeed, the national newspaper journalist to mention newsgroup use was an *Observer* journalist, who was a freelancer when he practised it. He regularly monitored traffic in Islamic newsgroup sites, and has published at least one story as a result, ironically about the activities of the newsgroup itself and the power struggle for the control of it (Bright, 1995).

Searching for contacts
This activity was undertaken more by journalists from the national and regional press than by freelancers or specialists, although with only six practitioners identified, it is not possible to claim there use is typical or representative. Also, the uses mentioned (seeking medical advice about long-range diagnoses, aboriginal art information, talking to Middle Eastern affairs experts) tended to be anecdotes about colleagues' use. New Media workers, who exploited the medium in all the ways indicated, tended to look at computer related sites for story ideas and technical support as well as to find contacts. To give an example of the latter, one online journalist said, 'I was looking for a specific piece of software and found it through questions to an appropriate newsgroup'.

In addition to seeking out experts, eyewitnesses were also sought from newsgroup messages. There has been much literature published which shows how those involved in making the news have used the Internet. Bacard (1993), for example, described how dissident Chinese students used 'computer networks' to communicate directly with the outside world when other media were being routinely censored by the authorities, and Press (1991) reproduces an email message from Moscow sent during the attempted coup in 1991. No concrete examples were offered by interviewees for the project, but one person indicated that he chatted to Czech dissidents 'in real time', but not for any reporting job. Another said he occasionally looked at messages originating from radical groups, although he regarded most of the material as 'a lot of rubbish'.

Gauging opinion

The use of newsgroups to gauge opinion simply involved either monitoring message traffic to obtain a feel for the current climate of opinion, or posting a message and judging opinion by the quantity and variety of answers. Both of these activities were undertaken, in two cases regarding the popularity of rock bands – Oasis and U2 respectively. The journalist (from a national broadsheet Sunday) who enquired whether the latter's popularity was waning, admitted that perhaps a U2 dedicated fans' newsgroup wasn't the best place for an unbiased objective opinion(!), although she did also use the Internet to find criticism, show reviews and much other material on the band to make a reasonable assessment.

Technical support

As with Web use, a minority – though a majority of New Media people – used newsgroups for technical support. One online editor occasionally puts up questions about computers generally or the running of his system in particular. On one occasion, for example, he was looking for a particular piece of software and found it through questions to an appropriate newsgroup. Another looks at those groups concerned with Mac: 'there are three good ones, where people discuss problems/solutions for their systems'.

Chapter 5

The Internet issues

As well as favourable comment, The Internet has attracted much criticism too, largely but not wholly, from information professionals. The main causes for concern are: its potential for overloading users with data, the suspect quality of much of its data and the negative impact it will have on much liked traditional information systems and services. As potential barriers to information seeking these issues were explored in the interviews and tested for more widespread comment in the questionnaires. However, it was generally, not our practice to prompt or prod people about these issues; we would always have preferred them to arise naturally as part of the conversation. Above all we did not want to plant ideas/problems in people's heads.

Information overload

Journalists already have to deal with far more information than they can ever hope to use. They are bombarded with information from every quarter. Journalists tell of receiving a hundred unsolicited faxes a day, of being inundated with post and of non-stop telephone calls. Vast quantities of information pour into a newspaper – and only a tiny fraction of that is used, but most of it must be 'tasted'. Plainly this is a problem, and takes up a lot of a journalist's day. But this is not the only problem that arises from the incoming information flood. With more and more material coming into a newspaper – and much of it now in real-time – there is a danger of journalists writing more and more of their stories at one remove. Trapped at their desks by the information flood there is the risk that their views on events become progressively institutionalised – seeing education issues, for instance, from the (second-hand) perspective of the educational institutions who provide the information – the unions and educational authorities – rather than from those people on the ground – the parents, individual teachers and children. Under these circumstances, then, what room would there be in the journalist's busy day for the Internet – yet another source, and not just one that dispensed information, such as FT Profile, but one that doubles as a communications channel; and will the Internet represent another step down the road of second-hand journalism?

The overall findings

Despite a multitude of diverse comments, it does seem that information overload is not the major problem or issue for journalists that we might suspect. In fact, many of the journalists we spoke to plainly had problems in understanding why we were bothering to raise the issue in the first place. One journalist pointed out that every time a new communication medium comes out the overload cry is raised: 'When they introduced Reuters in the nineteenth century people said they couldn't cope then'. For different reasons, 'overload' is not encountered by either novice or experienced users. Those – the majority – not familiar with different search engines, advanced searches, directories and subdirectories, and other layers of the system, happily use only the default search engine, take minimal care over their query terms and are unfazed by obtaining 20,000 hits. Their usual practice is to scan the first ten, follow a few links and, if no positive result is obtained after ten or fifteen minutes, switch off and turn to a different source.

Advanced users, on the other hand, do not worry about information overload for other reasons. They choose the search engine to fit their query – UK Plus, for example, for strictly British topics – follow directory subcategories, and use Boolean operators or other advanced search options where available. Again, where too many articles are obtained, a sensible time limit is adopted and the search terminated. They have little sympathy for the overloaded: if you put a search phrase into a search engine and it is not specific enough you get overload, but whose fault is that? In fact, for some advanced users, the Internet, with its baskets and tailor-made feeds, offers the tools and solutions to overcome information overload. Information overload is a cliché – as always people manage, spread things out, get technology to help them overcome it.

Even the negative comments we received about overload were largely made by heavy Internet users, and often then only after the topic of 'information overload' had been raised by the interviewer. In fact, around only 10% of all users complained about this problem, and on only two occasions was the issue raised – unprompted – by users themselves. Similarly, there were many 'Yes, but …' answers, where such problems were acknowledged, but then were quickly followed by remarks indicating the positive aspect of having this volume of information available. Forty per cent of users gave such answers. Non-users were more critical, of course, with around a third talking of overload as being a (potential) problem. Their major concern was with poor quality material on the Internet rather than being overwhelmed by information – something which we shall pick up later.

It was surprising, given the prominence accorded the issue of overload in the professional information literature, that librarians did not appear to regard the issue as being particularly noteworthy: 'Overload is hype. If you put a search phrase into a search engine and it is not specific enough you get overload – but whose fault is that?' Similarly: 'If you put in a very generalised query you are just going to get bombarded with information and most of it irrelevant probably. It's up to you to structure that query ... there are good search tools on the Internet nowadays.' Others dismissed overload on the basis that it was all part of the librarian's role to confront and solve the problem: 'It is the library's role to filter, sort, establish relevancy, quality, appropriateness.'

Only a small minority of librarians considered overload a problem associated with the Internet. This is what one of them said: 'You can do a search and it comes up with many thousands of items but you don't know within that thousands of items as to whether something might be useful to you. It is a problem. If you could do specific searches and have more sophisticated searching techniques then you could overcome that.' Those who took this attitude compared the Internet unfavourably with online services: 'There is too much dross. It can take a long time to find things, whereas with LEXIS-NEXIS you can do so in minutes.'

Reasons why information overload is not considered a problem

If journalists are complacent about overload it is because they are quite used to it. Wallowing in information is nothing new and it is something they are quite prepared for. The request 'Give me everything you've got on ...' is far from uncommon in journalist-information worker exchanges[5], and more than one journalist said that 'you can't have too much information'. Indeed, far from a cause for concern the quantity of information was itself thought to be a cause for celebration, regardless of any retrieval problems: 'There is a fantastic amount of information available ... you can access wires, you access libraries, you access information all around the world ... in an office ... or at home ... it is quite fantastic.' A majority of users cited this as a major positive attribute of the Internet. Those who did so tended not even to mention 'overload', by that or any other name. Amongst this group there was scant sympathy for those who dared raise the question of overload: 'There is always a lot of griping or whinging going on when anybody introduces anything new'.

---

[5]To which librarians at *The Guardian* reply: *Impossible, you can only have a selection.*

Table 12
Information overload and the Internet

	National and regional journalists		Specialist and freelancers		New media journalists		Total journalists		Librarians		Total	
	No.	%	No.	%	No.	%	No.	%	No.	%	No.	%
Those considering overload a problem: users	8	20	1	17	2	40	11	28	4	15	15	23
Those considering overload a problem: non-users	17	43	2	33	0	0	9	23	1	4	29	44
All those considering overload as a problem	25	63	3	50	2	40	20	51	5	19	44	67
Those considering overload as not a problem: users	9	23	2	33	3	60	14	36	1	4	15	23
Those not considering overload as a problem: non-users	4	10	1	17	0	0	5	13	5	41	10	15
All those not considering overload as a problem	13	33	3	50	3	60	19	49	12	44	31	47
Why overload *isn't* a problem:												
Extra material obtained from Internet minimal	4	10	1	17	0	0	5	13	2	7	7	11
Worth hunting through Internet to find valuable info.	2	5	1	17	2	40	5	13	2	7	7	11
Quantity is good in itself	4	10	0	0	1	20	5	13	5	19	10	15
Internet is unobtrusive (you can turn it off!)	1	3	1	17	0	0	2	5	2	7	4	6
Accessibility of obscure documents	1	3	0	0	0	0	1	3	1	4	2	3

Why overload is a problem												
Time taken to retrieve relevant information	7	18	2	33	0	0	9	23	3	11	12	18
Poor search engines	3	8	1	17	0	0	4	10	3	11	7	11
Too much information	5	13	0	0	0	0	5	13	5	19	10	15
Poor quality	4	10	0	0	0	0	4	10	2	7	6	9
Wider issues (i.e. too much information in society)	4	10	4	67	2	40	9	23	1	4	10	15
Solutions to overload												
Selectivity (i.e. only Government sites)	17	43	6	100	3	60	26	67	1	4	27	41
Use of bookmarks	10	25	3	50	2	40	15	38	14	52	29	44
Adoption of time limit	3	8	2	33	0	0	5	13	12	44	19	26
Limiting hyperlinking	2	5	0	0	0	0	2	5	7	26	9	14
Advanced search strategies (truncation etc.)	2	5	2	33	0	0	4	10	5	19	9	14
Total mentioning overload: users	22	55	3	50	5	100	25	64	12	44	37	56
Total mentioning overload: non-users	18	45	3	50	0	0	14	36	15	56	29	44
Total mentioning overload	40	100	6	100	5	100	39	100	27	100	66	100

*In all cases percentages figures are of the total in each category mentioning overload specifically

N.B. Some respondents gave more than one example of overload not being a problem; and others contradicted themselves, first saying it was a problem but then insisting this did not matter because of …. Therefore the figures in the table have to be treated with some caution.

There were other reasons why the Internet was not a cause for concern when it came to overload:

1. The extra material yielded from the system was relatively small compared to what was already available: 'Any one of the Sunday papers contains enough words to provide almost the complete text of Dickens. *The Guardian* every day is the equivalent of *Our Mutual Friend*..... But we read *The Telegraph* and *The Times* and we listen to *The Today Programme* and *The World Tonight* as well and we catch *Newsnight* later on. You throw in the Web – that's nothing.'

2. It was worth hunting through trivia to find valuable information: 'Searching the Internet is a bit like the toy shop Hamleys – if you want a Dinky toy which is on the third floor you know how to get to the third floor but en route there are various goodies which side-track you. and I think of the Internet as being an area the size of Africa in which there are a huge number of things going on which are of no use to me whatsoever, but if you know which parts of Africa to look at you will probably find valuable elephant tusks and things of this kind.'

3. The Internet is unobtrusive: 'You can sit it in a corner and tell it not to disturb you and it won't'. This observation, although only made by a minority of interviewees, nevertheless highlights an important distinction between the Internet and other information and communication channels. The telephone or the fax machine, for example, disgorge information regardless of the need or situation of the receiver and often, of course, at most inappropriate times. The Internet, on the other hand, can be called into action whenever required – people only use it when they have an information need.

4. The ease with which you could access documents on the Internet more than compensated for any problems associated with finding too many of them. The quantity and variety of information on the Internet clearly implies the presence of large numbers of documents difficult to obtain from other sources, a major attraction for librarians, for whom the Internet (as discussed in the chapter on displacement of other sources) played the role of provider of information unavailable elsewhere. 'Journalists are working to tight deadlines – the time that it might take you to get in touch with a research unit of a university somewhere and get hold of a particular publication [on their behalf] could go into days or even weeks – that's no use in this sort of environment. But [you can] go to the Web and find their page and get it in seconds. So there is a positive side to overload.'

Why information overload is a problem for some

Non-users were not convinced: the very fact that half mentioned information overload in disparaging tones indicated that this was an important reason for their avoidance of the Internet, although lack of access was also a complicating factor. Complaints were not only levelled at the excess information available, although that was a primary concern, but also at the Internet search engines – there was little confidence in their abilities to sort the wheat from the chaff; and there were also the worries about the time it would take to sort and filter the documents retrieved.

Too much information
For some, principally non-users, the basic problem was simply, 'there is too much information on the Net'. Other comments in this vein were these: 'You don't want to know all sorts of interesting things, you want to know what's relevant'; 'You can just be swamped by information'; and 'It creates more work than it reduces, I think'. Some interviewees said there was too much full text information which reduced its quality. This is a surprising complaint – the complete manifesto of the so-called 'Unabomber' and long tracts by the Tupac Amaru revolutionary movement in Peru, both posted on the Net, were prized by those who came across them. One journalist who did not want to read full text said that, as with Dickens' Mr Gradgrind, all he wanted was 'facts, facts, facts'. Another explained that he wanted a 'spin' when reading information, which was impossible from such prime sources. He compared raw text to newspaper cuttings, which he preferred every time: 'Newspapers make better judgements about what is news than any Internet server ... you want to know what's relevant and you have to read so much turgid stuff [on the Internet]'. On a similar theme a magazine journalist maintained that information on the Internet was 'all the same. She continued, 'With a book you know you have come to the end of a chapter, with the Internet you cannot see what is before, what is after, how much there is to go ...' It was all much of a muchness for her – a sea of information.

Poor quality of information
Of course, the question of overload is inextricably linked to that of quality and authenticity of Internet information: 'There is masses of absolutely useless information out there and all sorts of very strange people setting up sites and having various conversations ... these days anyone who produces a paper or research project will put it on the Net as well so you can probably find theories proving and disproving everything and get completely tied up in knots.' Interestingly, the speaker here was Hannah Pool of *The Guardian*, who is a heavy Internet user, exploiting particularly sites of overseas news-

papers and magazines for the Jackdaw column in the paper. There are still some journalists, however, who doubt whether the Internet yields any quality information at all. Thus a freelancer who writes frequently for *The Herald* in Glasgow, maintained that 'unfortunately the Internet is still run by the baseball-cap-turned-backwards brigade tossing puerile jokes into the ether'. The quality issue is examined in detail in the next chapter.

Inadequate search engines

A minority of both the librarians and journalists who considered overload a major impediment to Internet use mentioned Web search engines. The bluntest – and most typical – comment was that they were 'indiscriminate'. Another journalist complained that the 'hit list isn't graded in any useful way and that it would often be quicker to consult a standard set of reference books'. This view is also shared by a number of librarians who expressed concern about information overload. One had grave suspicions that the search options offered had very little bearing on the results – where Boolean searching was a feature, for example, documents were retrieved containing terms prefaced by the NOT operator, or, conversely, lacking one of two terms requested by an AND command. Another said that overload could only be overcome if the search facilities offered more transparency and sophisticated techniques.

Time factors

Just as many Internet users claimed that information retrieval on the Internet saved them time, so others (approximately a sixth of journalists – not all of them non-users) said, in effect the very opposite: the time taken to acquire and evaluate information from the excess offered by the Internet inhibited their use: 'If I use Profile I'm in and out in five minutes and five minutes is a long time for me on Profile. In that time I've got precisely what I want and downloaded it and out. Well I can spend ten minutes on Yahoo or whatever search engine I'm using. It will turn up 3,658 references or whatever, and there's no way of knowing what those references are.'

Another journalist – patently speaking for many of his colleagues – explained how the amount of material he had to read anyway every day left him with no time to look at the Internet at all: 'It's all very well having this information but the time one devotes to reading hasn't increased ... I get up at 7.00 every day and go out to get four broadsheets that I read ... unless I get up at 6.00 I can't devote more time than I do to actual 'reading' or 'information covering' time, so if I was to take advantage of the Net I would have to change my lifestyle.' This appeared to be a common theme amongst non-users, even those who were interested in the possibilities the system offered: 'I would love to take advantage of the training we are offered by the library – but if I don't have time for that – and I don't – then what use can I make of the thing itself?'

There was some evidence to suggest that even those who were heavy users of the Internet employed it less than they would have liked because of worries over the time it would involve. One interviewee even considered it an advantage not to have the desktop access that he had enjoyed in a previous academic job: 'In my old job [I spent] a lot of time just surfing. [Now] I don't have a terminal to work on, I don't actually click on it and go for a wander. I go over [to a remote terminal] when I know there will be something on the Web that will be useful ... to the sites I already know about. Another said that they would 'actually like ... [the] self-indulgent pleasures of wandering around the Internet,' but cautioned, 'I think every journalist knows that stage where you have simply over-researched a story and you have the makings of a ten volume book to boil down to five hundred words'.

Over reliance
Having so much information on tap from the Internet brings its own dangers to the journalistic process. It could 'eliminate the prime journalistic function of selection and evaluation of information. It will just be poured in'. The editor of *The Guardian* explains: 'Information is so readily available that sometimes it just gets fed unthinkingly into copy and I think that will be a danger especially in investigative reporters using it, as they get sort of dazzled by the information they can pull off it. A lot of this will go undigested into stories because journalists are so amazed that it is all there.' This can lead to problems: 'One journalist obviously used the Internet to pull down all these sort of lists of companies and all this sort of information about what some individual was doing in Italy but it was a completely incomprehensible story because he just sort of dazzled the reader – just look at all this stuff that I have been able to get, I have all these connections and all these companies and subsidiaries.'

The wider context
There was some consideration of information overload in a wider context, both with regard specifically to the Internet, and to information systems and dissemination generally, all of it being negative. What really concerned journalists were the bigger and wider issues: the way information systems were impacting on their industry and the society they serve. One *Guardian* reporter claimed that 'information just overwhelms people – it makes them aware that their ability

to change anything is zero. What's the point of knowing about things if you can't change anything? Who needs all that information?'

Some journalists also pointed to the fact that more information sometimes meant less knowledge. In this context they were worried about what they felt was the increasing 'dumbing down' of the news by 24 hours of news bombardment from a vast array of channels where currency and immediacy took precedence over detail and analysis. They feared a world full of 'information malnutrition', where people were simply unable to digest information. The result of so many news and information channels coming on to the market was 'fast and fleeting' information. Veronica Hallwell of *The Guardian* pointed to the irony that with dedicated TV news channels, and Internet information providers, newspapers will become more features driven, although people won't migrate to these new sources in great numbers, resulting, again in many receiving less current affairs information. The increased speed with which this new environment was forcing journalists to work compounded the problem.[6]

Overload solutions

Ways of dealing with information overload, although many and various, were generally what might have been expected, with information professionals taking the lead in employing retrieval skills, journalists simply choosing to look at a few potentially good sites from a hit list, and New Media professionals either denying that overload existed or claiming that the Internet was actually a cure for it rather than the cause.

With the Internet being famous for its 'user-friendliness', and web browsers being as intuitive as possible, it is surprising to discover that many journalists were unaware of the search engines it has spawned that incorporate various advanced search techniques. There is, indeed, evidence that some journalists, even fairly heavy users, were not even aware that there were different search engines. Lacking training, time and, possibly, motivation to experiment, they blissfully use the default option, type in a few terms and examine the resulting hit list. Many librarians, on the other hand, indicated that they did make use of, for example, truncation, phrase searching and Boolean logic[7]. Indeed,

---

[6]Even in the one year life of the project, for example, BBC has introduced its 'News 24' cable channel and Internet site, and digital TV, on the point of being launched as the project came to an end, promises over 200 channels of entertainment, news and documentaries.

[7]All of these facilities are provided by, for example, Alta Vista, Yahoo, and many other search engines.

using advanced search techniques or refining searches was the almost universally cited method librarians gave to overcome information overload: 'I've started being much more discriminating – I use phrase searching and advanced searching. I have started to use that more and more and use a combination of phase searching using inverted commas and Boolean searching because just throwing a couple of words at it and expecting it to come up with about ten or fifteen results is ridiculous. You just seem to get an awful lot of rubbish. I quite like the search engines like Excite where they say you can click on this bit at the side which says "Choose more searches like this", so if you find something you do like you can try that and it is more like relevancy ranking.'

Despite the often disparaging remarks made by librarians about the search skills of their journalist colleagues, many journalists were quite satisfied with their ability to retrieve information from electronic sources. The commonest tactic adopted by the heavy users – learned quite quickly it seems – was to be specific: '[The Internet] doesn't overload me because I am normally quite specific about what I want so I refine my search … it's easy enough to locate what you are after' and 'When I ask a stupid question on the Web I can see immediately how stupid I've been, but in the case of World Reporter you actually have to go through another level to see.' For the majority of journalists, however, the most popular solution was to be selective by choosing specific known sites. As indicated in the chapter on Web use, the majority of journalists tended to use only 'official' sites such as those of rival (or their own) newspapers, companies, institutions etc. By adopting this approach they overcame the problems both of filtering information from unmanageable hit lists and of authenticating the data they lifted from the Internet. Interestingly, the way these self-same journalists handled the overload that came with FT Profile searching was to conduct personal and corporate name searches (Nicholas and Martin, 1993).

The 'bookmark' facility used to save favoured locations was cited by nearly everyone as a major benefit even where, as in the case of national newspapers, this was a communal file as few individuals had their own terminal. Although creating individuals' own 'folders' is perfectly possible, this has not been undertaken to any large scale in the libraries visited (*The Guardian* being the main exception), which, in a way, reflects the laid back approach taken by many in the media business. In one library, a member of staff's penchant for lip balm information was celebrated by an entry under a 'Strange Junk' bookmark classification. Where individuals had their own networked PCs, the use of bookmarks was equally extensive. At *Sunday Business*, for example, a journalist had all the electronic national daily papers in one folder, specialist financial publications in another, and other directories of business or economic information – just as in a hard copy filing cabinet. The concept of the bookmark and its time saving and overload preventing qualities are generally understood. Indeed it is probably the most appreciated of all the World Wide Web's retrieval devices (almost invested with magical qualities) as this discussion between interviewer and newspaper editor shows:

Interviewer: *News International are developing at the moment this sort of idea of the intranet – the dedicated thing where what's interesting, what's useful, is sifted out and made more easily available to the staff.*

Editor: What and pooled – all the best bookmark sites?

Interviewer: *That's right. It is like having a centralised bookmark which News International have invested a lot in and it goes as far as contacts – everything being pooled – so when you log on there is a menu within News International and that will include favourite bookmarks and that sort of thing which does half the search work for you*

Editor: *That sounds wonderful.*

Another method employed to minimise the amount of noise obtained from Internet searches included adopting a self-imposed time limit on searches – the favourite figure being between ten and fifteen minutes per search and limiting the extent of hyperlink 'hopping'. These were mentioned by only a minority of both journalists and news librarians, but fieldwork observation indicated widespread adoption. Both illustrate a very common attitude towards the Internet – if relevant information can be found early on then that's excellent. If, on the other hand, it fails to yield anything of value, then that's no problem. It is generally regarded as a 'bolt-on extra' anyway.

For the New Media journalist, the Internet was itself the solution to Internet overload. One young male freelance IT journalist, pointing to an empty corner of his office, said, 'That used to be piled up with paper – press releases, stuff to read, publicity ... now I get my press releases on a special email account, which I can keyword search ... I use the Web to get information on companies ... electronic information has helped me organise everything.' As discussed in the chapter on the impact of the Internet on working practices of journalists, techniques such as SDI (known by these pioneers as 'baskets'), including intelligent agents which find the information you want and rank it for you, were much appreciated by this group – and a few IT journalists from the traditional press. 'What could solve information overload more completely than tailor-made newsfeeds?' According to Richard

Withey (1997) this information sorting process may become, paradoxically, so accurate that efforts are already underway to build in an element of serendipity for the people – journalists for instance – who cannot define their interests that closely

Quality of information

Assessments of the quality of information or the authority of a source may be subjective, but, nevertheless, quality figures very highly in the mind of the journalist. Broadsheet newspapers in particular are held in high esteem by their readers and to ensure that they do not diminish that by using inaccurate sources, journalists always seek to cross-check the data. Journalists and newspaper editors have to stand by what they publish, they cannot use the source as an excuse. Though some still do that – for instance, amongst journalists, the BBC is very well known for laying off a story to another source, typically the tabloid newspapers – in the main they make sure the information they use is accurate and authoritative. However, it does not mean that they implicitly trust even authoritative information. Unpublished documents and oral sources of information have always posed special problems for journalists in terms of their authenticity or accuracy. So, given the problem is not new, but arguably much bigger now, how do they, and their intermediaries, the news librarians, approach the Internet? After all, popular perception is that the Internet is riddled with poor quality, unauthenticated and subjective data.

In fact, the majority of journalists were phlegmatic about the quality of data you get on the Internet and the problem of verifying it. It concerned, rather than worried them, but no more than information obtained from other sources. And they had ways of getting around the problem. This was true for broadcast journalists as well as print ones. Journalists are well-used to evaluating information. 'Users must question the data they get from the Internet, they must evaluate and not take it as read. They must apply the normal rules of common sense.' This evaluation process is more intuitive than investigative, as the expression 'common sense' suggests. It's their job and they have been trained to do it. From long years of experience journalists obtain a 'feel' for the authenticity of the data. Plainly the Internet does not present anything unusual here, although there is a suspicion that they are not fully aware of the pitfalls of the Web. After all, telephone information must be even more circumspect when quality of data is concerned, yet few people question its provenance. Indeed, at one newspaper a hoax story was believed because it was telephoned in – the traditional route into newspapers for this kind of information. In fact, a number of journalists said how they were pleasantly surprised by the high quality of much Web data: 'The data was quite reassuring ... if you were a medical correspondent and you didn't avail yourself of that you would be bonkers ... I am sure if you were a defence correspondent, the same would be true and if you were an environmental correspondent it would have to be true.'

Whether the quality of the data was seen to be a problem with Internet data depended on several factors:

- job role and the different information needs that arise from that role;
- experience and knowledge of the Internet;
- attitude towards the nature of journalism and what constituted a newspaper.

Those who appeared to be most worried, approximately a fifth of all Internet users, were all either in positions of considerable authority or wrote on subjects that required particular attention to the veracity of data. Other journalists, such as features writers, seemed generally aware of the problem but many pointed to the problems of authenticating other sources such as information from personal contacts, paper cuttings etc., claiming that the Internet was no less reliable than these channels. A minority claimed that as newspapers were not academic journals there was less obligation on them to be 100% accurate. Many freelancers, and those with wide-ranging story briefs, who looked for initial leads from Web material, did not worry about authenticity as the fact checking process came later, when other sources were consulted.

The principal method by which quality problems were overcome or circumvented was – as we have already learnt – to choose trustworthy sites in the first place. As described in the chapter on Internet use, journalists predominantly used government or academic information from the Web, or accessed sites of other institutions and organisations of good repute. Only a tiny minority mentioned the problems associated with fake sites or of a genuine site being hacked (despite the recent publicity over the Labour party web site, which had suffered just this). Those looking at radical, alternative or 'unofficial' information from the Net – the minority – also claimed that their choice of site type obviated the need for verification. What was being sought was the opinions, or the facts according to the radical etc. organisation. The other method by which journalists established the quality of Internet data was the time-honoured one of checking the information against other sources. Typically, New Media journalists preferred to verify Web information on the Web – by emailing the Web master of a particular site for further details.

Influential factors

Job role and information needs

Journalists perform many roles, and hold a variety of posts. Indeed, a good number of journalists have nothing to do with the reporting of news. They are variously involved in criticism, comment, analysis, the obtaining of gossip, production of various forms of listings, management and a number of other tasks which may require information of various types in various quantities – from hard facts to whimsical speculation, from government report resumes to hype or innuendo. Clearly, then, the quality question is tied in with the nature and type of information required.

Looking first at the job role and position of the user (or non-user), editors figured strongly amongst those who appeared to hold strong views on the authenticity of data. These people were, of course, preoccupied with the reputation of their papers for which they had some responsibility. This comment was typical of many: 'It may be all right for the [named local paper] to do that [take unauthenticated data from the Internet] but not for quality journalists working for a quality paper'. Concern for the good practice of their staff in the changing information arena was also expressed: 'If you were researching Shell's record in Nigeria and you came across ten different sites, how would you evaluate one set of information against another and quite possibly the better looking one, the luminous one, might be … you will have to teach, especially the younger ones [journalists], how they evaluate what is reliable and what is not reliable.'

Those whose subject fields required particular attention to the veracity of information – crime, business and science are cases in point – were also aware of the problems. Some had concerns peculiar to the type of data they handled. This quote is from a leading crime correspondent: 'There is a problem with inaccurate information and particularly in my field that could be very dangerous because we run into problems of libel and we run into problems of contempt. It is obviously less dangerous in other areas of reporting like say the environment or arts. Reporting crime, if you get bogus information or inaccurate information about people's convictions or about crimes, then you are in trouble and I am wary of the Internet for that reason.' The reasons for City journalists being reluctant to use email (and even fax machines) – because they want to protect their sources – has already been mentioned.

Science reporters are another group who have stringent quality and accuracy requirements. Thus, the science editor at *The Guardian* regularly consults sites such as The NASA Pathfinder mission, The

American Association for the Advancement of Science, The Global Seismology Unit, other research institutions, universities and laboratories etc. in pursuit of quality information. He unquestioningly accepts that the information from such bodies will be accurate and reliable (whether conveyed via the Internet, hard copy press release or any other means) and is prepared to incorporate it straight into his stories: 'If I read an article in *Nature* or *The Journal of the Medical Association* then it is not an unreasonable assumption that the guy knows what he's talking about and that his colleagues believe he knows what he is talking about.'

Journalists from the departments for whom factual and accurate information was essential to their work often consulted web sites of other newspapers, magazines and journals of all descriptions. These were invariably described as 'official' sites – or trusted might have been a more accurate description – and as such the material found accorded a high degree of accuracy. Journalists have always placed newspaper cuttings in high regard and the fact that they now consult the Internet for this information matters not at all. The following quotes make this point: 'The things I ... [look at] are mostly newspaper articles from respected publications like *The Washington Post* ... I don't have any qualms about using [the Internet]'; '[I use] reasonably authenticated sources: magazines, publications ... and reports. I don't know what you mean [by 'authenticity']'; 'I am very wary of trusting the Internet – that's why I only go to newspaper sites.' That is not to say journalists trust newspaper sites (or cuttings, for that matter) implicitly. Thus one US journalist working in the UK said the British press was 'very unreliable', and others pointed out, almost as a justification for using the Net, that Profile and other online databases contained numerous factual errors: 'Profile [repeats] mistakes because you don't get corrections. If you run a story and there is a mistake in it and then the next day you run a correction that correction will not actually appear in Profile[8]. You will actually pull out the original article and then you repeat it – there's the danger. You could ask a Profile user about authenticity – it wouldn't occur to them that it wasn't [authentic].'

Government, company and academic sites were also heavily used and highly regarded. Interestingly, no doubts at all were cast on the veracity of the former, despite the low esteem in which the public – and journalists – generally appear to hold politicians. It was acknowledged that sites of commercial organisations had to be treated with some caution (they are going to make their own product look good), although, as one interviewee put it, they aren't going to put out lies.

---

[8]This is not quite true – they are published but not linked to the original story.

Journalists are not always seeking the truth. There is a high demand for the controversial, gossip and plain dirt. Thus, the fact that the Internet contains information of dubious, but interesting, quality is a journalistic plus for some journalists. In particular, features journalists and those charged with producing articles of unusual 'human interest' or of a generally lighter nature tended, as might be expected, to be less preoccupied with the quality of information problems. Indeed, in a lot of cases they are looking for information and angles regardless of its authenticity: 'A good example of someone who used the Internet very cleverly was *The Standard* with all the kind of series about Diana and so on. *The Standard* did a great pull of every theory off the Net and ran every Diana theory and broke them down into subdivisions and categories – you don't have to believe it but it's great journalism. Where would you do that without the Net? How would you know what the theories were? The Net offers all sorts of possibilities for that.'

With sites such as the infamous Drudge Report, a scandalous political site, features and general news reporters are bound to be tempted at least to scan the material – and the latest Clinton scandal had them queuing up to use the site. Drudge set up on his own without any journalistic qualifications or credentials, posting news onto a web site. *Wired* magazine noticed and then hired him, and America Online soon followed. His attraction was his knack for beating the mainstream press to some big stories, and there are claims (Stevenson, undated) that he even beat the networks by five minutes on 'the Diana story'. *Time, Newsweek* and *USA Today* (amongst others) have all profiled him. Drudge is the epitome of a 'non-official' news provider whose very independence (he has turned down 'six figure offers' to maintain this) paradoxically gives him authority.

Although, surprisingly, the sites like Drudge were mentioned by only a small minority of interviewees, alternative news and opinion outlets were particularly popular with freelancers, who were most likely to surf web locations as diverse as commercial sites, personal home pages, pressure group notices, sites of overseas political parties etc. to obtain leads. For these writers the information found acts as a catalyst for further investigation. The information is not taken raw from the World Wide Web, edited and placed directly in the article, as is done with respectable sites. But the site is used to fuel further inquiry. Thus the authenticity question is tackled further down the line with this type of use, when the potential leads acquired from 'surfing' are followed up by making personal contact or making other enquiries. Only one freelance journalist expressed any concern with the authenticity of Internet data.

Journalists seeking ópinion rather than facts – amounting to a little more than one tenth of Internet users – saw the authenticity/quality issue differently. Thus, the online editor for ITN, for example, is interested in Middle East affairs and monitors the newsgroup traffic of relevant Islamic and other groups, much as Swett (1993) recommends for the Central Intelligence Agency. The information he gleans is 'authentic' almost by default, if you make the logical assumption that the participants in these electronic discussions are legitimately interested in the subject area, and thus represent genuine strands of opinion. Thus, where the Internet is used as a kind of person locator, be it an expert in a particular field, a victim of a particular crime or sufferer of an unusual disease, authority doesn't seem to be an issue. Journalists use the information to arrange face-to-face or telephone communication, and use their subject knowledge and interviewing skills to evaluate the contact.

Librarians' approaches to quality and the Internet were also dominated by the nature of the information required (and the source of the query). Information specialists, like journalists, also used the Internet to access government, commercial, institutional and academic sites, as well as to consult the world's press. Many librarians also use the Internet extensively to research pop music artists, films, 'showbiz' and television programmes – as one interviewee put it, 'the entertainment side of things rather than serious news things'. As described in the chapter on use, there seems to be a much greater tendency on the part of this group to use the Internet for researching material unobtainable elsewhere. Some librarians go further, describing the information they seek from the Internet as 'offbeat', 'cult', and 'weird'. Many librarians said there was less need to try to authenticate such information.

Nevertheless, fewer librarians than journalists were relaxed about the quality issue, and there was a general feeling, sensed particularly in informal off the record conversation, but also openly declared in taped interview, that it was the library staff who had to counsel the journalists in relation to this matter. They were taking on their professional shoulders the corporate responsibility for accuracy and quality. Hence the emphasis of *The Guardian*'s information professionals on how to authenticate sites in the training package offered to journalists. It was hard not to sense a slight resentment from journalists when such matters were being mentioned – plainly many thought this was their patch – as the following (online) example shows. A journalist wished to write a story comparing what scientists and newspapers regard as the main current issues. The former was available in a scientific journal which had undertaken a survey of research publications. Newspaper coverage was intended to be established by an article count from FT Profile. When the librarian pointed out that this was too crude a measure, as some retrieved articles may not have the keyword issue as a central theme, the journalist asked for a 'rough figure.' This was refused, as it would have been too rough. After much haggling, the journalist said, in effect, *This is journalism – its not meant to be exact; all right, tell me what you think the main scientific stories have been*! The librarian gave a few guesses, and the journalist took his leave, muttering, *That's all I wanted to know*! Sure enough, the following day they were presented as an authoritative list.

Another librarian described a reporter's disappointment when reluctantly deciding not to use information from a Northern Ireland Loyalist group's web site they had found for him, because of the librarian's cautions. It had no contact number or email, and the URL appeared, as the librarian had to point out to him, to be a personal one. 'He had to authenticate that stuff – but he couldn't.' Those information professionals who were less worried about the issue felt that their responsibility ended at providing the information and the source: 'These sort of questions [authenticity, validity] are part of the programme maker's brief'; 'We know about the problem of authority, the reporter knows about it and it is up to the reporter'. By regarding the ultimate responsibility for proof as one to be borne in the newsroom and not the information unit, librarians, it might be argued, are in a stronger position to use the Internet in responding to queries, although in fairness, the overwhelming attitude among librarians was that they should do their utmost to ensure that all information passed to journalists was authoritatively sourced.

Experience and knowledge of the Internet
Not surprisingly those journalists well experienced in using the Internet were more aware of its limitations. Perhaps used to being fed on a diet of wire and other online services considered of high quality and current, many occasional Internet using journalists had clearly not even considered the issue with regard to the Internet. The following remarks illustrate this: 'You've hit a query above my head on that. It hadn't occurred to me to doubt the authenticity'; 'I've never thought about it'; 'I don't know exactly what you mean [by authority]. Something very solid, like Reuters News Agency, that's all right ... I wouldn't give the same level of trust to a claim by some Iranian exile saying that 74 members [of his opposition group] have just been shot in the back of the head] ... it has to do with the general credibility of the source ... the Internet is only a vehicle.'

The question often is really whether a site purporting to be, say, the White House really is what it claims to be. It appears to be this that respondents have not considered and a direct consequence of the limitations on their knowledge and experience of the Internet – a point reflected in Internet training sessions at *The Guardian*, described elsewhere in this report.

Other users were equally untroubled by the authority issue by virtue of another factor in the equation – their familiarity with their subject or with the news-making people they work with. This was mentioned particularly by specialist journalists. For example, one interviewee heavily involved in Middle Eastern affairs (and an Arabic speaker) is prepared to use communiqués posted onto the Internet by various disparate political and religious groups. He said he knows their aspirations, beliefs and workings and the kind of language which they use to articulate these. It would be no problem for him to identify false association with any particular faction. Similarly, science writers know their subject and, apart from having an abundance of web sites of prestigious organisations to choose from, are well capable of judging data from other, less authoritative, sources.

Another factor is the accessibility, or lack of it, of information from alternative sources. Some information is not only difficult to acquire but even more difficult to verify. Information staff at *The Guardian*, for example, have been required to find experts in 13th century Mongolian history and medieval Arabic languages which they have achieved via the Internet. Authenticating the credentials of such experts may be difficult, but the chances of material used being challenged for inaccuracies are small.

The nature and role of newspapers
Newspapers are not academic journals and thus do not require the same levels of proof and referencing, and this of course colours their views on the authority issue. While this was specifically mentioned by only four journalists in the sample, it is important nevertheless in that the ideas expressed were very similar and, given the general attitude towards the question of authority, probably representative. Putting it in its crudest terms, one *Guardian* journalist explained, 'In journalism, citing one source is considered plagiarism, and two, academic research'. The Scottish Media Group information manager explained it in more measured tones. Explaining that there was a marked contrast between, for example, medical research and newspaper reporting. Someone engaged on the former, investigating the effect of a certain drug, is required to consult and evaluate all appropriate literature and proceed with due consideration of all the evidence documented therein. A journalist researching the same thing, on the other hand, may be happy to read two or three medical reports, and interview a few patients or users. There isn't the same onus on the reporter to apply equal scientific rigour to his research, nor to obtain

the same degree of descriptive accuracy. In the case of the doctor or other medical researcher, omission of one piece of evidence could result in dire consequences for future patients.

This rather liberal attitude towards the authority question is further typified by a story recounted by the information manager of a leading national broadsheet. Researching the cost to the UK of the BSE disease she uncovered a mass of figures from a MAFF web site, including the price of slaughter, medical costs and many other statistics, presented in huge tables of information which she printed out. Realising the journalist would be less than pleased with this mass of data (a clear case of information overload) she also undertook a FT Profile search and found an article with one figure which exactly represented the information required: 'Whether someone on the other paper had done all the calculations or not I don't know, but faced with all those reams of figures on the one hand, and one lump sum on the other, I know which one the journalist chose to use – rightly or wrongly!'

Finally, it is not surprising to learn that it is also quite OK to pass the buck: 'We state explicitly in our articles that the information came from the Web: that way we are covered'.

Problems in authenticating data

The above, then, are the factors affecting journalists' and librarians' approaches and attitudes towards the quality of Internet data. Those seeking facts tended to 'visit' sites of well known and authoritative bodies; others, seeking opinion on a subject, did not even consider authenticity an issue. Nevertheless, some concern was expressed – largely by non-users, regarding the abundance of unsourced material posted onto the Web. Difficulties associated with email communication were also cited. The first of these was the biggest obstacle: 'If you found something on the Net you would be a bit sceptical about taking it as true because there is no way of verifying it'. The now famous TWA-800 flight story, where veteran American newsman Pierre Salinger used what he described as a government document to claim Navy gunners accidentally shot down the ill-fated aircraft while conducting missile tests, was cited several times. The document was originally posted onto the Internet and passed to Salinger by a French Intelligence agent (Noveck, 1996). It has since been discredited, although Salinger apparently continues to believe his original theory (Schmid, 1997) and a recent book on the subject (Sanders, 1997) supports him.

The TWA story may be a good example of a second problem cited by journalists concerned with authenticity. This is the 'Chinese whispers' effect, where one story is taken by various people and repeated, with each new author citing the previous ones to lend an air of authenticity, despite the fact that all accounts came from one dubious origin. This aspect of the Internet was mentioned in connection with travel information, the journalist, an ex-freelance, pointing out that in this field there has always been a problem. He claims that the Internet has made the situation worse, to the extent that one ends up reading almost word for word the same information, opinions and descriptions from several different sites.

The problem of authenticating email was mentioned by a small minority of journalists (along with other problems associated with this medium outlined in the chapter on communication via the Internet). One respondent summed up the disadvantages of this medium over that of personal contact: 'As journalists, we are still very conditioned to ringing a human being and asking it and hearing it. I suppose this is one of the things one worries about with the Internet. We are very used to going on tones of voice. Somebody speaks to you and you think he is lying or somebody speaks to you and you think he is telling the truth. Whereas with the Internet you lose that whole layer of context completely. You can't see people shifting and clicking their thumbs and just looking a bit evasive.' Of course, this also applies to the phone.

Tactics in authenticating data

The major reason why the majority of journalists do not regard authority as an issue is that they simply do not access sites they consider to be untrustworthy. Apart from this expedient, the tactic cited by the vast majority of journalists (over 90% of those discussing the topic) was to check or double check everything (there is some doubt as to whether they actually do this). Ironically, this partly explains why some journalists avoid using the Internet in the first place: 'I haven't had personal experience but I would imagine if you found something on the Net then you would be a bit sceptical of taking it as true because there's no way of verifying it'. New Media journalists mentioned using the phone as the method of verification so often it became almost like a mantra. Interestingly, this included phoning the Web master – as if they would admit that their information was of dubious quality!

Few people admitted to using the Internet alone. Many journalists either only used the Internet where the information was already known to them in a general way and confirmation or additional details was sought or, alternatively, as a first step for some background information researched in more detail later from other sources: 'The Internet points you in the right direction and then you check it out [elsewhere]'. Whatever the information source – and the Internet is no different in this respect – sources have to be double-checked – or triple checked in the case of Time Life. Indeed, at the latter organisation journalists claim to have so many checks and balances that inaccurate material is soon exposed.

Displacement of other information sources and systems

Never before – not even with the coming of online – have existing information sources been so challenged as they have been with the arrival of the Internet. No information retrieval system has ever been so widely available, so comprehensive, so flexible or easy to use as the Internet. It offers huge opportunities for rationalisation and consolidation of the communication system. The amazing variety of uses to which it can be put, and the quantity, depth and breadth of information provided, not only from its millions of sites, but also from use of chat groups and other communication channels, leads to the obvious question: what will happen to the existing electronic, hard copy and oral information sources? Will more work (and leisure) time simply be allocated to information seeking, to ensure the full utilisation of the Internet, or will other sources and systems be displaced to make room for it. Indeed, will some of these sources actually join in the process and replace (and re-invent) themselves, as *Yellow Pages* has done, by transferring their online service to the Internet? These were all issues we wanted to explore in the interviews.

Internet take up was relatively low among journalists, so talking of displacement may appear premature. However, many of those who did use it did so to retrieve information from a great many different web and other sources. At first sight, then, it would appear that at least within this group, if not within the news industry as a whole, a migration from other sources might have taken place, with Internet enthusiasts switching from traditional sources to the new medium. In fact, nothing could be further from the truth, with even the New Media gurus admitting that this has not happened. Indeed, no other communication medium or information systems seems to have lost out to any great extent as a result of growing Internet use. If that had happened it might have explained why few complained about information overload: they had simply picked up one source and dropped another. In fact, some interviewees reported that their use of other sources has actually gone up as a result of the Internet – it has simply made them handlers and processors of even greater quantities of information than they were before.

More often than not the Internet seems to reduce one type of use of a source whilst increasing its use in another way – leaving usage levels at what they were but having slightly changed their nature. Telephone use is a good example of this. These days Internet-using journalists and information professionals rarely phone the press office of a company for a copy of a press release or annual report; instead they visit the company's home page and download the document – it's easier to process it that way, and as one journalist said, 'the press office is always open'. In this case the Internet has resulted in a decline in phone calls. On the other hand, the suspect quality of some information on the Internet leads journalists to cross check-information over the phone, thus increasing its use. What seems to have changed is *when* the telephone is used: instead of phoning first, they now phone after they have gleaned some information from the Internet.

Where there is evidence of real displacement and not just changing usage patterns, the displacement is patchy and minimal, except at various locations such as New Media laboratories where Internet use is constant. Hard copy, online and CD-ROM have all been affected in some small way. Overseas newspapers are now being purchased less, with so many freely available on the Net. A minority of respondents, generally librarians, indicated that they used some book material less, and organisations were visited where either there was no library or that the library was little used for hard copy consultation. Most claimed the effect of commercial online hosts had not been repeated, and that the core of books left would continue to be required and used. Online itself *was* beginning to suffer, partly because of database swapping between various newspapers and partly because of thrifty Internet use. The pricing policies of FT Profile and NEXIS were considered to be unsustainable in the future, both because of this title exchange and due to the ever-increasing amount of cheap information sources becoming available. But even where this is no swapping going on – as in the case of *The Guardian* – online bills were plummeting (thus the NEXIS bill was down 50%). CD-ROM, never too popular in the newsroom, was also suffering a small decline, where information was available on the Web. *Yellow Pages* and *Hansard* were both accessed more on the Internet, but, because of a general distrust of the permanence of Internet sites, libraries were not removing paper forms of these publications. Finally, it seemed that fax would be elbowed aside by email in the not too distant future.

Why there is little displacement (so far)

A number of factors were identified:

- the Internet 'filled the gaps' in other sources;
- it provided preliminary information to be confirmed by other sources (stimulating a knock on effect);

- there is a mistrust about the permanence of Internet sources;
- and, for users and non-users alike, other sources meet information needs far better than the Internet.

The first factor was the most commonly expressed, mentioned by over half of those who spoke about the subject. Respondents invariably said it was used as 'an add on bonus', or a 'supplement'. One journalist said it 'accessed the parts other systems failed to reach'. At Time Life sources on the Internet were never the sort that would have been kept in the past, even when available in other forms (such as hard copy cuttings), and therefore do not displace anything. The Internet was seen as a follow up source when others failed. Observation sessions showed that at large traditional libraries where there was either a multitude of alternative sources – such as at News International – or where an Internet using culture hadn't developed (*Scottish Daily Record*), cuttings and/or online services were generally consulted first, and then the Internet. The situation was different at *The Guardian*, where often it's a case of consulting the Internet first and last.

In many cases the Internet has exactly the opposite role. It provides instant preliminary information to be augmented later from traditional sources. The extent of Net use for background information has been described in the chapter on web use. More than a third of Internet-using respondents mentioned this practice. The principal method of authenticating such Internet data was found to be consulting other sources – the very ones which, of course, would have been displaced! Similarly, the same source was contacted after information had been acquired from the Internet – information about companies being a good example, where phoning (and the perhaps consultation with more extensive hard copy PR material) followed from initial Net research.

The above are both good examples of the way Internet research affects the way other sources and communication channels were exploited rather than the degree to which they were displaced. Instead of a reduction in their use, working patterns have been affected, with the order of the various journalistic activities changed. Email is another good example of the way an extra facility does not necessarily eat into usage of existing systems. Although some journalists used email to communicate with their various contacts, this was often to ask them to phone later or to arrange face-to-face meetings, thus not replacing or diminishing either of these channels. perhaps, this was partly because of the lack of security of centralised/terminal-based email.

One prominent New Media journalist said that there was no proof that any significant displacement had ever occurred regarding information sources. Rather the appearance of one information source inevitably stimulates information seeking in general, with the result that other sources are actually consulted *more*. Echoing the example above, he claimed, that despite email, 'snail mail' continues to prosper; despite TV, more books are sold each year. In his case he reads more books because of the Web – he has found some sites where excellent and current book reviews are posted, and is thus persuaded to buy the publication.

Only a small minority of respondents indicated that the Internet did not actually provide for their information needs, and so it had not displaced anything, although, of course, it may be that, with the low Internet take up, a large body of journalists take this view. A City correspondent at *The Guardian* indicated that in his department there were plenty of other sources available to consult, and that they were hardly information impoverished. The very low Internet take up by him and others on the City desk at *The Guardian* seemed to confirm this. An economics reporter, also on *The Guardian*, said that statistics such as unemployment figures were also only available from other sources. A similar claim is made by interviewees on regional papers – they require information from the local council and local politicians, who do not (yet) have a presence on the Web. Even relatively heavy Internet users were not blind to the qualities of traditional sources – especially the much maligned cuttings files. Thus, a senior editor at the Press Association said that 'our reporters use the Net frequently, though of course it varies from person to person. Most would use it at least once a week,' but 'because it is so random it is still not as useful as a good cuttings library. Unlike most newspapers, we still use traditional cuttings; we cut a wide range of papers every day, and have, I think, about 14 million cuttings. We use these in preference to an online service like Profile. Our reporters use the cuttings library all the time. I still take the view that on screen all text looks the same – you don't know if they are worthwhile or not. Whereas cuttings you can judge. Your eye is guided, you know the ones that are no good.'

A final reason for the low displacement is a general distrust of the Internet, both in terms of information continuing to be posted and whether such information will remain free. An example is that of *Hansard*, available originally in hard copy, later on CD-ROM, and currently also on the Internet. Although journalists and/or librarians from at least four organisations use *Hansard* on the Internet (*The Guardian*, News International's main site, *Times Supplements* and *Sunday Business*), only at the latter was there no hard copy access. As outlined in the case studies, *Sunday Business* set out to be an almost exclusively online paper. The information manager at *Times*

Supplements, says he doesn't trust anything on the Internet one day to still be on it the next. *The Guardian* information unit has been considering cancelling their hard copy subscription for many months but staff were rather wary of doing so for the same reason. There were even comments by two librarians that the Internet version was badly organised and hard to search, and another said that as the previous day's *Hansard* transcript arrived in the newsroom at 2.30 the following day, there was little advantage in consulting the Internet for this record.

What is being displaced?

Given the generally low level of displacement to date, what sources are being affected, however slightly, by the Internet?

Hard copy

Hard copy generally, which might have fallen victim to the Internet on a large scale, is being affected, but only marginally. The lack of substitution may be because the real erosion took place in the wake of the online revolution in the 1980's, with a residual 'rear guard' of core books such as *Who's Who?* surviving. Even Internet enthusiasts value a good reference book, particularly if it is close to hand. Although a minority of interviewees gave specific examples of certain hardback publications that were no longer consulted – government reports; certain directories – very few spoke of the large scale replacement of this source. A Time Life journalist told of the reduction in space the US office library occupied 'from the whole floor to fitting snugly into a conference sized room, using the phrase 'shrink space information' in connection with the Net. The only respondent to claim that book research was no longer undertaken in her office was unable to say that this was simply because of the Internet. However, other specialist journalists and freelancers – those without extensive information sources available at their workplace – report using libraries less, and the head librarian at *The Daily Telegraph* reports that journalists at her publication are so adept at retrieving information from the Internet that it has pushed out many other sources and ways of doing things. New Media organisations such as VirginNet acquire, manipulate and disseminate all the information that passes through there hands exclusively in electronic form.

Far more common in the mainstream press (though not, as has been mentioned, at *The Telegraph*) however, was the comment, typified by a Herald information professional, that, 'Yes, we still use books – these [pointing to a particular shelf] are in almost daily use ... we still rely quite heavily on books'. Later she indicated that journalists too at *The Herald* still used hard copy, revealing that 'We've also got a locked cupboard with the more valuable books for obvious reasons. We've got the key.' The Reference Library manager at News International, provides a good example of the continuing appeal of books. She was given a trial password by a sales representative to access Encyclopaedia Britannia on the Internet (which would normally be charged): 'I must admit I never got round to actually trying it out, and that goes to show that I would still go to the hard copy – I know where it is, exactly where to look and I don't have to faff about.'

Hardest hit of all hard copy sources (and indeed, of all others too) may be overseas papers and magazines. These are not only free on the Internet but current too – *The Washington Post*, for example, appears in full text and, of course, is available for reading here as early as it is in the States. As outlined in the chapter on web use, nearly 40% of Internet using print journalists use the Internet specifically to access online papers. Both the perusal of the original web versions ('Having the big US papers hanging round the office is a thing of the past – we get them all off the Web.') and Internet digests of them ('Slate ... has a very good daily Washington column and a digest each day of the American press ... and is now doing a digest on it of all the European press.') are replacing the hard copy charged article. There is some evidence to show that information professionals in the broadcast media are also searching free newspapers on the Web before or instead of going to FT Profile. The (now ex-) librarian at London Weekend Television recounts the story of an Irish Times sales representative who failed to convince her or her library colleagues to subscribe to the publication, because 'at least 15% was available on the Internet'. Nevertheless, many librarians, particularly at News International, possibly because of its tabloid titles, report that journalists continue to prefer hard copy cuttings, and it seems safe to assume that UK papers – if not the foreign press – will continue to be bought daily, regardless of the Internet or online electronic cuttings services.

Although there are so many examples of newspaper archives on the Internet – *The Washington Post* and *The Wall Street Journal*, for example – they are, of course, not searchable as one entity or in a standard form, and no interviewees indicated that they use hard copy paper cuttings less as a result of the Internet. A displacement of cuttings was undoubtedly a result of the introduction of online in the 1980s, but there appears to be a continuing demand for information in this medium, so that organisations such as News International still cut papers every day for hard copy consultation by journalists.

Online services
Just as Web newspapers have led to a diminution of hard copy newspaper buying – particularly with overseas titles – so there is some

evidence of the displacement in the use of online services due to this new information source. Various interviewees speculated that the presence on the Internet of, for example, the full text of *The Washington Post*, various regional US titles, *The Daily Telegraph* archives etc. 'must make a difference to online sooner or later ...' although often here too it is a case of the Internet accessing information unobtainable elsewhere. Patrick Ensor, editor of *The Guardian Weekly*, for example, notes that many *Washington Post* stories on the Web aren't sent to the syndication services, so now they check both the wire feeds and the Net – an excellent example of how the Internet is being seen as a complement to traditional sources. As a clear example of the (slowly) changing information environment, it was only at the very end of the project that librarians at *The Guardian* confirmed with few doubts that online services were beginning to feel the Internet effect, with bills down consistently over recent months. Earlier lower costs had in fact been run up for one or two months, only for them to then spring back up to its previous (or even higher) level.

It is also likely that the internal database swapping that is now the norm between several titles (but not *The Guardian*), who upload electronic text of each edition onto a common database, is having a greater impact on online hosts than the Internet: 'Yes, we spend a lot of money on Profile. We are trying to cut back because we have got our own internal database which has got a lot of titles on it now. *The Mail* and *The Independent* are on there as well. We are trying to cut back on our Profile use ... [but] I can't see how the Internet could come close to providing a service that Profile provides.' Despite this reservation, one newspaper group reports a 75% reduction in their online bill partly as a result of this free swapping of internal databases. Even news agencies do not appear totally invulnerable – *The Daily Telegraph* foreign editor estimates that half his staff use the Internet. That they no longer subscribe to Reuters may be significant. Many doubted that, with all the digital competition mounting up, in the form of internal databases, the Internet and other news providers, online services could continue to charge such rates as they do.

CD-ROM

CD-ROM was never popular with journalists because of its lack of currency; nevertheless, none of those mentioning CD-ROM in the newspaper medium considered that there had been any displacement. Again the feeling was that the Internet simply complemented information obtained from this source: 'We have a dictionary of quotations on CD – if I can't find what I want on that I have a click around the Web just to see if there is anything'. CD-ROM was also favoured – but not by everybody – over the Internet because of its comprehensiveness: 'The electronic [web telephone] pages are very good but it is not comprehensive, whereas we have got telephone directories on CDs which are 99% comprehensive, so I would always trust them over the web site'. Interestingly, however, the use of Web directories was the most common retrieval activity mentioned by librarians in questionnaire returns, where displacement wasn't explicitly mentioned.

In the broadcast media CD-ROM does appear to have suffered as a result of the Internet. Here too, it seems it had never really been too popular – respondents mentioned its inflexibility and the inevitable delay in the availability of reissues – and many broadcast libraries had never made much use of the information supplied in this format. Casting it aside, therefore, in favour of the Internet, as has occurred almost totally at the London Weekend Television library, is not a surprising development.

Migration of sources themselves to the Web
Yellow Pages was one of the most frequently mentioned sites consulted over the Internet, generally by people who had used its online version, but by some who had been used only to the hard copy. So many now preferred the Web to the online site (there were criticisms that the latter was difficult to use) that there was some speculation that the online version had, in fact, been converted for Web dissemination and no longer existed – thus, in a sense, displacing itself. *The Guardian*'s science correspondent talks much of this development, citing in particular NASA's policy of displacing hard copy information releases by issuing all its bulletins and other material only on the Internet. With many other organisations issuing press releases on the Internet, even if not exclusively so, there was a general feeling that Internet access to these was beginning to replace traditional online sources: 'Sometimes you can get press releases quicker on the Internet than you can on the messenger services'. Although the vast majority of Internet sources were either electronic versions of material available in other formats (web newspapers, for example) or material that never appeared, or would appear, in any other form (bulletin boards, personal web home pages), the migration of information that traditionally appeared in one form to the Internet, with the original source terminated, looks likely to provide a major impetus to Internet use in the future.

There is a sense amongst many of the people we spoke to that we are on the threshold of bigger changes, greater displacement – and that where we point to small changes now they will inevitably become bigger.

Changes in work practices

The question of how the Internet was impacting and would impact in the future on individuals' work patterns (and on the news industry itself) was possibly the widest and most open question asked in the project. The chief area of interest was the changing relationship between the newsroom and information unit with the advent of mass end-user searching, push technology etc., and the consequent implications this would have for the information professional. Also of interest was whether the flexibility afforded by the Internet both to access remote information and communicate on a one-to-one and one-to-many basis would affect time spent in the office and interaction with colleagues.

Broadly, the answers, comments and observations offered regarding the issues showed that the canvas was, in fact, even wider than had been suspected. Journalists were expected and (gently) encouraged to discuss their views on retrieving remotely located information rapidly and without recourse to an intermediary – their approach to the new communication channels offered by the Internet and the way these may affect their story research, and their attitude to the possibility of teleworking. Librarians were also asked for their views on this too. It turned out, however, that their concerns went far beyond these issues, important and wide-ranging though they were. Their preoccupations were, instead, with the dissemination of information via the Internet, rather than its retrieval, and the consequent future of their profession. Principal amongst their concerns for the future was what they regarded as the dumbing down of news, occasioned partly by the increasing influence of marketing people and accountants. One spoke of a generation fed on instant news 24 hours a day and suffering information malnutrition – in other words, fast news having the same lack of substance as fast food. The increased speed with which they had to work because of the advances in computerised editorial production was also a big topic. Much was said also regarding the future of the hard copy newspaper, the nature of Web journalism and the degree to which web papers would be read. Apart from the odd vague comment that 'I expect I will use the Net in the future', the system as an end-user research tool and the implications of that on their working practices never really engaged any except the New Media Internet disciples – and librarians, of course.

By contrast, information professionals did look at the issues in the way anticipated, both in terms of what these were perceived to be and in the way they were regarded. Their main interests were with the possibilities afforded by LAN intranets, both in their construction and in improving their professional work. The main talking point here was the hope that intranet databases and web sites would reduce the number of trivial, fact based queries received – something they had hoped that commercial online would deliver, but patently did not – and allow a more investigative role for librarians. A minority also expressed interest in the potential for involvement in greater journalist training. Most librarians, however, did not feel their job would change in any major way as a result of Internet use, and there were certainly no worries about job losses amongst intermediaries as a consequence of greater end use.

Key areas of change

End-use

There appeared to be a general feeling, at least amongst journalists themselves, that it was only a matter of time before most of them began to use the Internet, although there were doubts about whether this would be in a big way, and, unlike the big bang that many have suspected, many seemed to think their use would develop slowly and gradually: 'The Internet is bound to come into the office. I suppose sooner or later I will be using it – if I'm shown. I certainly don't need it yet.' There was universal agreement that before any mass end use could take place the facilities had to be there for instant desktop access. This was even acknowledged by one leading broadsheet editor who, despite his awareness of the lack of access for his staff, said they are 'bonkers' if they don't use the Internet. 'I think it does take some time and until you get a reporter with a terminal on his own desk it is not likely to catch on'. There were, however, few comments to suggest that those currently using the system would actually extend their range or sophistication of use. Rather, there would be greater consultation of sites already known, or similar sites, and a readiness to use the Internet over other sources not so easily to hand: 'Yes, I would definitely [use the Internet more, given easy access]. I would subscribe to new news services or specialist outfits ... on a particular country or particular issue. I realise that more and more things are going on the Web and I should get better geared up to accessing it.'

There was a general feeling amongst librarians that end use would not increase significantly – journalists were lazy, they didn't feel it was their job to do online searches, they wouldn't have time to learn the Internet, were a few typical comments. There was, indeed, much criticism of journalists' ability to retrieve information: 'They search in a haphazard way; they do not know what to do with 33,000 hits they get when they input 'Tony Blair' into the system ... they are successful maybe 10% of the time'. Even the editor of a national broadsheet daily, very enthusiastic about the Internet, had reservations about the online search skills of some of his staff: 'You just know from the size of the bills. [One journalist] comes up with bills of £700-£800 a month and you know that is just because he isn't searching properly'. As with online use, Internet use looks set to plateau at quite a relatively low level of sophistication

Non-Internet users – very much the majority of journalists – although feeling the Internet would play an increasing role in the newsroom, generally did not show much enthusiasm about using it in the future. Many were simply non-users of all information systems, as the following quote from one national paper journalist illustrates. Of the Internet he said, It's a nightmare ... there's too much information ... if you've got to do three or four stories in a day you just can't spend the hours deciding which server might have which bit,' and of online, 'All the services are there but it's quicker to ... ask someone up here [in the library] who is really good at knowing where [the information] might be'. Other non-users did not consider that they would use the Internet in the future because of their negative perception of it or because they felt there would be no need: 'It's overhyped ... I am wary of it'; 'We have all the resources we need already'.

The lack of anticipated future Internet use was reflected equally with regard to email. Although external email is already available from the desktop at many titles, its potential use would be extended by users being able to send messages via web site mail links. There were no suggestions that this facility was eagerly anticipated or that it would be used to any great extent.

One leading New Media expert is not at all surprised by the current low Internet take up or lack of commitment to its future use. As far as he is concerned the Internet is in its infancy. His own research into past technologies shows that it takes forty years for a technology to come to fruition – horse ownership peaked in 1931, decades after the invention of the motor car. Nevertheless, he regards the Internet as 'the big one', with online being a cul-de-sac by comparison.

Role of the information professional
Just as there was little indication in the research findings that end use was about to explode, so little change was anticipated regarding the role of the librarian and the relationship between the information professional and the end-user. With so much misinformation and misconception around we might expect a very mixed response on the part of libraries to the Internet. And, indeed, this is exactly what we find. Some have used it as a launch pad to enter new territory – training, research, web design and end-user support for instance – whereas others – essentially those already marginalised by the previous rounds

of IT – have become even more marginalised, more isolated and more removed from the mediation role.

Those who have already embraced the end-user in the previous online wave, created by the entry of full-text databases into the market, and followed the migration of information from the library to the user's desktop, were proving to be the quickest of the mark. Their closeness to the user, and the credibility they obtained from being associated with the introduction of IT earlier on, has put them in the ideal position to provide Internet training, documentation and advice. For them the Internet is providing the professional growth and opportunities that online/CD-ROM promised but never really delivered. Examples are the Internet training courses currently being developed by the Research and Information Unit at *The Guardian* and the construction of an intranet at News International. The former, in addition to outlining search techniques, organising bookmarks and introducing various sites of potential interest, includes tips on how to evaluate and authenticate data. 'Library lunch' seminars have also taken place, introducing journalists to information issues surrounding the Internet. The intranet at News International, is an impressive catalogue both of useful external web sites and internal HTML-coded databases. Included are chronologies of famous people, birthdays, stories grouped by theme such as 'Care in the community murders', and even metric to imperial conversion tables. Library staff feel their status has increased as a result of its introduction, and believe that their jobs will become more interesting in the future when journalists become familiar enough with the intranet site not to have to ask them basic fact type questions that can be quickly answered by the journalists online and from their desktops.

More often than not this seems to have been the case. However, a number of libraries have boxed and coxed and failed to take a strong lead. The more traditional the library the more they appear to be losing out. Some libraries have opted to concentrate on their archival role – editing the electronic feeds, and have largely dropped news research. Librarians have become inputters, database editors; they work round-the-clock but have very little contact with their users. The line of work is however profitable with the selling on of electronic data to other news providers. It is journalists who use the Internet and not them. They watch journalists search the Internet and internal databases and wonder how they get on – always suspecting that the answer is poorly. But they do not have the time, nor apparently receive the encouragement, to do anything about it.

The Net's 'we are all librarians now' culture has not really been embraced by journalists. A minority of journalist respondents spoke about the selective dissemination of information (SDI), the use of which would widen their exploitation of the Internet. However, this was more with regard to the dissemination of news to the public via web papers than with such services being employed by and helping journalists in the future: 'People do not go to the Net for a depth read … how many people read all of a newspaper? The information [will be] filtered for them … individuals can adjust the length and depth of stories'. One of the few comments to relate this possibility to journalists themselves was: 'I fully expect the Internet to improve its own accessibility … and actually generate those programmes which will actually point stories that you want to read straight at you. I can see the day when I will be using search engines on the Internet which point stories to me which I need for my work without me having to go out and look for them'.

The fact that few journalists mentioned SDI in any guise testifies to the general lack of relevance to them of such services: 'I don't tend to write about the same things and you do not know what you want until you see it' and poor quality of those developed so far: 'Customised news services haven't helped me in any way'. Indeed, for at least one journalist the lack of filtering is a positive advantage. She has got to know the (Russian news) sites that will give her the information she wants without any SDI help, and says, 'One of the great attractions is that they are unmediated – no English journalist has provided any filtering … there is much more detail'. Filtering, or push technology, or any other expression indicating some form of SDI service was, surprisingly, spoken of by few librarians. Those who did so were generally unimpressed: 'Baskets are crap. There is a huge problem associated with them. You have to spend so long teaching the intelligent agent that it is not worth it. What you get is usually too much – and rubbish.' Interestingly, however, questionnaire returns indicated that about 25% of librarians did not have an opinion about this issue; of those who did indicate a particular view, a small majority said they disagreed with the statement that 'there is no future in push technology'. It appears that when they are in open conversation, intranets and training occupy their thoughts more than SDI, but when required to give an opinion, many do see some role for this technology

Push was, not surprisingly, enthused about by New Media workers, though with these people too the emphasis tended to be on the end-user as member of the newspaper reading public rather than as researching journalist. There was, nevertheless, some mention of the latter: 'Streaming information and filters is a solution to overload – otherwise they [journalists] will miss things. Journalists who say they do not know what they are looking for so cannot stream are lazy – by browsing that broadly you are going to miss lots of stuff'. The principal advantage of SDI cited by New Media people was in the area of customised web newspapers. Once this subject was touched upon, the whole debate widened beyond the initial remit of the research, to the way newspapers would react to the information superhighway and the migration of news to the Internet, interactivity between newspapers and their readers, and the nature of journalism itself. Regarding SDI, much play was made of apparent evidence that, in addition to sales decline in the newspaper industry (for which there is hard evidence) that those that are bought are being read less – 'The traditional newspaper is not suited to the crowded lives we all live. We want the headline clicking features of the Net'; 'How many people … read all of a newspaper … everyone [will have] potential access to all news information but the information [will be] filtered for them, by them and intelligent agents'; 'Intelligent agents, the real intelligent ones, are on the way. They will be with you from birth and anticipate your every information need.'

This enthusiasm wasn't shared by all new media journalists. We will leave the last words on push to the creative director of VirginNet: 'Push is just like rain – it comes when you don't want it.'

The dumbing down of journalism

Various journalists – unprompted – mentioned a number of factors which they felt, when put together, were leading to a lowering in the standards of what they wrote. Not all of this was to do with the Internet, but most of it was due to the phenomena of which the Internet was a part – electronic information dissemination, seeking and processing, and its attendant problems. The essential problem was that there was too much information, in too short a time and in too short a space. A number of journalists claimed the quality of their journalism was suffering for reasons connected with the proliferation of information: 'With online and the Net you cannot physically look at every story – there are too many and it takes too long … in the old days I used to pride myself with the fact that I read every cutting on a topic so I knew everything and did not repeat anything. And it is possible to read a hundred or so cuttings at one pass. It's so easy to discount things with cuttings…. Today I'm content to look at just a few – and I have no idea whether these are the best few.' In other words, the masses of information available with online and the Internet had the effect of narrowing, rather than broadening, the focus, and forcing almost arbitrary selection. This, and ever tighter deadline demands ('Most of my stories have to be completed in thirty minutes, but sometimes I have five minutes to research and five minutes to write.') results in stories being less well researched today than previously. This would lead to problems for consumers as well as journalists: 'People are bombarded by information sources, but these sources are purveying soundbites ... [they] belong to the information family but are shallow – and that is all most people get ... just as growing numbers of people are suffering from malnutrition as a result of an incessant diet of fast food, so people are suffering from information malnutrition from the fast and fleeting information they only ever obtain.'

Similarly, journalists were more worried about the impact of news SDI on their readers than themselves. There was, however, the feeling that by being able to choose the subjects about which one could receive news, and the breadth and depth of that news, a certain information impoverishment would result. One journalist recoiled from the possibility that some people would only ever hear sports news ('That scenario horrifies me') and another complained that already people were seeing 'news events without context – they see them as discrete, isolated, only exploding 'now' events. There is the double jeopardy of untutored minds exposed to a flashing sea of web pages'. One New Media specialist spoke about research his organisation had undertaken showing that of 2,000 people 'visiting' their news Web site per month, only one tenth of that number clicked individual headlines for further information.

There seems to be a paradox here which was not lost on a number of respondents. The Internet has improved information supply, and has given users access to documents, discussions and individuals that would have been almost impossible in the past. Not surprisingly, it is felt that news dissemination generally will gradually migrate to the Net because of its instantaneous nature and ease of distribution. This was borne out particularly in the questionnaire responses, where over fifty percent of all correspondents agreed with a statement to this effect. At the same time, and perhaps because of this, there are forces – accountants and marketing people – who are pressurising for less in-depth news and more features in newspapers. Indeed, some interviewers claimed this process had already began. With less news content in newspapers, journalists will simply not require the information that is available on the Net and elsewhere, exactly because it is available from those sources. One journalist takes all this to its logical outcome – as the press leans more and more towards features, lifestyle, leisure etc., eschewing in-depth current affairs coverage, people will need to get their news from elsewhere. However, they won't be bothered to use the Internet or multi-channel TV for this purpose, but, rather, for recreational purposes. Thus the Internet may be responsible, despite its incredible depth of information, for dumbing down the news!

Finally, several journalists cited the reduction in the number of foreign correspondents as a sign of the diminishing dedication of newspapers to delivering quality reporting. One cited the 'shrinking band of news gatherers', a vivid contrast to the burgeoning market in news dissemination, and lamented the lack of investment in this area. Also the reduction in the power of the editor hasn't helped: 'Once kingpins, they are now on the third rung under accounts and marketing. We are led not by editors but by user surveys.'

Working at home
There was little enthusiasm to take up the possibility the Internet gave for working at home. Indeed, of the interviewees who spoke on the subject, only one wished to spend more than one or, occasionally, two days at home. Much was made of the teamwork necessary to bring out a newspaper: 'Producing a product in which every section compliments every other section can only really be done if you've got people in the same office talking to each other and saying, 'Don't forget to do a cross-reference from that story to the book review ...'''. As noted in the chapter on email, there was even reservation expressed about internal message systems inhibiting the discussion of ideas, spontaneous information seeking and other interaction with colleagues.

Other reasons for the lack of enthusiasm centred around problems related to technology, although those citing these also mentioned the importance of being with colleagues. Only one interviewee gave technical reasons for not working at least some of the time at home: 'I tried working from home [but] I have been reluctant to spend a lot of money on printers and paper fax at home because it seems to me that it is technology that is on its way out.... If I had Internet access at home and if all the people I needed were accessible on the Internet (they're not) I could certainly see myself working more at home. A lot of the work I do, particularly features stuff, is a lot easier to write at home.'

It seems that, even with the technology, there are problems in working away from the office: 'I have an arrangement which I negotiated to work one day a week from home but recently I haven't been doing that because I have got a brand new computer with Windows 95 which is absolutely terrific but unfortunately the office software, which is very outdated – MS DOS programme – doesn't work properly on it, so I can't get into the system here to get messages and to pick up PA copy which is extremely frustrating.... So because of that I am hesitant about working at home because I know I am going to be disadvantaged in a way, which is a real nuisance.'

New Media people take far more advantage of the possibilities for remote working. One freelance multimedia journalist said that not only the Internet but IT generally has revolutionised his working practices. His company consists of three partners, plus others hired on a freelance basis. Because of the IT facilities they exploit, the company does not even have an office. All three work from their respective homes, communicating by email or phone. Faxes arrive at a special mailbox they all use. If one of the group is out, any phone calls to that location automatically get diverted to one of the other numbers. Any reports etc., can be passed around for amendment by the others. The 'absurdity' of paying £500-£600 a month renting an office when there is no reason for all three to be in one physical location was pointed out with some relish.

Differences of opinion

During the course of the many interviews we conducted with journalists, a number of strongly worded – and, possibly, contentious – remarks were made. We have quoted many of these in at appropriate places in the text. However, we also wished to establish the extent to which the views contained within them were shared by media librarians. Twenty one remarks were reproduced and sent to librarians as part of a questionnaire. Table 13 provides the results of this exercise. The main findings were:

1. Few librarians strongly shared the journalists' views. In fact, in only one case did librarians as a whole strongly agree with the journalists – and that was in regard to a remark (no. 15) that highlighted the importance of librarians as filterers: 45% of them strongly agreed with the view expressed. The surprise, perhaps, was that not more of them concurred.

2. Librarians were, however, far more likely to mildly agree with the journalists' remarks (10 cases) than mildly disagree with them (4 cases).

3. Librarians only strongly – and universally – disagreed with one remark (no. 8) – and that, interestingly, was one that suggested that journalists would end-up tied to their screens. 84% of librarians felt strongly that this would not turn out to be the case.

4. The remark that had them most split was no.6 – 'A global, easy to access/publish system scares the newspaper industry to death'.

Table 13
Extent to which librarians agreed with journalists about the Internet

Opinions expressed by journalists	Strongly agree		Mildly agree		Mildly disagree		Strongly disagree		No opinion		Total	
	No.	%	No.	%	No.	%	No.	%	No.	%	No.	%
1. When journalists get 100% access only 20% of them will refuse to use the Internet but only 20% will use it as a force for good/change.	2	5	13	32	3	7	2	5	21	51	41	100
2. There will be a cataclysmic change (because of the Internet) in the way society works.	6	15	15	38	10	25	7	18	2	5	40	100
3. With the Internet there is no excuse for not knowing anymore.	2	5	13	31	11	26	12	29	4	10	42	100
4. The Net will change the face of journalism.	9	21	20	48	5	12	4	10	2	5	42	100
5. Newspapers will be increasingly features driven and the news will migrate to the electronic media.	3	8	17	43	8	20	6	15	6	15	40	100
6. A global, easy to access/publish system scares the newspaper industry to death.	4	10	9	23	13	33	10	26	3	8	39	100
7. I couldn't do my job without the Internet.	4	10	11	26	11	26	18	43	0	0	42	100

Statement												
8. With so much information flowing around the Net and what with this two-way dialogue you do not need journalists to go out and gather information anymore.	1	3	0	0	5	13	32	84	0	0	38	100
9. From just scanning cuttings I know what kind of story they are without me having to read them. I know the tabloids from the broadsheets, I know the popular article from the specialist one That is faster than anything the Internet can do.	9	23	11	28	9	23	10	25	1	3	40	100
10. The sites are not updated as much as you would like.	3	8	24	63	4	11	3	8	4	11	38	100
11. With the Internet you could go on and on never reaching the end – with a book you know you have come to the end of the chapter; with the Internet you cannot see what is before, what is after, how much there is to go.	6	15	17	44	6	15	5	13	5	13	39	100
12. If I want to find out something I get on the phone … with email it's like sending it out into the wide blue yonder.	1	3	7	18	16	41	12	31	3	8	39	100
13. If there is a problem on the Internet, the Internet is also likely to offer a solution.	7	19	6	16	11	30	2	5	11	30	37	100
14. Instant access is the key attraction of the Internet for me.	12	29	18	44	7	17	1	2	3	7	41	100

Statement												
15. The librarian's role is to protect the end-user from information overload – by filtering, sorting, establishing relevancy etc.	19	45	18	43	2	5	2	5	1	2	42	100
16. Information just overwhelms people – it makes them aware that their ability to change ganything is zero – what's the point of knowing about things if you can't change anything?	1	3	4	10	10	26	23	59	1	3	39	100
17. There is no future in push technology – its all so arbitrary and random.	0	0	4	10	8	20	17	43	11	28	40	100
18. Those worried about overload don't turn on (their Internet connection) in the first place.	5	12	10	24	10	24	4	10	13	31	42	100
19. People are suffering from the fast and fleeting information diet they only ever obtain.	1	3	12	32	13	34	3	8	9	24	38	100
20. I just want the facts from a Web site, not the graphics or other trimmings.	6	17	15	42	5	14	8	22	2	6	36	100
21. I use the Internet to find the quirky, offbeat or obscure.	10	27	11	30	7	19	6	16	3	8	37	100
22. The Internet is vastly overrated as an information tool.	2	5	10	26	17	44	10	26	0	0	39	100

Most agreed with:

Opinions expressed by journalists	Strongly agree		Mildly agree		Mildly disagree		Strongly disagree		No opinion		Total	
	No.	%	No.	%	No.	%	No.	%	No.	%	No.	%
The librarian's role is to protect the end-user from information overload – by filtering, sorting, establishing relevancy etc.	19	45	18	43	2	5	2	5	1	2	42	100

Most disagreed with:

Opinions expressed by journalists	Strongly agree		Mildly agree		Mildly disagree		Strongly disagree		No opinion		Total	
	No.	%	No.	%	No.	%	No.	%	No.	%	No.	%
With so much information flowing around the Net and what with this two-way dialogue you do not need journalists to go out and gather information anymore.	1	3	0	0	5	13	32	84	0	0	38	100

The one that had them split:

Opinions expressed by journalists	Strongly agree		Mildly agree		Mildly disagree		Strongly disagree		No opinion		Total	
	No.	%	No.	%	No.	%	No.	%	No.	%	No.	%
A global, easy to access/publish system scares the newspaper industry to death.	4	10	9	23	13	33	10	26	3	8	39	100

Chapter 6

The Case studies

The purpose of the two case studies is to provide a coherent and detailed picture of the impact of the Internet on a particular organisation – and to set the discussion firmly in a particular news environment. Two very different case studies have been chosen: one a very established and traditional news organisation (*The Guardian*) and the other a news organisation that is very much a child of the nineties (*Sunday Business*). The differences are deliberate: *The Guardian* is a big, quality national newspaper of some repute, that has had a long and successful experience of the introduction of information technology, whereas *The Sunday Business* was a very small, new and specialist newspaper that tried new solutions to succeed in a very competitive market – and used technology to help it succeed. (Unfortunately it folded during the life of the project).

Case study 1: *The Guardian*

The Guardian is a national quality broadsheet daily, sistered with the Sunday paper *The Observer* which operates from the same building in Farringdon Road, London. The paper is unusual in at least two respects. It is one of the few nationals not to suffer a decline in readership over the last few years, and it is the only one to be free from proprietorial pressures, enjoying the common ownership of a trust. The Research & Information Unit (which serves both papers) is open-plan, situated on the same floor as the features and sports sections of *The Guardian* and three floors below *The Observer*. It is fairly accessible, though the library staff themselves would prefer to be situated on the same floor as *Guardian* news and nearer *The Observer* – from which their main customers come. The open-plan set up, common in newspapers, though less so in newspaper libraries, is significant in that it reflects the attempts the information unit has always made to be a pro-active force in news researching. The Information Manager has always been interested in the relationship between journalism and librarianship and 'is very conscious of how the two professions overlap' (Sylge, 1996). It is no surprise, then, that the training of journalists in using the Internet is a current priority and several librarians report working more closely with journalists since the arrival of the Internet terminals at the paper. This, of course, was also true of the arrival of online.

Introduction of the Internet at *The Guardian*

The development of Internet use at *The Guardian* has been sporadic and although the Research and Information (R&I) Unit was not slow to become aware of its value, there was a delay in obtaining access. The first moves towards editorial access came in late 1992 (before Alan Rusbridger was appointed editor), when key members of the editorial staff were given modem connections. For a while facilities seemed to appear arbitrarily, with the R&I becoming increasingly agitated both at their poor equipment and at being excluded from the developments – this happened with FT Profile too, so 12 years on and little noticeable change in information policy at *The Guardian*. There is one difference though between Profile and the Internet: while the former can be accessed via the Atex editorial system journalists use to key in their stories and access working files, the Internet cannot be. For Internet access they have to use the smattering of PCs spread through the building. This is very significant to the discussion below.

With the Information Manager describing the link as 'vital' to their working (and self-respect), R&I were finally given a modem connection in April 1993 and one member of staff was detailed to get to grips with it. The difficulties with the modem link, however, were enough to dissuade all but one other librarian, from getting too enthused. Nevertheless, enough was being written about the Net by 1994/5, including an enthusiastic endorsement from Harry Evans, a former *Sunday Times* editor now based in New York, to persuade the Information Manager that more formal training was needed for all the staff. Slowly the odd journalist was beginning to ask questions about the Internet, one columnist wondering, confusedly, if they knew of this new 'massive database somewhere, where you could access all sorts of information on virtually any subject'. However it was not until early 1997 that the ISDN link was installed in R&I by a new and sympathetic IT director – it is significant that the prodding was not coming from editorial. All other links were rationalised at the same time. It was the establishing of the ISDN link that allowed use of the Net to take off in R&I, demonstrating how important speed and dependability of access count. Answering reporters' queries with reference to the Net now became the norm. Daily papers are dependent on speed and connection via the modem link at R&I's busiest time, mid to late afternoon, was just too slow. And with the easier access came increased interest from all the staff, so that today all members of the R&I staff use it on a regular basis and two people have responsibility for training journalists.

Facilities
Despite this enthusiasm expressed about the Internet in the R&I unit and, indeed, also emanating from the Editor (Alan Rusbridger), Internet use at *The Guardian* is low – with probably not more than one in ten journalists being active users. The lack of terminal access appears to be a major inhibiting factor preventing the Internet's greater exploitation. For journalists there is one terminal in home news and one in City news. There is some individual access for senior staff: The Editor, Deputy Editor and other leading figures, for example, have terminals. A terminal in the features section has recently been removed, although this may, apparently, be a temporary loss. Significantly, none of the access points for general use are connected to printers. Journalists do have access to online services from their own desks through the Atex system. This facility appears to be occasionally used by the majority of journalists. Even those who do use this service regularly complain that it is not always accessible, as only two passwords are available for all the journalists in the building. The situation is far better for information staff – there are two terminals in the library. Previously one operated through a modem, and the other direct line. Now, however, in preparation for the construction of an Intranet at the paper, both terminals have ISDN connections, but only one printer.

The training of journalists
Internet training at *The Guardian* began in 1997, not long after the installation of the ISDN line. There was a history of training courses being run by the R&I department which had started thirteen years previously to cope with journalistic end use of FT Profile. Early courses were fairly basic how-to sessions but in line with a perceived development of their role as trainers the library staff up-graded the training course following a conference at the European Centre for Journalists in Maastricht where other American newspaper training courses were studied. It was at this stage that the training metamorphosed into a rather more expansive, evaluatory course, with explanations as to how to recognise the provenance of URLs, how American and European URLs differed, using an amalgam of this US information and some home-grown ideas too. Journalists were advised to approach evaluation structurally along the suggested lines of authority, accuracy, objectivity, currency and coverage, as the following paragraph, taken from notes used by the information staff, shows:

Authority: is it clear who or what company is responsible for page; check for addresses/tel nos (email can be forged; what are aims, qualifications, purpose or nature of company/person/organisation)

Accuracy: are sources for factual info clearly listed for verification;

check for spelling and grammatical errors as these indicate lack of quality control and can produce inaccuracies in info.

Objectivity: be aware of biased info; is info free of advertising; if any advertising on page is it clearly differentiated from factual content;

Currency: are there any dates on page – when material was written; when page last revised; how regularly updated; is there archive of older material

Coverage: is site completed; is it clear how deep or wide coverage of subject is; are there links (Martin et al, 1997)

The course was designed to last about an hour and was given on a one-to-one, voluntary basis, running through email, mailing lists and list-servs, newsgroups (where reporters were warned that their email address clearly indicated their company and that they should be wary of expressing views thought to be representative of *The Guardian*), Internet Relay Chat, searching and search engines. Journalistic advice was also offered, namely that they should re-evaluate with every link and that online interviews should always be followed up by telephone to try and make sure they were genuine. Bookmarking was also covered and trainees were given a list of bookmarks pertinent to their field. In March 1998, and following an interview with *The Guardian*'s editor for this project (who had expressed a need for such information), the course was revised once more to increase the advice given on search engines, which were best for what, which offered Boolean, which didn't and so on. This information was organised into a table and attached to the training guide given to reporters.

In the summer of 1997 the R&I unit ran a group 'how-to' session. The feeling among the library staff, however, was that whilst this may have been the quickest method of creating widespread interest in the Net, it was not the best method of training; one-to-one was thought to be better. By July 1998 – and in spite of frequent adverts on the in-house electronic bulletin board (news-wir on Atex) – only 51 reporters from both papers (total number in excess of 300) had presented themselves for training. Evidently, in the absence of Net access from the desk-top – and the lack of printing facilities with some of the PCs – it was not thought worthwhile to go to the second floor to train. Once the Atex system has been replaced by either a Mac or PC based system, this thinking might be revised.

It is currently proposed by editorial management that Internet training will become compulsory when the new PC-based editorial system is introduced in 1999/2000. However, despite the R&I unit's past efforts it is not naturally perceived as the agent for this training.

Users

With respect to Internet use by journalists, *The Guardian* is probably about mid-table (with *The Times*) in a league of those national dailies visited. Higher use was reported at *The Independent* and *Daily Telegraph*, less at *The Herald*, and none at all at *The Mirror*. As with other similar papers, use was heaviest in the 40-49 year age group, reflecting the ease of access of senior figures at the paper. Indeed, for men the modal age was 50 plus, which included the Assistant Editor and Science Editor who both have desktop access, and three others, at least two of whom have access at home. As with the overall sample, there was no evidence of an army of young bright and enthusiastic journalists clamouring to use the Internet and forcing management to provide the necessary access, although young staff were interviewed who used the Internet and would appreciate desktop access. The Editor is a strong proponent. As may be expected at a paper such as *The Guardian*, he seeks to run the paper in a way that allows his staff to have their say, and has held a series of lunches towards this end, not forgetting to promote the Internet at the same time: 'At the end of every session I got them all to put their hands up and say whether they were using it or not.... At the end of every lunch I said, "You are all bonkers if you are not using it. It ought to be an absolutely standard tool."' He has also sent round an email to all staff using similar language and sentiments. Perhaps not surprisingly, Alan Rusbridger considers himself to be the most prolific user of the Internet on the paper, with the exception of another senior figure, Assistant Editor Victor Keegan (although actually science correspondent Tim Radford is probably the biggest user, employing it 'every day, all the time', for a wide variety of purposes).

At the other end of the staff hierarchy, Internet use was inhibited, more by access problems than attitude. Younger reporters were perhaps a little more enthusiastic about the system than at other papers. This was illustrated by Jackdaw researcher Hannah Pool, who found the Internet invaluable for searching the foreign press and was lucky enough to be able to do so by having a (communal) terminal very close to her desk. Its removal 'made me realise just how much I rely on it'. A minority had actually used the Internet more in previous jobs – at a university, as a freelancer etc. – and said their use would be greater with easier access.

In terms of use by different departments or news desks there does not appear to be one section that uses it significantly more than any other (apart from Science, about which Tim Radford says, 'I am the science editor, that sounds as though I have got a staff but I haven't – there's just me.'). The sports editor indicated that his reporting staff, who, by the nature of their jobs, are not required to be in the office a great deal, tend to use email more than others might, and work more from home. Web use appears to be highest in the offices of *The Observer*. As a weekly paper, staff have more time to work on stories, to research and, consequently, time to experiment with the Internet. Even here, however, access was difficult: 'We have one Internet terminal for the whole of the newsroom ... access is absolutely appalling. We are supposed to be receiving and disseminating information all the time and we are hamstrung by the fact that we don't have decent access.' Although one interviewee, an Assistant Editor at the paper, considered that use tended to be extensive but by just a small minority of journalists, there were certainly more users volunteering to be interviewed, a greater awareness of the potential and a realisation that the Internet would play a bigger role in news gathering in the future than elsewhere.

By contrast, Internet use on the City desk was minimal. Yet high levels of commercial online searching go on – largely in respect to FT Profile. One interviewee was unaware that there was a terminal in that area, and another wasn't sure where it was located. Interviewees claimed that sometimes it was not used for weeks, and there was a general feeling that the paper had enough information sources without recourse to it – online makes them feel self-sufficient. Amongst the interviewee sample, one economics reporter/researcher and a personal finances reporter were users – the former a light user, inhibited by the lack of desktop access, and the latter a great enthusiast who used it a lot at home. The lack of use by their colleagues, and the feeling generally in the department that there was little need for the Internet, contrasts markedly with the attitude and use pattern at *Sunday Business*, which made heavy and constant use of both free and paid services on the Internet, and also the findings of other studies. MORI (1997), for example, found in questionnaire responses that 81% of business and financial journalists have access to the World Wide Web at work (although the degree of access was not asked) and 39% had looked at web sites of various companies.

Regarding gender of Internet users the picture is mixed. Considering only journalists, fewer women were interviewed – indicating in itself a possible lower take up among this group – but of those (eight) all but one were users. This contrasts with twenty nine males, among whom only twelve were active users. It may be that women non-users were more reluctant to be interviewed or, on the other hand, that any female sample would have resulted in a high percentage of users. It is even possible that the nature of the reporting jobs that women happen to have at *The Guardian* lends itself to Internet use.

It was a case of near universal acceptance in the information unit. Ten permanent staff are employed. Most of these have a particular area of responsibility – two for the Internet, one for online searching, one for uploading the electronic feed of the paper to the online host, one research co-ordinator etc. etc. Four graduate trainees are also recruited annually. Access in the library is not a problem – two terminals between fourteen potential users – and its use is coming to be seen as more and more an integral part of the information seeking process. Only one librarian claimed 'I have survived very well up to now without it', the others all being users to a greater or lesser degree. With such universal adoption it is, of course, impossible to make any comment regarding age or gender, regarding Internet take up – except that library staff tend to be female.

Use: The Web

The general feeling among those who use the Internet for information seeking is that it is employed, as by journalists at other national newspapers, for consulting online newspapers, official sites of well known organisations and government produced web documents. When asked how his staff used it, Editor Alan Rusbridger said, 'My sense is for raw information, such as, I guess, Hansard. So it would be used quite frequently as a searcheable site for text ... things like government statements, legal documents, legal rulings where they are available.... If you were a medical correspondent and you didn't avail yourself of [the vast amount of information on the Internet] you would be bonkers. I am sure if you were a defence correspondent [or] an environmental correspondent [this] would have to be true also.'

Of his own use, he gave as a specific site example, Slate online magazine: 'I look at that most days because it has got a very good daily Washington column and it has also got a little digest each day of the American press ... and Alexander Chancellor is now doing a digest of all the European press so that is quite interesting to look at'. Specific subject areas were also given by him: 'I have done quite a lot of work on privacy and defamation through the Net – picking up rulings from South Africa and Australia and ... writing leaders on the regulation of the Internet ... download[ing] the entire Supreme Court judgement on the Common Decency Act in America.'

Guardian librarians also used the Internet for weighty, 'official' information. However, as found with other newspapers, they also tended to search for the weird and wonderful. As mentioned in the chapter on Internet use generally, this is not surprising, as even end-user journalists are likely to pass to the information unit the kind of queries they can't satisfy by traditional means. An excellent example is described by one of the biggest Internet using librarians: '[An amazing story] that I got involved in … [on which] I spent the whole day on the Internet was the mass suicide – the Heaven's Gate thing. When I came in at 11.00 I had a department asking me what was this Heaven's Gate thing. So I went down and I think somebody had already tried doing a search and couldn't find it using one of the search engines they use. I tried a different engine and found [it] straightaway and was using it all day until I couldn't take it any further. It was quite spooky knowing that the people that had designed it were all dead.'

It is rare for journalists on the paper to use sites for which money has to be paid, although the *Miami Herald* site was used to download a particular article, for which the journalist requiring the piece used his own credit card.

Displacement
Even at *The Guardian*, where Internet use is lead from the top in both the journalist and information sides of the paper, it was still seen very much as a complement to other information sources, and as a 'second port of call', to be explored when other more traditional sources fail to yield the required information. Nevertheless, accounts indicate variously that The Internet has replaced some hard copy publications (such as Yellow Pages, which is now on the Web) and press release messenger services (Victor Keegan, Assistant Editor, reports that sometimes the Internet has these first). It has been reported that, since data collection ended, the Internet has become increasingly a port of first call for information professionals on the staff.

There is some debate about whether online database use has also been displaced to any great degree. NEXIS, for example, could be used a little less now because some US newspapers upload substantial sections of their publications onto the Internet. *The Wall Street Journal*, indeed, makes its full text available and includes a search facility for its own current archives and a 'Search the World' service where reference materials and web resources for more than 220 countries are listed. The bill for using NEXIS sometimes appears to be lower than might be expected (such as in April and May 1997) but then it climbs again (as it did the following month), making assumptions about displacement difficult to sustain. As mentioned earlier it was only in the very last weeks of the project that *The Guardian* Information Manager declared that there was sufficient evidence to conclude that the use of online was, indeed, finally being affected by web searching.

Use: Email
There is an extensive and widely used internal messaging system, but external email is probably used by, at the most, half of all journalists. Not surprisingly, of course, those in the New Media unit are heavy

email users. Despite some interest by certain reporters, the telephone and personal contact were much preferred. Only a third of *Guardian* journalists mentioned using email – almost exclusively to message colleagues or contacts overseas – and only a small minority spoke with any great enthusiasm about the medium. One journalist described it as being an easy way to communicate: 'You can have half a conversation without having to go through the preliminaries or having to be polite'. Ed Pilkington, now Foreign Editor (then Editor) of *The Week*, said it has made things more convenient for him because he can 'get people to send articles in by email, which is really good'.

More typically, however, were remarks indicating low use or a dim view of the channel: 'I only email a couple of people'; 'I like using the phone – I've got a good phone manner but I don't know if I've got a good email manner'; and, 'I like to make one quick phone call and sort everything out like that'. Indeed, even where there was enthusiasm, many criticised the system set-up. One interviewee described the Atex front end as 'slow and cumbersome', another as being 'very tricky to use', and a third as 'extremely clumsy and time consuming'. When one Observer reporter, who had waxed lyrical about the benefits of email, suddenly realised he was being asked about using it from his office terminal he started back, saying 'Oh no, I wouldn't use it here....' When approached about these attitudes, the information manager was surprised. Acknowledging that external email went first to the IT department before being forwarded on, rather than going directly, she said that nevertheless it was 'Very easy. You open a file, type your message, put "email-sys" in the appropriate box and hit "send". That puts it to IT who do the rest.'

There may be confusion between the internal Atex system and email. With the former, messages go to an electronic box from where they can be retrieved by the recipient. As all editorial staff are connected to this system, they are 'messaged' and not 'emailed'. Non editorial staff, however, are not on Atex and are therefore emailed, albeit internally. Another complication is that lengthy attachments are stripped off at the IT department stage, as they tend to crash the Atex system. Therefore these have to be sent to an IT address and collected. Finally, the system does not include a subject header line, so the content of messages isn't known until they are opened: 'You are working [and] then you see "message pending" and you think this is something terribly important ... [so] you stop what you are doing and store it and look at it and all it says is "Thanks" – usually "tks"'. Mail sent to the IT department (readers' letters, and emails to the Jackdaw column, for example, are automatically routed there) are allocated a code: 'The actual message is preceded by something between 10 and 15 lines of, let me call it, pre-code. To me that is an immense waste of time and resources. You have to get through this and you have to scroll it up before you actually get to the message.'

Most recently, the R&I unit has begun to use it to communicate with the Editorial sections of the paper; before it was a case of typing out letters.

Use: Newsgroups
Bulletin boards and newsgroups were not utilised by *Guardian* journalists or librarians. One librarian expressed interest, but felt that he did not have the time to undertake what would essentially be an experimental effort, taking an unknown period of time to obtain information from dubious sources. Another said that he had tried several times to acquire information from newsgroup message traffic, but that it was difficult to find an appropriate discussion group, and virtually all of the information was banal or unsuitable in other ways. One interviewee thought that it was not possible to access newsgroup messages from the library terminals, and others had never considered this potential resource. Only one journalist mentioning newsgroups. This was Martin Bright, Education Correspondent of *The Observer*, whose use is described in the chapter on Internet communication.

Conclusion

In many ways, *The Guardian* gives the impression of being a newspaper on the brink of a sudden explosion in Internet use. The Editor and one of the Assistant Editors are both keen proponents and heavy (if novice) users themselves, and every encouragement – other than suitable access points – is given to other staff to indulge. The R&I unit exploit the Internet constantly, and have several staff members capable of running training programmes (although only two are charged at present with doing so). Although the pool of current users is probably no greater, percentage-wise, than is the norm for the national press, the users tend to be influential figures, and as many as one third of non-users are keen to learn or to practice skills already acquired. Another healthy sign is that there is evidence that any gender differences are flattening out. What is changing too is that management has finally made a financial commitment to provide high quality universal access. Editor Alan Rusbridger, has long realised that 'until you get a reporter with a terminal on his own desk, it is not likely to catch on'. And this now looks as though this will happen – by January 1999 in fact. When this happens, the paper will become a leading light in journalistic Internet use, befitting its image of a progressive and innovative publication.

Case study 2: *Sunday Business*

Introduction

For a number of reasons, not least the fact that the paper ceased publication during the life of the project (and has since started again), *Sunday Business* was unique among the media organisations involved in the fieldwork. It was a specialist publication, created to satisfy a hitherto neglected niche in the market – the business person with an appetite for financial news even on a Sunday. Although journalists from other specialist titles were interviewed, *Sunday Business* was the only such paper researched in depth. Ironically, however, the principal difference between this paper and the others was its youth – it survived for just over one year, being founded as recently as 1996. This meant it began life when the so called 'Information Revolution' had already started, a fact of great significance in terms of IT equipment installed and the information seeking practices of the journalists on the paper.

IT provision at *Sunday Business*

Uniquely among those newspapers visited, *Sunday Business* reporters were all given PCs internally networked and with Internet access. There was no library or information officer, nor any hard copy information provision, be it in the form of books, reports or cuttings – a big contrast to the tabloid dailies (but not *The Mirror*), which still, as noted elsewhere in this report, devour clippings. Approximately half of the journalists had used the Internet before starting at the paper and those who had not ended up doing so almost as a matter of course after a very short while. Another distinguishing feature was the very tight financial budget operated under. This was important as it necessitated economic information seeking – hence a degree of Internet use that went off the scale relative to other titles. Almost needless to say, *Sunday Business* was in a class of its own in terms of IT provision and the general computer literacy of the staff.

Internet Access

Giving all those involved in the editorial process Internet access was not originally deliberate policy on the part of the *Sunday Business* directors. Information Technology manager Derek Beecroft had to convince Executive Editor Tom Rubython of the advantages of desktop access. He wanted to make *Sunday Business* 'the first PC-based newspaper system.... Everything ... is run on PC. He wanted it to be a showcase about how a newsroom should be so he could sell the same sort of system to other people. We are probably fairly well set up in terms of we've all got Pentiums and email to the desk.' 'All' includes one PC for every journalist, sub, editor and everybody else involved in the newsmaking process. It has taken less than a year for this access to be considered so normal that one journalist declared, forgetting (or ignorant of) the degree of IT provision on show at other newspapers: 'If you've got a mainframe, dumb terminal and you've got these Atex systems it would be just a nightmare.'

To illustrate the point further, it was revealed that even the receptionists were also networked, and made full use of the facility to alleviate boredom when there was little activity in the foyer. Staff on duty during the late afternoon and evening were, apparently, particularly liable to succumb to the temptation to 'surf the Net'.

Internet use

The quantity and quality of financial information *Sunday Business* staff managed to access free from the Internet was truly impressive and Internet use was extensive. This ranged from data collection, in depth research, browsing for story ideas, lifting pictures and graphics, and using email both for making contacts, seeking information from experts and delivering copy.

World Wide Web

Given the low budget of the paper it is no surprise to learn that the Internet was worked to the full, although it has to be said that there is evidence that other specialist publications have not taken quite so readily to the Internet. At Financial and Business Publications, for example, staff are warned against reliance on the Internet. The heavy exploitation by *Sunday Business* also contrasts starkly with the normal information seeking behaviour in the City/Business sections of national papers. Even at *The Guardian*, a relatively progressive title in IT outlook (if not provision), the Internet was very rarely used to find financial information, and few staff were aware of the material available. Indeed, some were only dimly aware of the presence of an Internet terminal in the vicinity, and considered that it had nothing to do with them.

It is worth examining in detail the kind of free data available and accessed at *Sunday Business*, demonstrated to the researchers during fieldwork at the paper, as it is illustrative both of the extent to which the system was worked to produce information, and the possibilities for other titles in the future, currently relying on expensive subscription or other charged services. Before doing so, however, it is worth mentioning that not all staff used all the resources available: 'Although I used ESI, Moneyworld and III, I'm not sure how many of the others did – we all tended to have our own sites to go to, depending on which beat we were on'.

Naturally *Sunday Business* journalists also used paid services, but these also tended to be over the Internet. They will be considered later in this report.

Free information sources
Firstly then, the following was obtainable from a site known as The Interactive Investor (*http://www.iii.co.uk*):

- Unit Trust performances over specified time periods (so, for example, the top ten Far East unit trusts over the last five years could be accessed, downloaded and then converted into graphical format which would later be credited as with any other source, and used to illustrate an article);
- online forms for calculating personal taxation; and
- other personal finance news, including interest rates for various savings accounts etc.

Moneyworld (*http://www.moneyworld.co.uk*) contains similar data, and also covers what *Sunday Business* reporters described as 'the two biggest financial stories of the day', which they found extremely useful. Another site widely used at *Sunday Business* was created by a company known as Electronic Share Information (*http://www.esi.co.uk*). ESI was founded in 1993 with the aim of offering private investors 'easy, instantaneous access to the type of online price information and services previously available only to major investing institutions' (Electronic Share Information, 1997). It does this 'by means of the highly cost-effective channel provided by the Internet' (*Ibid.*). The company points out that professional investors 'have long had two important advantages over the private investor: access to real-time stockmarket prices along with comprehensive information about the companies they want to invest in and online dealing facilities' (*Ibid.*). It is worth looking at the services offered by Electronic Share Information because they illustrate clearly the extent of financial information on the Internet and, therefore, what other papers are missing by not utilising the medium. Briefly, then, the service allows access to stocks and shares, including share prices updated eight times daily (a paid service also exists, as outlined later, in which prices are available in real-time); and information on companies (a 'vast range', including company news, analytical information and forecasts). UK listed shares can also be bought and sold directly over the Internet through ESI.

Bloomberg is another financial service accessible through the Internet and used at the paper. Information available includes world equity indices, top US mutual trusts, mortgage calculation etc. Much of the company information provided is also free – this is in the form of 'Hoover's Company Directory Search', a database of over 10,000 of the largest public and private companies in the US In addition to basic information on the company, each listing contains links to the company's stock quote, stock graph, SEC documents, financial data, and more.

Other popular sites consulted were online versions of other newspapers and news services such as UK Plus, Profound and PointCast. The latter is described as an 'Internet news network' The service broadcasts national and international news, stock information, industry updates, weather from around the world, sports scores and more, from sources such as CNN, *Time*, *People* and *Money* magazines, Reuters, PR Newswire, BusinessWire etc. Many US 'local' newspapers are on PointCast, including the *Los Angeles Times*, *New York Times*, *Boston Globe* and the *San Jose Mercury News*. Because it is supported by advertisers, the PointCast Network is free. Also, it provides a personalised news service whereby the source (such as CNN etc.) can be chosen. Filtering by subject is also a feature, although it does so in what was described as 'a limited way' only.

Other magazines, particularly US titles, were accessed over the Internet. Use included both in-depth research and browsing for story ideas: 'We also often researched stuff on US magazines … the leisure reporter might look on catering, hotel, etc. magazines in the US for ideas and the IT reporter read *PC Week US*, *ComputerWorld* etc… We didn't buy US magazines, or only rarely. But some reporters used such publications extensively on the Net.'

As in other organisations, the Web was also used as an online telephone directory: 'First of all if I'm looking at a particular company I can just do a search. More importantly, if I'm searching for stories I'll come up with a pile of stories – I'll see that Mark Christopher or Cater Allen has been quoted on a piece about money markets…. I'll think right, that guy's been quoted, I'll go and talk to him…. I could do this with a phone book probably but there is a site called Moneyworld.co.uk. There is another one called Find.co.uk and there's others – iii.co.uk – all have databases of financial services companies so you can find the company you want. Which I could do I suppose by calling Directory Enquiries but sometimes you don't find them.'

Even the picture desk would retrieve material from the Internet, although quite often the quality wasn't sufficiently good for images to be usable in the paper, regardless of whatever copyright problems that may have resulted from this practice.

Paid information sources

As mentioned earlier, paid information over the Internet was also used where necessary. As has been mentioned, ESI offers such a service. In fact, they have two levels of information provision costed at different rates. The appendix outlines the information available to subscribers of each, known as 'bronze' and 'silver'. Bloomberg also offer a more comprehensive financial information service for paying subscribers, and was used by some Sunday Business staff, notably Derek Beecroft.

As may be apparent from the description of the various sites and the information it is possible to retrieve from them, the Internet appears to have a different character with respect to financial data than to information it yields on other topics. One Sunday Business reporter said it was excellent for specialist and 'focused' information, which would be very useful for freelancers who may not have access to newspaper funded databases or clippings. This is interesting because the overriding view of the Internet from the majority of interviewees using (or not using) it for other kinds of data is that it is vague, unstructured and informal. It was indicated, however, that 'you have to know where to look'.

Email

Sunday Business was an email newspaper – everybody used it, and most staff checked their 'inbox' several times a day. Indeed, the production editor was said to be 'always on email'. Unlike at other papers, it was used primarily for external communication – elsewhere it tended to be used either principally or exclusively for internal messaging. At *Sunday Business* the office was small enough to make it easier, and one suspects more satisfying, to go and talk to colleagues in person.

The heavy email use lead, not surprisingly, to journalists building up folders of addresses. These were used if, for example, information was required about a particular subject. Mailshots would be sent out to groups of recipients known to be experts in the particular field. One reporter explained: 'I sent out this email this morning to 30 odd people just saying, "Anybody got any information on this?" Say I'm going to do a story this week about Self Invested Pension Plans and it is quite a specialised area and if I didn't have the Internet I'd probably phone two or three large PR companies like Lansons [or] Dewe Rogerson, whereas with the system I use I'd hit all of them with an email in much less time than I could make one phone call. Also, maybe there is a little company out there that I don't often deal with that has a client that does just this.' In another case forty three people were emailed for advice about the experience of building societies changing to banks. Several email and telephone replies were received, some fittingly during the course of an interview for this project, making the story research a lot easier than it would have been.

Although generally submitting material by fax when the paper first started, by the end of its life staff, even freelancers, routinely delivered copy via email. Indeed, its use became so prevalent that when the system went down it spelt disaster for everyone. On one occasion two people were 'desperately waiting for copy' when exactly this happened. In the end the private CompuServe account of one of the journalists had to be used to allow the stories to get to the office rapidly and in electronic form. Listservs were not used by *Sunday Business* reporters, although this was due more to a lack of time to explore the possibilities rather than disinclination: 'If I found relevant listservs directly to personal finance I would definitely sign up for them but I don't know the existence of any at the moment. Again it's time, because I've not been able to go to a course and somebody ... – say you are in personal finance you can do x, y or z.... I've had to find it out myself. I'd just know loads more if I had the time.'

Newsgroups

Although no examples of the use of newsgroups were discovered specifically at *Sunday Business*, at least one journalist had used the facility before. This was at *PC Week*, and was to research 'virus' stories, where a lot of information could be found on the 'alt.comp.virus' site. Journalists said they would use newsgroups more, but the system was 'not set up for newsgroup site setting' and they were difficult to access. Also, the predictable problem, again, of time constraints was mentioned, confirming findings from elsewhere that this aspect of the Internet is the least used because the time required to find useful information within the endless stream of text is regarded as simply not viable. Here is a group of IT-literate people who publish weekly, and yet they still do not use newsgroups.

Training

Unusually, about half the staff had already had previous experience of the Internet before being employed by the paper, many of them as freelancers. There was, however, no recognised system of training for the other fifty percent. Although that could be said for virtually every other publication studied, the predominance of IT makes that perhaps more significant at *Sunday Business*. The responsibility fell to those journalists *au fait* with the system who would show prospective users how to search the Internet as and when circumstances demanded and time was available. As journalists became familiar with basic Internet searching, they would begin also to find out about saving HTML files, converting to text, cutting and pasting onto a word processor document etc. Again, advice was asked by individuals about these possibilities from whoever happened to be available.

Issues

Information overload

It was considered so convenient to have Internet connections at their desktops that journalists at *Sunday Business* were hardly worried about having potentially too much information. As has been described, a number of very valuable, information-rich sites were known and bookmarked, so they became the standard first ports of call and not, as at many other locations, a 'last resort'. When word searching was undertaken this was often directed, with UK Plus topic categories being used; searches undertaken on *Wall Street Journal*, *Daily Telegraph* or *Euromoney* magazine archives, or other specific searchable sites such as Companies House online 'search rooms'. These targeted searches meant that overload did not even arise, let alone be considered a problem. Also, the time saved in not searching through hard copy magazines easily compensated for any difficulty with 'too many hits' from a keyword search.

Displacement of other sources

Paid sources, other than those available through the Internet, were used by *Sunday Business*, despite the full exploitation of the World Wide Web. These included ICV and Reuters, although use of the latter was strictly limited. Other sources were also available: 'Originally we used M.A.I.D. over the Internet. But the deal fell through and we switched to FT Profile. But we had a limited deal and were encouraged to use the Net wherever possible to get information. Each month our time on FT Profile would run out and once it was gone it was tough luck.'(Plainly there was a place for commercial online services).

As the Internet was available from the birth of the paper, patterns of use of these other sources do not seem to have changed much. Those journalists in the area of financial information before they began working at the paper reported that it is the hard copy sources that have been replaced by the Internet. It was pointed out that with sometimes only eight journalists to bring out a forty one page edition it just wouldn't be an option any more to go off to the London Business Library etc. This removal of one hitherto extremely rich information source was not lamented: 'I know that if the Queen Mother dies today I could actually write a piece on brain surgery ... I could do that as a freelance without having access to a library now. I can do it here without having access to a library. I can also put a feature together in an awful lot shorter time. I will sometimes do a search, say it was brain surgery, find a whole pile of stories, actually cut and paste them into the Word document I'm working on. So I can be writing a story at the top and referring to stuff at the bottom for the background. Which is quite phenomenal in terms of the research you can be doing.'

Similarly, the fact that the paper didn't have its own library was not a cause for concern: 'Have you been to News International, for example? You have to go down six floors or something into the library, find what you are looking for and photocopy it and then go back to your desk and half an hour has gone. I could probably have done that here in ten minutes.'

Chapter 7

Conclusion

It is all too easy to be misled into seeing the Internet as the first big IT wave to hit the media – New Media journalists (and students) are particularly guilty of making this assumption. But it was not – there have, in fact, been a succession of waves: the introduction of computerised editorial systems in the early eighties was followed by full-text online searching a few years later; in turn this was quickly followed by the arrival of CD-ROMs in the late eighties – albeit this more a ripple than a wave – and then internal online databases arrived in the early nineties (although not in *The Guardian*'s case), preceding the Internet by a matter of years for some and months for others. Each wave has served to 'soften up' journalists and librarians for the next wave – each wave has made its mark – and frequently its effect has not been felt till some 5-10 years after its initial appearance, thus complicating any IT impact analysis as a result.

Take-up and impact

What we discovered was not what we were led to believe from the published literature – especially that emanating from the United States. Far from being in the vanguard of the Internet revolution, the media appear to be nothing more than followers; far from finding the media awash with Internet users, it was sometimes more a case of find the Internet user. (Media) hype has preceded reality by some margin in most things related to the Internet; and in a few instances never looks like ever materialising. Plainly nobody is going to take a leap off the information high board when they are so well provided with information and communication services. The situation varied throughout the media – and it was interesting that freelancers – the least well provided for in information terms – should take to the Internet with some enthusiasm. However, on average it was unlikely that more than one in five journalists used the Internet. In this it was no different to FT Profile – and there are still many more journalists at papers like *The Times* and *The Guardian*, where the service is piped to their desks, who do not use it than do. Low and patchy use can be ascribed to the poverty of Internet access (and the dead weight of the Internet-unfriendly editorial systems) in much of the media – by academic standards they have a long way to go. The decisions are now being made to move to PC/Mac based editorial systems, so undoubtedly access will improve significantly over the next few years.

It is not simply a matter of access though, and even at the IT-aware Press Association, where the Internet can be used from the editorial terminal, it was thought that journalists used the Internet about once a week – hardly a revolutionary pattern of use. The richness of exist-ing information provision, a little suspicion of the new resource (on quality and quantity grounds), a lack of training/awareness and a shortage of time were the other contributing factors. And, to be fair, with all these factors stacked up against the Internet – taken together with journalists' innate conservatism – you might not expect anything other than a low and variable turn out of Internet users.

The early leaders

If the lack of Internet take up in the workplace was unexpected, another surprise was the characteristics of those who have taken the Internet route. Far from being the stereotypical young and male, most are experienced journalists well into their thirties and forties, and in some media companies women outnumber men. This runs counter to all that we have been led to believe. But here too there are good reasons why it is so. One reason is that people in these age bands, having emerged successfully from the scramble to get established in their early careers, can now both experiment at work (certainly it was mainly those in authority who had desktop access in their newsrooms) and have the resources and wit to use home PCs with Internet access. Secondly, it was the 'older hands' who saw the introduction of online ten to twelve years ago, assimilated it into their journalistic practices and are now viewing the Internet in much the same light. This finding is broadly in line with that reported in *The Times* Interface: most web users are in the 35-to-45 age range (*Times* Interface, 1997).There is, however, one area of the media where Internet users do conform to type – and that is in the New Media companies (VirginNet) and units (like that one which runs *The Guardian*'s web services). Here journal-ists are young and male indeed, and pronounce this fact by playing loud rock music in the workplace (confirming Simon Jenkin's worst fears about the future of journalism).

As was the case with the introduction of full-text online services during the mid eighties, the Internet leaders tend to be the editors, the subject specialists – especially IT – and the foreign journalists (Nicholas et al, 1987), all journalists with the incentive, need, time and resources to exploit the new technology to their benefit. The one group who were active onliners but who have yet to show interest in the Internet are the City desk journalists at *The Guardian*. Yet, operating in a near identical field, the journalists of *Sunday Business* used it extensively. The explanation probably lies in the fact that the former group, well-cushioned in financial terms, is so well catered for by commercial services – FT Profile, Datastream, Reuters etc. – that the Internet can offer them very little indeed.

Uses

'Visionary' CAR journalists/librarians in the USA describe posting questions on newsgroup lists, email facilitated real time interviews, investigative reporting from the Web and much more. We see few signs of such innovative and adventurous Internet use; there appears to be an information conservatism (or a good deal of information commonsense?) amongst journalists in the UK. Where the Internet was being used, it was being used in a very limited way. When given the powerful, comprehensive, freely available ultimate end-user tool – that is, the Internet – the tendency is to stick with what you know, what is familiar (newspapers. and official sites – something which Garrison (1997) also found) and do just the simple things (fact checking, background information). The tendency, then, is to use the Internet as a cuttings collection.

The finding that librarians *do* exploit the nooks and crannies of the Internet for the obscure, unusual or 'unofficial' information points to a kind of information adventurism and a higher level of searching skills. Despite the huge number of newspaper sites the Internet now hosts, librarians, in stark contrast to their journalist colleagues, spurned them. Indeed, the majority of those interviewed – but not those from *The Guardian* – were doubtful even that use of online services such as FT Profile would decline significantly, and only then more because of mutual text swapping between titles than as a result of papers on the Web. FT Profile's multiple newspaper searching cross-referencing facilities and its greater retrieval speeds was the main reason. Similarly, despite generally good Internet access in information units and, of course, librarians being professionally trained information specialists adept at using electronic systems, only three out of fifty one interviewed in-depth described the kind of interactive and communicative use of the Internet exemplified by the BBC *Panorama* researcher who sought opinions on rail transport from user group message flows. Of course, time and volume factors are important here, because *Panorama* has a narrow brief and more than a week to prepare its stories.

Attitudes and expectations

Few journalists use the Internet, but even fewer have made up their minds about it. The Internet and the issues it confronts are so enormous that this must be seen to be inevitable. It would be difficult to be logical or consistent towards it, and why, anyway, should we expect a coherent, logical approach to information and communication – after all, logic does not govern many other aspects of life. As a consequence, the data collected was sometimes difficult to square. Journalists interviewed might say one thing and then go on to contradict themselves later on. Thus they might have said they were not worried by overload and then when quality was mentioned they talked about how they screened out vast quantities of data. But this is not a flaw in the data for this is surely information life as it is – as captured by the open-ended interview rather than that processed via the structure – and perceptions – of the questionnaire designer. Users are still in a spin about the Internet and have plainly not fully made up their minds yet, if they ever will.

Librarians and their position

The arrival of every new technology is normally greeted with a flurry of articles writing the obituaries of the library/librarian – and it is interesting that similar things are starting to be said about newspapers/journalists (Nicholas and Frossling, 1996). There is no sign of this happening (for either group). In particular, the situation with librarians and information professionals could hardly be more different. For this group Internet use tended to be universal and heavy. Hardly any of them felt that the new technology was a threat to their jobs, more a case of increased work and opportunities. This appeared to be another instance – full text databases was the last one – where librarians have employed and pioneered the new end-user technologies to their own advantage. Those librarians that had used previous waves of IT to enhance their relationship with the end-user were the biggest beneficiaries – using the Net not just to increase the effectiveness of their searching, but also to extend their domain, by engaging in training, and – in the case of *The Guardian* – to re-badge. So the Net increases the muscle of the existing technologically vibrant information services, but it also provides new companies, like *Sunday Business*, with the opportunities to dispense with the need for a library altogether. Job opportunities are created on the one hand and lost on the other.

If not libraries then surely some other information system or source is going to be elbowed aside by the Internet? The answer has to be not as yet. No other communication medium or information system seems to have greatly lost out as a result of growing Internet use. If that had happened it might have explained why nobody was complaining about information overload: they simply picked up one source and dropped another. Web sites seem to stimulate the greater use of other sources. However, the writing appears to be on the wall for commercial online services. They are naturally in the frontline and are perhaps the exception. Usage is being depressed but only partly by the Internet. The 'free' swapping of internal databases amongst major newspapers is a major factor here, resulting in the case of one newspaper group in a 75% reduction in their online bill. There is, however, increasing evidence that thrifty information professionals are searching some of the Internet's free newspapers before going to FT Profile – and *The Guardian*, which is not part of the swap arrangements, is already seeing some of their online bills plummet by 50% as a direct result. Most worryingly for the hosts, new markets, like freelancers and contractors, a rapidly expanding group, blanch at the very prospect of paying what they see as an unacceptable level of online costs, and are increasingly drawn to the Net because they see it as a free online and library service. More often than not though, the Internet *both* reduces and increases the use of a source, leaving usage levels at what they were but having slightly changed the nature of use. This is particularly the case with the telephone. Email has yet to take the media by storm, but when it does – as it surely will – fax's days must be numbered too.

The Internet issues

Given our national traits, it is probably to be expected that we would concentrate not on the opportunities provided by the Net, but by the problems that arise from its use. In this connection, the authority and permanence of much of its data has been questioned, the volume of data available and even its impact on the traditional sources of information merits unfavourable comment. It is difficult to be sure, because non-users were under-represented in our study – and they might well have had contrasting opinions – but few journalists were overly concerned with these issues. Thus the merest suggestion that the Internet would overload their capacities to select and filter information was ridiculed by many journalists. There was something very wimpish about the whole notion of overload – it had connotations of poor journalistic techniques. More information was generally seen as a cause for celebration. Also overload was not going to be a problem because: (1) the extra material yielded from the system was relatively small compared to what was already available; (2) there was nothing new in hunting through trivia to find valuable information; (3) the Internet is fairly unobtrusive – you don't have to search it, unless you want to; (4) the ease with which you could access documents on the

Internet more than compensated for any problems associated with finding too many of them.

Most journalists were also pretty phlegmatic about the so-called poor quality of some of the data you get on the Internet and the problem of verifying it. It did not especially worry them because it was felt that the good journalist instinctively doubts the quality of all information, is trained to 'second source' everything (they don't always of course), and therefore sees the Net as another source to be checked. Journalists have a 'feel' for the authenticity of the data, judging it from long years of experience. Doing this is no different, and no less prone to error, in dealing with, say, telephone calls than it is with the Internet. After all, telephone information can be even more suspect when quality of data is concerned, yet few people question its provenance. Anyway, the problem rarely arises because most journalists search the Net to find out some official information from an official site. And when they are not, they are actually looking for dirt, the controversial etc. – in which case the suspect quality of the Net is not a factor! However, journalists for whom the authenticity of data was especially important – editors, crime and financial reporters, and librarians, who plainly felt that they had a protective role to play here – took the quality issue more seriously. It has to be said though, that a number of librarians felt that journalists did not worry about quality issues because they were simply unaware of them.

The contrast with the United States

The situation portrayed in the US – albeit by rather dubious question-naires – could not be more different. New media journalists – advanced guard or lost patrol – come closest. And their love affair with the Internet has a lot to do with the fact they work online. But will CAR succeed with the print and broadcasting journalist? It has to be said that some journalists – and librarians – practice CAR without ever mentioning the word. However, there are obstacles: generally news-papers in this country would not allow a story to be sourced entirely on the Web; amongst journalists there is a definite preference for primary rather than secondary data – of course, some Web data is primary; plainly CAR can only thrive in an environment where infor-mation is liberally and generously placed in the electronic public domain. This is a long way from happening in the UK

The future and the changing times

Finally then, for most of the people we spoke to the Internet was nothing revolutionary – evolutionary would be a more accurate description, and it was certainly not a panacea for all their communication and retrieval ills. However, what was there was a palpable sense that major changes were in the air – for good and bad – and that we were just a few yards down the Internet road that would continue for miles. The signs of this change were indeed there in the cases of the New Media companies we investigated. New companies plainly found it easier to adapt and adopt than the traditional media companies that were saddled with, in the words of News International's New Media Director, 'Renaissance baggage'. Freelancers, too, were another group who appeared to have been (information) enfranchised by the Net.

It is clearly early days – and we would certainly see things changing in the not too distant future. But what we have learnt will not be lost as a result. It is plain, for instance, that the Internet is not the knight in shining armour for the media, it's more Jekyll and Hyde. It offers, but it disrupts, it gives and it takes away, it provides opportunities but it also provides opportunities for competitors. What will firmly push journalists towards the Net is if news migrates from hard copy to the Web, if the batch process model turns to a tailor-made one. We have the model/example of the New Media journalists. Within journalism a division has opened up as never before – it is whether the division will turn out to be a crack or a fault line.

According to our admittedly snapshot data, Simon Jenkins (1997), the archetypal Luddite journalist, got it more right than wrong when he proclaimed that the Internet but was a niche service, but he is surely wrong when he says that it will strut the stage for only a short time. All technologies are talked up – by the purveyors of hardware and software, by information professionals looking to enhance their job – but the reality is that impacts are always slower and more gentle than that and that existing communication and retrieval technologies refuse to fade away – and are in many cases re-energised by the new, incoming technology. In many ways then, the Internet in the newsroom is, if not a sleeping giant, certainly one whose faculties have not all been awakened yet. It has definitely arrived, and with more than a whimper – but not (yet) with the expected bang.

Final observations

- The Internet debate has been diminished by too much short-termism. Too often the wisdom (and mistakes) of the past are overlooked. The Internet has a long online pedigree and we know a good deal about how such systems are received and how users search them. And much of what held true for FT Profile, holds true for the Web.

- The undue emphasis, by Internet disciples and developers, on its (sometimes phony) access and speed of delivery qualities, ignores the fact that there are around ten other equally important aspects of information need – the need for processed data, subject data, current data, quality data, data in the right quantities etc. (Nicholas, 1996). Unless such characteristics are fully addressed, the use of the Internet will be seriously proscribed. There is a particular problem with currency and speed of delivery being confused. Just because you can get to a site on the other side of the world in seconds does not mean that it is bang up-to-date – and invariably it is not – and as a result users are being shortchanged.

- The Web has legitimised the systems-driven approach to information life: the user is too often the impediment, too often the simple fool. Thus Nora Paul's reaction to the information that journalists' in the UK were reluctant to give up the cuttings collection they found so useful was that they would have to be weaned off the bottle (Paul, 1997). The defence for this remark would no doubt be: why should information professionals spend precious hours a day selecting cuttings and filing cuttings that are (individually) rarely looked at and in many also made available electronically but in a different context? A defence that would be understood by the journalist, but not agreed with.

References

(NOTE: Electronic citation format follows that recommended by Shields and Walton [no date] plus document production or revision date where referenced and the date of site visit, both as suggested by Walker [1996])

Anonymous (1995) 'Computer links strengthen German Neo-Nazis.' Unclassified US Army Intelligence Report 15.12.94 (cited in Swett, 1995)

Anonymous (1997) 'Pierre Salinger: Hook Line and Sinker awards.' *http://www.math.uiuc.edu/~tskirvin/home/daemons/kotm/salinger.html*

Bacard, A. (1993) 'Electronic democracy: can we retake our nation?' *The Humanist* July/August, pp 42–43

Barlow, M. (1997) 'Online classified ads: the UK experience.' Paper delivered at NetMedia 97 (London: NetMedia 97 Conference Proceedings)

Batty, M. and Barr, B. (1994) 'The Electronic Frontier: Exploring and Mapping Cyberspace.' *Futures* 26(7), pp. 699–712

Bright, M. (1995) 'How Brenda fell out with Cynthia and started the world's weirdest Islamic holy war.' *The Guardian* 4 March, p. 27

Cerf, V. (1997) 'Computer Networking: Global Infrastructure for the Twenty-first Century' URL *http://www.cs.washington.educations/lazonska/cra/networks.html* (visited 1.4.97)

Chapman, P. (1997) Remarks made at the steering group meeting of the Journalism and the Internet project, 10 December 1997 (Peter Chapman is Information Manager at Newsquest North East).

Clement, D. (1997) 'Online advantages for journalists.' *Press Gazette* 18 April, p. 15

Clements, R. (1997) 'Times sets its site even higher.' *The Times* Interface, 9 April, p. 3

Cole, P. (1997) Personal communication (Peter Cole is Head of the Department of Journalism, University of Central Lancashire)

CommerceNet (1996) 'CommerceNet/Nielsen Internet Demographics Recontact Study – March/April 1996.' URL *http://www.commerce.net/work/pilot/neilsen-96/exec.html* (visited 1.4.97)

Computer Intelligence (1997) 'US Children now have PCs at home.' *Computer Intelligence* 31 March. URL *http://www.viamall.com/vw/studimpurrar.html* (visited 8.4.97)

Coy, P, Hof, R. D. and Judge P. C. (1996) 'Has the Net finally reached the wall?' *Business Week* 26 August. URL *http://www.business-week.com/1996/35/b3490107.htm*

Cronin, M.J. *Doing Business on the Internet: How the Electronic Highway is Transforming American Companies* (New York: Van Nostrand Rheinhold, 1994))

Digital Kids (1997) 'Digital Kids Report: US kids online' URL *http://www.jup.com/jupiter/release/mar97/kids.shtml* (visited 8.4.97)

Drayton, H. (1997) 'The Communications Industry – the impact of the new media electronic telegraph,' in *Impact of Communications Revolution, Canada-UK Colloquim,* Keele University, 23-26 November, 1997

Driscoll, M. (1997) 'Trust me, I'm a guru.' *The Sunday Times,* 18 May, p. 15.

The Economist. (1992) 'The PEN is mighty.' *The Economist,* 1 February, p. 96

Feola, C.J. (1994) 'The NEXIS nightmare.' *American Journalism Review* 16(6), July/August, pp. 39–41

Furner. (1997) 'IR on the Web: an overview.' *Vine* 104, February, pp. 3–13

Garrison, B. (1995) *Computer Assisted Reporting* (Hillsdale, N. J.: Lawrence Erlbaum Associates).

Garrison, B. (1996a) 'Online services and the Internet: Computer Assisted Reporting in Newsrooms in 1995.' URL *http://www.miami.edu/com/car/online96.htm* (visited 22.4.97)

Garrison, B. (1996b) 'Newsrooms flock to the 'Net.' URL *http://www.nicar.org/uplink/mar96/gar.html* (visited 24.4.97)

Garrison, B. (1997a) 'Online newsgathering trends in 1994–96.' URL *http://www.miami.edu/com/car/stpete.htm* (visited 22.4.97)

Garrison, B. (1997b) 'Computer Assisted Reporting Story and Project Topics in 1995–96,' a paper presented to the newspaper Division, Southeast Colloquium, Association for Education in Journalism and Mass Communication, Knoxville, Tennessee, March 13–15 1997 URL *http:/www.miami.edu/com/car/knoxvill.htm* (visited 21.3.97)

Garrison, B. (1997c) 'Computer assisted reporting project: 1997 Research questionnaire.' URL *http://gehon.ir.miami.edu/com/car/quest97.htm* (visited 21.4.97)

Garrison, B. (1997d) 'The Web in the Newsroom 1997.' URL *http:/www.miami.edu/com/car/spj-97/index.htm* (visited 12.3.98)

Gilster, P. (1997) *Digital Literacy* (New York: John Wiley and Sons)

Gray, M. (1996) 'Internet statistics: growth and usage of the Web and the Internet.' URL *http://www.mit.edu/people/mkgray/net/* (visited 2.4.97)

Greenslade, R. (1997) 'Red sales in the sunset.' *The Guardian* Media section, pp. 8–9

The Guardian. (1997) 'Editorial: coming out of the digital closet.' *The Guardian*, 8th May, p. 8

Hilgemeier, M. (1996) 'Internet growth.' URL *http://www.is-bremen.de/~mhi/inetgrow.html* (visited 2.4.97)

Hobbes, R. (1996) 'Hobbes' Internet timeline v2.5.' URL *http://www.isbremen.de/~mhi/inetgrow.htm* (visited 1.4.97)

Huizer, E. (1997) 'Internet domain survey January 1997.' URL *http://www.sec.nl/persons/huizer/internet.growth.html* (visited 4.4.97)

Internet Informer (1997) 'NET is booming.' *Internet Informer* URL *http://www.mmp.co.uk/mmp/informer/netnews/HTM/326nle.htm* (visited 8.4.97)

IT Link. (1996) 'Who's really on the Internet?' *IT Link* January/February, pp. 6–7

Jarrett, C. (1998) 'Internet use at *The Guardian*.' Talk to post-graduate degree students, City University, 26 January 1998

Jenkins, S. (1995) 'The death of the written word.' *Journal of Information Science* 21(6), pp. 407–412

Jenkins, S. (1997) 'No plugs, no wires, no rivals.' *The Times* 4th January, p. 16

Keegan, V. (1997) 'What a web we weave.' *The Guardian* G2, 13th May, p. 2–3.

Kehoe, C., Pitkow, J., and Morton, K. (1997) 'Graphic, Visualization, & Usability Center's (GVU) 8th WWW User Survey.' URL *http://www.gvu.gatech.edu/user_surveys/survey-1997-10/.#exec*

Knight, K. (1997) 'Royal web site beats Spice Girls for hits.' *The Times*, 7th May, p. 6.

Lawson, R. (1996) 'Exploding the anorak myth.' *Digital Publishing Strategies*, November, p. 5

Leiner B. et al. (1997) 'A brief history of the Internet.' URL *http://www.isoc.org/internet-history/* (visited 1.4.97)

Line, M. (1974) 'Draft definitions: information and library needs, wants, demands and uses.' *Aslib Proceedings* 26(2), p. 87

Liu, J. (1996) 'Understanding WWW search tools.' URL *http://www.indiana.edu/~libresd/search/* (visited 4.4.96)

Long, M. (1994) 'We are the world.' *Net Guide*, December, pp. 55–56

Lynch, C. (1997) 'Searching the Internet.' *Scientific American*, March, pp. 44–48

Marr, L. (1997) Doctoral thesis transcripts and notes, and personal communication with the author (Liz Marr is Senior Lecturer at the Department of Information Science and Sociology at Manchester Metropolitan University)

Martin, H. et al (1997) *Internet Training for Journalists* (London: *The Guardian* [internal document for information staff])

Middleberg, D. and Ross, S. (no date) 'The media in cyberspace IV: a national survey.' URL *http://www.mediasource.com/study/CH01.HTM* (visited 2.4.98)

MORI (1997) 'Business and financial journalists on the Internet.' (Survey results faxed to present authors)

Motorola (1997) *The British and Technology* (London: Hill and Knowlton [press release])

Nicholas, D. (1996) *Assessing Information Needs: tools and techniques* (London: Aslib).

Nicholas, D., Erbach, G., Pang, Y.W. & Paalman, K. (1988) *End-users of Online Information Systems* (London: Mansell)

Nicholas, D. and Fenton, D. (1997) 'The Internet and the changing information environment.' *Managing Information*, January/February, pp. 30–33

Nicholas, D. and Frossling, I. (1996) 'The information handler in the digital age.' *Managing Information* 3 (7/8) July/August, pp. 31–34

Nicholas, D. and Martin, H. (1993) 'Should journalists search themselves? (And what happens when they do?),' in *Online Information 93: proceedings*, pp.227–234 (Learned Information).

Nicholas, D. and Martin, H. (1997) 'Assessing Information needs: a case study of journalists.' *Aslib Proceedings* 49(2), February, pp. 43–52

NOP (National Opinion Poll) (1997) 'Internet Surveys: one in twenty five British households now linked to the Internet.' URL *http://www.nopres.co.uk/surveys/Internetsurveys.htm*

Noveck, J. (1996) 'TWA Flight 800 – Pierre Salinger's News Conference on the US Missile – Pierre Salinger Claims Navy Missile Shot Down TWA Flight 800 Friday, November 8, 1996.' URL *http://webusers.anet-stl.com/~civil/govliestwaflight800salingr.html*

Nua Internet Surveys (1997a) *http://www.nua.ie* (visited 20.5.97)

Nua Internet Surveys (1997b) *http://www.nua.ie* (visited 11.6.97)

Oldfield, C. (1997) 'Small firms miss the Net message.' *The Sunday Times* Business, 18th May, p. 2

Outing, S. (1997) 'A decade of online newspapers – lessons and trends.' NetMedia 97 Proceedings

Owen, T. 'Hanging on to the telephone.' *Information World Review*, January 1997, p. 24

Paul, N. (1996a) 'Computer Assisted Journalism: The Four Rs of CAJ.' URL *http://www.facsnet.org/report_tools/CAR/carfourr.htm* (visited 8.4.97)

Paul, N. (1996b) 'Computer Assisted Research: Ready Reference.' URL *http://www.facsnet.org/report_tools/CAR/carready.htm* (visited 1.4.97)

Paul, N. (1997) *Computer Assisted Research: A guide to tapping online information*, 3rd edition (St. Petersburg, Fla.: Poynter Institute)

Paul, N. (1997b) Comments made during talk 'New emphasis on traditional roles for news librarians.' NetMedia, City University 04/07/97

PAULEY J (chair) (1996) *Tomorrow's Broadcast Journalists: A report and recommendations from the Jane Pauley Task Force on Mass Communication Education* (Greencastle, Indiana: Society of Professional Journalists)

Pitcow, J. and Kehoe, C. (1996) 'GVU (Graphic, Visualisation and Usability Centre)'s 6th WWW User Survey.' URL *http://www.cc.gatech.edu/gvu/user_surveys/survey-10-1996/* (visited 20.4.97)

Pitcow, J.E. and Recker, M.M. (1994) 'Results from the first World Wide Web user survey.' URL *http://www.gatech.edu/pitkow/survey/survey-1-1994/survey-paper.html*

Press, L. (1991) 'Wide Area Collaboration.' *Communications of the ACM*, December, pp. 21–24

Rackiewicz, C. (1996) 'Internet growth: work displaces home as the driving force, according to new INTECO research.' URL *http://www.inteco.com/pu961205.html* (visited 2.4.97)

Rheingold, H. (1993) *The Virtual Community: homesteading on the electronic frontier* (New York: HarperCollins)

Ross, S.S. and Middleberg, D. (no date) 'The media in cyberspace III: a national survey' URL *http://www.mediasource.com/study/CH01.HTM* (visited 2.4.97)

Ross, S.S. and Middleberg, D. (1997) 'The media in cyberspace IV: a national survey' URL *http://www.mediasource.com/cyberstudy/INTRO.HTM* (visited 16.3.98)

Saunders, J. (1997) 'The Downing of TWA 800.' Excerpt at *http://www.accessone.com/~rivero/CRASH/TWA/sandersbook.html*

Schmid, R.E. (1997) 'TWA 800.' URL *http://www.pufori.org/news/*

nws0515976.htm

Scott, S.D. (1995) 'The technological challenge for curriculum and instruction.' *Journalism and Mass Communication Educator* 50(2), pp. 30–40

Semonche, B. (1993) *News Media Libraries: a management handbook* (Westport CT: Greenwood Press). Extract at *http://sunsite.unc.edu/journalism/caj.html* (visited 1.4.97).

Semonche, B. and Raitz, B (1997) 'The news librarian's role in Computer Assisted Reporting,' in *News Media Libraries: a management handbook*, edited by B. Semonche (Westport CT: Greenwood Press, 1993). Available online at *http://sunsite.unc.edu/journalism/caj.html* (visited 1.4.97)

Shields, G. and Walton, G. (no date) 'Cite them right! How to organize bibliographical references.' URL *http://www.unn.ac.uk/central/isd/cite/* (visited 7.4.97)

Stevenson, S. (1998) 'Invisible Ink: How the story everyone's talking about stayed out of the papers.' URL *http://www.cspc.org/drudge/invisibl.htm*

Swett, C. (1995) 'Strategic Assessment: The Internet.' URL *http://www.latnet.lv/INET96/el/el_2.htm* (visited 8.4.97)

Sylge, C. (1996) 'An interview with Helen Martin, Chief Librarian.' *Managing Information*, January/February, pp. 22–23

The Times Interface. (1997) 'Everyone knows about the net.' *The Times* Interface, 23 April, p. 2

Tseng, G., Poulter, A. & Hiom, D. (1996) *The Library and Information Professional's Guide to the Internet* (London: The Library Association)

Varn, R.J. 'Jefferson Boom or Teraflop?' *Spectrum*, Spring 1993, pp. 21–25

Walker, J.R. (1996) 'MLA-style citations of electronic sources (endorsed by the Alliance for Computers and Writing).' URL *http://www.cas.usf.edu/english/walker/mla.html* (visited 8.4.97)

Weinberg, S. (1996) *The Reporter's Handbook: An Investigator's Guide to Documents and Techniques*, 3rd edition (New York: St Martin's Press)

Wells, W.D. & Gubber, G. (1996) 'Life Cycle Concepts in Market Research.' *Journal of Marketing Research*, November, pp. 355–363

Appendix 1

Media organisations surveyed

Anglia Television
> Total (questionnaires):
> 2 librarians

Ashton Weekly
> Total (interviews):
> Unspecified number in a group of 24 trainees

Associated Electronic Newspapers
> Total (interviews):
> 1 Managing Director

BBC
> Total (questionnaires):
> 4 librarians
>
> Total (interviews):
> 1 Resources Development Manager
> 14 librarians
> 2 researchers
> (17 librarians in subsequent tables)
> 7 journalists
>
> Major observation site

Blackpool Gazette
> Total (interviews):
> Unspecified number in a group of 24 trainees

British Sky Broadcasting
> Total (interviews):
> 1 librarian

Chorley Guardian (weekly)
> Total (interviews):

Unspecified number in a group of 24 trainees

City University, School of Journalism, London
    Total (interviews):
    1 Journalism lecturer

CNN (Cable News Network)
    Total (interviews):
    1 librarian

Coventry Evening Telegraph
    Total (questionnaires):
    2 librarians

Daily Telegraph
    Total (interviews):
    1 librarian
    4 journalists

    Total (questionnaires):
    1 librarian

    Observation site

Darlington & Stockton Times
    (Telephone interview and subsequent email exchange with
        journalist.)
    Total (interviews):
    1 journalist

Eastern Counties Network
    Total (interviews):
    1 librarian
    1 Editor (New Media)
    1 Manager (New Media)

Eastern Daily Times
    Total (interviews):
    1 journalist

Express
    Total (interviews):
    1 journalist

Finance and Business Publications
> Total (interviews):
> 1 journalist

Financial Times
> Total (questionnaires):
> 1 librarian

Freelance
> Total (interviews) freelance interviews:
> 6 journalists (3 New Media)

FT Profile
> Total (interviews):
> 2 marketing and customer care managers

The Guardian
> Total (interviews):
> 14 librarians/researchers
> 28 Journalists
> 8 Editors (or Deputy Editors)
> 2 Journalists – New Media
>
> Total (questionnaires):
> 1 librarian
> 2 journalists
>
> Major observation site

Harrogate Weekly
> Total (interviews):
> Unspecified number in a group of 24 trainees

Herald (Glasgow)
> Total (interviews):
> 5 librarians
> 6 journalists (including 1 Editor)
> 1 journalist (New Media)
>
> Total (questionnaires):
> 5 librarians
>
> Major observation site

The Independent
    Total (interviews):
    1 Journalist – Editor

Independent Television Commission
    Total (interviews):
    1 librarian

    Total (questionnaires):
    2 librarians

Independent Television News
    Total (interviews):
    1 journalist (online editor)

Lancashire Evening Post
    Total (interviews):
    Unspecified number in a group of 24 trainees

Lancaster Guardian
    Total (interviews):
    Unspecified number in a group of 24 trainees

Liverpool Daily Post
    Total (interviews):
    1 journalist (editor)

London News Network
    Total (interviews):
    1 librarian

London Weekend Television
    Total (interviews):
    1 Editor
    2 librarians

Manchester Evening News
    Total (questionnaires):
    2 librarians

Microscope Magazine
    Total (interviews):
    1 journalist

The Mirror
> Total (interviews):
> 1 librarian
> 4 journalists

New Scientist
> Total (interviews):
> 1 journalist

News International
> Total (interviews):
> 15 librarians
> 50 journalists
>
> Total (questionnaires):
> 10 librarians
>
> Major observation site

News Online
> Total (interviews):
> 1 Manager

Newsquest Northeast
> Total (interviews):
> 3 journalists
> 2 librarians
> 1 New Media
>
> Total (questionnaires):
> 2 librarians
>
> Major observation site

Newsquest Wiltshire
> Total (questionnaires):
> 2 librarians

The Observer
> Total (interviews):
> 7 journalists
>
> Major observation site

People
> Total (interviews):
> 1 Journalist – Editor

Press Association
> Total (interviews):
> 1 Deputy Editor in Chief

Redwood Publishing
> Total (interviews):
> 1 journalist

Reuters Financial TV
> Total (interviews):
> 1 journalist

S4C Cardiff
> Total (questionnaires):
> 2 librarians

Scotsman
> Total (questionnaires):
> 3 librarians

Scottish Daily Record
> Total (interviews):
> 1 journalist
> 1 New Media
> 5 librarians/researchers
>
> Total (questionnaires):
> 1 journalist
> 1 librarian

Spenborough Weekly
> Total (interviews):
> Unspecified number in a group of 24 trainees

Sunday Business
> Total (interviews):
> 1 Journalist (repeat interviews)
>
> Major observation site

Time Life
>Total (interviews):
>4 journalists
>2 librarians

Time Out
>Total (questionnaires):
>2 librarians

Times Supplements
>Total (questionnaires):
>1 librarian

United States Embassy Press Office
>Total (interviews):
>1 Journalist
>1 Librarian

University of Central Lancashire
>Total (interviews):
>1 Journalism lecturer (repeated interviews)
>
>Total (questionnaires):
>1 Journalism lecturer
>1 Business Information Manager
>31 Journalism students

VirginNet
>Total (interviews):
>3 journalists
>1 librarian
>
>Observation site

Wolverhampton Express and Star
>Total (questionnaires):
>1 librarian

Yellow Advertiser (Basildon)
>Total (interviews):
>Unspecified number in a group of 24 trainees

Yorkshire Evening Post
>Total (interviews):
>Unspecified number in a group of 24 trainees

Appendix 2

Guidelines for interviewers

Ideally information on the Internet should emerge from general questioning about the job and the impact (or potential) of the Internet on it. However, if the topics below do not come up users should be gently and slowly lead towards them. The thrust of the interview is how the Internet is changing needs/the information seeking/communicating process (if at all) and how (if at all) that is changing the relationship between user and information professional (and other information systems/sources – face-to-face, libraries etc.). It is possible that change is not happening yet, but might be beginning to – and that is where the depth interviews are so important. Inevitably the questions overlap and answers to any specific question might feed many off our lines of enquiry. Their perceptions of what we want/are asking is as important data too. What follows is nothing more than a very rough shopping list.

Information sought

1. Background data
Gender; job role; department; would like age-band too, but ... (i.e. under 30; 31-40; 41-50; 50+); computer competency/experience (staff development/training).This data is sometimes volunteered, sometimes prompted for or sometimes summarised.

2. Use/non-use
Volume, frequency, pattern, growth; session length; first use; future use. Plainly if the interviewee is a non-user then should trigger a different line in questioning. There is a need to establish quite clearly what it is that is being used when interviewees say that they are using the Internet (e.g. CompuServe) as a channel to search commercial and non-commercial hosts/databases. Because journalism does not confine itself to the office it is important to ask about home use as well.

3. Nature/purpose of use/reasons for non-use
What it is used for/to find – communicating with others (email); fact-finding; browsing around for an idea etc.; trawling around for profiles; obtaining press releases; investigative research; playing/recreational. Might be best obtained by asking them to

recount things that they have done with the Internet recently – whether that is typical. Could be good to get a few case study uses – from librarians and journalists – for example: *Started with a specific search in two or three search engines, downloaded files to read later (or immediately online), continued browsing after seeing an interesting topic not thought of initially, moved on to recreational use for a time, checked to see what other colleagues/competitors were writing etc.*

Possible reasons for non-use – not available, nothing to offer, too slow, problem over verification of data etc. Then move to next non-use section.

4. Contribution; value of Internet data; satisfaction/degrees of success

The level of awareness is going to be important here. Are people who are aware of the possibilities more/less satisfied than people who are new to the Internet? Is their level of (dis)satisfaction related to their expectations?

5. Sources/sites visited

Could be linked to examples of searches. Interested if they trek all over the place, have favourites etc.; never go back to the same place again; Do they bookmark them, note them electronically or manually, how much information do they link to the URL in order to remember its importance, do they rank sites, do they categorise them, if so by what criteria – subject?

6. Searching methods

Do they use engines, bookmarks, search directly on sites; browsing; fact-finding/specific searches; number of terms they normally input; how happy with ranked output. It also helps to know what it is about a search engine they like in relation to their own perceptions, working practices etc., since some engines provide wider but less focused results and others are narrower and tighter this may reflect on the journalists themselves.

7. Impact on/relationship with existing sources/systems: hard copy, online and CD-ROM services

How is Internet use impacting upon use of other sources/communication channels? Must establish if they are an existing FT Profile searcher and user of newspaper's own database.

8. Overload

Is Internet use creating any problems here in terms of too much information. In fact this is a good question to get at the above

9. Impact on work

Has the Internet changed the way you work – do you do the job in different ways; do you do anything different; relate differently to people. Have your stories changed. Have your responsibilities changed?

10. Training
Have they had any/would they like any

11. Intermediary/library
Do they delegate the search

Non-users

1. Attitudes
Peering ahead and reasons for non- or delegated use the key here. Also get a feeling for whether they search computerised databases generally/library users etc.

2. Can do/won't do
There are those who can (in theory) but do not and those who cannot because they have no facilities. We need to find why the former do not: unaware; limited access; lack of training; no need; poor Internet resources, happy to delegate; we need to find whether second group would if they could. We also need to know something about awareness levels – journalists might know about the Net but not use it.

3. General attitudes towards the Internet
Even non-users will have attitudes towards the Internet – perceptions very important here. Some will have tried and rejected. Others might be future users. With non-users the questioning will inevitably be more general and futuristic; but we need to retain some reality in the interviewing – no wish lists. Asking about current constraints in doing the job and questioning whether the Internet could help might prove profitable.

4. Things that might get them using the Internet
Improvements in access/speed/training etc.

5. Non-judgmental
With non-users there is a possibility of them feeling that they should be searching the Internet – we could overcome the possible biases that come with this by asking such questions as: *There is a lot of hype associated with the Internet, I mean, is there really anything new here; a lot of people say that the Internet is a waste of time, what do you think.* Such leading questions should be used with care.

6. Others might search
Does anybody in their organisation search the Internet – who and why.

7. Profitable lines of questioning
A lot has been written about the way the Internet could reshape the industry – this could prove a good way to start the interview

8. Ask about other computerised information systems
Are there any online users amongst non-Internet users.

Appendix 3

Questionnaire schedule and raw results

1. Librarians questionnaire: Journalists, news librarians and the Internet
(A British Library funded research project);

Part One: Internet access and use;

1. Do you have access to the Internet at work?
No 3
Yes 38, plus 2 email only
(Base = 43 respondents)

2. Do you use the Internet at work?
No 7
Yes 36
(Base = 43 respondents)

3. How much use do you make of the Internet at work?
Use it all the time 12
Use it heavily sometimes 10
Use it occasionally 14
(Base = 36 users)

4. What kind of use to you make of the Internet? Please answer in the space below:

2	Web site creation
17	Subject searches/reference/background
2	Personal research
8	Email/mailing lists
11	Telephone nos./Yellow Pages/addresses/contacts
6 + 1(personal use)	Newspapers/ magazines
2	Software updates
2	Company information
5	Copies of documents/ journal articles/publications
5	Use as a final resource/ when information not in own archives
7	Contemporary pop, film, entertainment & literature sites
10	Government/political information (UK & foreign)
1	British Library OPAC
1	OECD Online
1	OPAC 97
6 (1 esp.	Associations/organisations sites LIS)
1	Chronological lists i.e. Nobel prize winners etc.
4	Picture resource
1	DFEE site
3	Usenet newsgroups
1	Story ideas
4	Press releases
1	Going to known Web sites
1	Maps
3	Browsing for useful journalist sites
1 + 1 (personal use)	Football/other sport
1 (personal use)	Travel/timetables
1 (personal use)	Shopping
1	Checking out new Web sites
1	Checking out courses on offer
2	Use as a last resort

Only one respondents answers per organisation used in Qs 5–7.

5. *Do journalists at your organisation have any access to the Internet at work, apart from through the library?*
Dont know
No 6*
Yes 13
(Base = 19 organisations)
*Including one respondent's comment: 'All programmes, including news, are commissioned, and therefore produced outside S4C. Journalists have no need to use the Internet through us.'

6. *Approximately how many journalists have access **on their own desk top**?*
None 1
A few (up to 25%) 7
Some (25-50%) 2
The majority 1*
All 0
(Base = 11 organisations with separate Internet access for journalists, not including two BBC institutions (News/Research Unit & Information Research Library) where journalist access was not known).
**Scotsman*

7. *How many journalists have access within their department or close by (do not include library terminals)?*
None 1*
A few (up to 25%) 3
Some (25 - 50%) 1
The majority 4
All 0
(Base = 11 organisations with separate Internet access for journalists.)
Plus 2 comments: Don't know.
**Scotsman*, where majority have desktop access

Part two: Opinions;

(Base = 43 respondents – although not all answered every question)
The type and quality of information on the Internet;

The sites are not updated as much as you would like.
Strongly agree 3
Mildly agree 24
Mildly disagree 4
Strongly disagree 3
No opinion 4

The Internet is vastly overrated as an information tool.
Strongly agree 2
Mildly agree 10
Mildly disagree 17
Strongly disagree 10
No opinion 0

I use the Internet to find the quirky, offbeat or obscure.
Strongly agree 10
Mildly agree 11
Mildly disagree 7
Strongly disagree 6
No opinion 3

I just want the facts from a Web site, not the graphics or other trimmings
Strongly agree 6
Mildly agree 15
Mildly disagree 5
Strongly disagree 8
No opinion 2

People are suffering from the fast and fleeting information diet they only ever obtain
Strongly agree 1
Mildly agree 12
Mildly disagree 13
Strongly disagree 3
No opinion 9

Information overload

Those worried about overload don't turn on (their Internet connection) in the first place.
Strongly agree 5
Mildly agree 10
Mildly disagree 10
Strongly disagree 4
No opinion 13
Comment: I don't even consider it an issue.

Information just overwhelms people – it makes them aware that their ability to change anything is zero – what's the point of knowing about things if you can't change anything?
Strongly agree 1
Mildly agree 4
Mildly disagree 10
Strongly disagree 23
No opinion 1

The librarians role is to protect the end-user from information overload – by filtering, sorting, establishing relevancy etc.
Strongly agree 19
Mildly agree 18
Mildly disagree 2
Strongly disagree 2
No opinion 1
Comment: 'Does a book on the Internet need an index?'

Ease, speed of use and delivery of the Internet;
If I want to find out something I get on the phone … with email its like sending it out into the wide blue yonder.
Strongly agree 1
Mildly agree 7
Mildly disagree 16
Strongly disagree 12
No opinion 3

Instant access is the key attraction of the Internet for me.
Strongly agree 12
Mildly agree 18*
Mildly disagree 7
Strongly disagree 1
No opinion 3
*Including the comment, 'Not in the afternoons!'

If there is a problem on the Internet the Internet is also likely to offer a solution.
Strongly agree 7
Mildly agree 6
Mildly disagree 11
Strongly disagree 2
No opinion 11

With the Internet you could go on and on never reaching the end – with a book you know you have come to the end of the chapter; with the Internet you cannot see what is before, what is after, how much there is to go.
Strongly agree 6
Mildly agree 17
Mildly disagree 6
Strongly disagree 5
No opinion 5

There is no future in push technology – its all so arbitrary and random.
Strongly agree 0
Mildly agree 4
Mildly disagree 8
Strongly disagree17
No opinion 11
Comment: Does this make the Internet closer to reality?

From just scanning cuttings I know what kind of story they are without me having to read them. I know the tabloids from the broadsheets, I know the popular article from the specialist one ... That is faster than anything the Internet can do.
Strongly agree 9
Mildly agree 11
Mildly disagree 9
Strongly disagree10
No opinion 1

The effect of the Internet on journalism/news librarianship & the newspaper industry

With so much information flowing around the Net and what with this two-way dialogue you do not need journalists to go out and gather information anymore.
Strongly agree 1
Mildly agree 0
Mildly disagree 5
Strongly disagree 32
No opinion 0
Comment: Why go to second hand information – cuttings – 50s technology!

A global, easy to access/publish system scares the newspaper industry to death.
Strongly agree 4

Mildly agree 9
Mildly disagree 13
Strongly disagree 10
No opinion 3
Comment: 'It should be seen as an opportunity.'

Newspapers will be increasingly features driven and the news will migrate to the electronic media.
Strongly agree 3
Mildly agree 17
Mildly disagree 8
Strongly disagree 8
No opinion 6
Comment: 'But plenty of investigative news, in which case I disagree.'

I couldnt do my job without the Internet.
Strongly agree 4
Mildly agree 11
Mildly disagree11
Strongly disagree 16
No opinion

The Net will change the face of journalism.
Strongly agree 9
Mildly agree 20
Mildly disagree 5
Strongly disagree 4
No opinion 2

With the Internet there is no excuse for not knowing anymore.
Strongly agree 2
Mildly agree 13
Mildly disagree 11
Strongly disagree 12
No opinion 4
Comment: 'There has NEVER been an excuse for not knowing.'

When journalists get 100% access only 20% of them will refuse to use the Internet but only 20% will use it as a force for good/change.
Strongly agree 2
Mildly agree 13
Mildly disagree 3
Strongly disagree 2

No opinion 21
Comment: 'Don't understand – journalists not able to have big decisions, but agree they'll use if access.'

There will be a cataclysmic change (because of the Internet) in the way society works.
Strongly agree 6
Mildly agree 15
Mildly disagree 10
Strongly disagree 7
No opinion 2

2. Student journalist questionnaire;

Part One: Internet access and use;

What is the extent of your current Internet use:

at work?		at home?	
Very frequently	19	Very frequently	1
Sometimes	8	Sometimes	1
Occasionally	5	Occasionally	6
Never	1	Never	25

If you never use the Internet please answer the non-users questions on the right, below.

Users
What kind of use to you make of the Internet? Please answer in the space below

_____
_____
_____
_____

_____
_____
_____
_____
_____
_____

Non-users
Does the Internet interest you?
No 0 Yes 2

Do you think the Internet could help you in your work?
No 0 Yes 2 How? Please indicate below:

_____
_____
_____
_____
_____
_____

Do you see your job changing over the next five years because of the Internet?
No 8
Yes 25 How? Please indicate below:

| |
| |
| |

Part Two: Attitudes towards the Internet

Please indicate the opinion, taken from interview transcripts, that most closely fits your own in the tickbox.

The Internet is vastly overrated as an information tool.
Strongly agree 3
Mildly agree 13
Mildly disagree 13
Strongly disagree 4
No opinion 0

People are suffering from a diet of fast and fleeting information.
Strongly agree 9
Mildly agree 8
Mildly disagree 9
Strongly disagree 4
No opinion 3

Those worried about overload don't turn on [their Internet connection] in the first place.
Strongly agree 7
Mildly agree 12
Mildly disagree 2
Strongly disagree 2
No opinion 10

The librarians role is to protect the end-user from information overload – by filtering, sorting, establishing relevancy etc.
Strongly agree 5
Mildly agree 12
Mildly disagree 3
Strongly disagree 3
No opinion 10

If I want to find out something I get on the phone ... with email it's like sending it out into the wide blue yonder.
Strongly agree 1
Mildly agree 8
Mildly disagree 15
Strongly disagree 8
No opinion 1

From just scanning cuttings I know what kind of story they are without me having to read them. I know the tabloids from the broadsheets, I know the popular article from the specialist one ... That is faster than anything the Internet can do.
Strongly agree 6
Mildly agree 14
Mildly disagree 7
Strongly disagree 1
No opinion 5

With so much information flowing around the Net and what with this two-way dialogue you do not need journalists to go out and gather information anymore.
Strongly agree 1
Mildly agree 4
Mildly disagree 5
Strongly disagree 22
No opinion 1

Newspapers will be increasingly features driven – the news will migrate to the electronic media.
Strongly agree 2
Mildly agree 16
Mildly disagree 4
Strongly disagree 8
No opinion 3

The Net will change the face of journalism.
Strongly agree 12
Mildly agree 16
Mildly disagree 2
Strongly disagree 2
No opinion 1

There will be a cataclysmic change (because of the Internet) in the way society works.
Strongly agree 4
Mildly agree 10
Mildly disagree 8
Strongly disagree 8
No opinion 3

The Internet is still controlled by the anorak brigade tossing puerile jokes into the ether.
Strongly agree 1
Mildly agree 12
Mildly disagree 10
Strongly disagree 5
No opinion 5

Im not sure the Internet would give me over and above the information Ive already got.
Strongly agree 1
Mildly agree 10
Mildly disagree 7;
Strongly disagree 12
No opinion 3

When email gets really established there will be an incredible amount of junk mail.
Strongly agree 17
Mildly agree 12
Mildly disagree 0
Strongly disagree 1
No opinion 3

FT Profile is quick and concise – the Internet can't compete.
Strongly agree 1
Mildly agree 3
Mildly disagree 4
Strongly disagree 1
No opinion 24

A brilliant information system has already been invented – its called the book.
Strongly agree 10
Mildly agree 10
Mildly disagree 3
Strongly disagree 3
No opinion 6

I simply do not have time to mess about on the Internet.
Strongly agree 0
Mildly agree 8
Mildly disagree 11
Strongly disagree 11
No opinion 3
Non-user 0

The following questions may be difficult for non-users. Please make use of the non-user option if you feel you cannot give an opinion.
There is no future in push technology – its all so arbitrary and random
Strongly agree 1
Mildly agree 5
Mildly disagree 6
Strongly disagree 6
No opinion 15
Non-user 0

The sites are not updated as much as you would like.
Strongly agree 8
Mildly agree 12
Mildly disagree 1
Strongly disagree 2
No opinion 10
Non-user 0

I use the Internet to find the quirky, offbeat or obscure.
Strongly agree 5
Mildly agree 14
Mildly disagree 5
Strongly disagree 0
No opinion 9
Non-user 0

I just want the facts from a Web site, not the graphics or other trimmings.
Strongly agree 4
Mildly agree 9
Mildly disagree 5
Strongly disagree 10
No opinion 5
Non-user 0

Appendix 4

Project Publications

Nicholas, D., Williams P., Cole, P. & Martin, H. (1997) 'The Internet: the users story.' *Managing Information*, November, pp. 28–31

Nicholas, D., Williams, P., Cole, P. & Martin, H. (1997) 'The Internet: it's early days, but there are some surprises.' *Aslib Proceedings*, 49(8) September, pp. 214–216

Nicholas, D., Williams, P., Cole, P. & Martin, H. (1997) 'The Changing Information Environment: the impact of the Internet on information seeking behaviour in the media.' In *Online 1997 Conference Proceedings*, pp.181–185 (Oxford: Learned Information Limited)

Nicholas, D., Williams, P., Cole, P. & Martin, H. (1998) 'Journalists – not true to type?' *Library Association Record* 100(2), February, pp. 84–85

Nicholas, D. & Williams, P. (1998) 'Journalism and the Internet.' *Research Bulletin of The British Library Research and Innovation Centre* 20, pp. 9–10

Nicholas, D., Williams, P., Cole, P. & Martin, H. (1998) 'Journalists and the Internet: how they use it, what they think of it.' In *NetMedia 98 Conference Proceedings*, pp. 248–251 (London: City University)

Williams, P. & Nicholas, D. (1998) 'Not an age thing! Greynetters in the newsroom defy the stereotype.' *New Library World* 99(1142), June 1998, pp.143–148

Williams, P. & Nicholas, D. (1997) 'Journalists, news librarians and the Internet.' *New Library World* 98(1137), August, pp. 217–223

Index